EXODUS

METHUEN'S OLD ENGLISH LIBRARY
General Editors
A. J. Bliss, Professor of Old and Middle English,
University College, Dublin
and
A. Brown, Professor of English, Monash University

METHUEN'S OLD ENGLISH LIBRARY

EXODUS

Edited by

Peter J. Lucas

Methuen & Co Ltd
11 NEW FETTER LANE LONDON EC4P 4EE

First published in 1977 by Methuen & Co Ltd
Copyright © 1977 Introduction, Notes, etc.
Peter J. Lucas

Typeset in Great Britain by
Preface Ltd, Salisbury
and printed by
the University Printing House,
Cambridge

SBN 416 17170 2

For
Angela

Dægweorc ne mað

Contents

Preface

Old English literature offers a unique opportunity to study early medieval Christian poetry. Some of the earliest poems may well have been written at a time when Northern England held the intellectual leadership of Europe. *Exodus* is one of these and is indeed one of the most outstanding poems in Old English. Stylistically it is perhaps *the* most outstanding Old English poem, showing a use of metaphor and a fusion of disparate concepts (such as abstract and concrete, literal and allegorical) unparalleled in Old English poetry. The poem focusses on the greatest of Old Testament events, the exodus from Egypt and the crossing of the Red Sea, which is interpreted both within the historical perspective of other Old Testament events (the Deluge and the Offering of Isaac) and within the allegorical perspective of the exodus to the Promised Land seen as the Christian's journey through life to the heavenly home. *Exodus* is thus an ideal poem with which to introduce students to the possibilities of an Old English poem reflecting allegorical exegesis of the Bible. This edition aims at making the poem more readily accessible, and better understood and appreciated than hitherto.

Exodus has appeared in a modern critical edition only once before, in the edition by E. B. Irving (1953). While this edition was a great step forward when it first appeared, and is still useful, it is now rather out of date, as the author's efforts to supplement it indicate. As the importance of the poem gradually came to be realized a need arose for a completely new edition which would take into account all the new work done on the poem since the early 1950s and sift the older evidence again. Many of the textual problems, formerly considered a barrier to the study of the poem, have now been overcome either through the application of new discoveries in the technical aspects of Old English poetry, or because the text can now be seen in the light of a considered view of the poem's literary import, (though naturally, as far as possible, an interpretation must be drawn from the edited text rather than vice versa), or because readings based on new emendations have been suggested. The present edition is the first modern critical edition of the poem to print the text in the order in which it occurs in the manuscript, and the first to have a section in the Introduction devoted to the metre. The Glossary is unusually full, citing all inflected forms as well as giving cross-references for the second elements of compound nouns and adjectives, the latter to facilitate studies of the poem's diction. A larger portion of the Introduction than is usual in such editions is devoted to the only manuscript in which the poem occurs because study of the manuscript helps to establish and define the text; in particular study of some of the punctuation-markers enables a clearer formulation of the nature of the lacunae than hitherto. In the course of these investigations into the manuscript I discovered that it was possible to establish its place of origin (Malmesbury), the first time that the place where a major codex of Old English poetry was written has been fixed with any degree of firmness. This discovery adds a valuable fact to the scant information upon which conjectures as to the poem's origin have to be based.

In the preparation of this edition I have had access to notes taken from lectures given by J. R. R. Tolkien at Oxford. Two of the emendations adopted in the text (280, 519) were, as far as I know, first suggested by him in these lectures and are therefore attributed to him in the Textual Notes. His comments or suggestions are also incorporated in the Commentary from time to time (notes to 33b, 38, 62, 142, 166, 275, 308–9, 344a, 575).

In the preparation of the Glossary I have drawn on a complete *index verborum* of the text made with the aid of the computer facilities available in University College, Dublin: see *Computers and the Humanities* v (1970) 106 no. L401, and *Computers and Medieval Data Processing* ii (1972) 39 no. 65. It is a pleasure to thank the staff of the computer laboratory for their co-operation.

I also have pleasure in thanking the many friends and colleagues who have helped me while the edition was in progress.

Professor A. J. Bliss (Dublin) first suggested to me that I might prepare an edition of *Exodus* for the Methuen Old English Library series and has made valuable comments on my work as it progressed. Dr R. B. Mitchell (Oxford) has discussed some of the textual problems with me and made comments on the Commentary. Mr M. B. Parkes (Oxford) was most helpful in discussing the manuscript with me and commented on the relevant section of the Introduction in typescript. Mr G. Pollard (Oxford) kindly sent me detailed notes on the binding of the manuscript. Professors J. E. Cross (Liverpool) and E. G. Stanley (Yale) made valuable comments on parts of the Introduction. Professor P. A. M. Clemoes (Cambridge) made material available to me prior to publication, Mr R. W. McTurk (Dublin) advised me on matters relating to Old Norse, and Dr M. J. Swanton (Exeter) sent me information about Anglo-Saxon spears. I have also benefited enormously from discussing the poem with students, especially Miss Ann Dooley and Mrs Rosemary Thomas. My greatest debt, however, is to my wife, to whom this book is dedicated: as a fellow medievalist she has listened patiently to many disquisitions on *Exodus*, often interrupting to point out absurdities. Any that remain are my own responsibility.

A travel grant from University College Dublin enabled me to visit Oxford and study the manuscript at first hand. My thanks are also due to The National University of Ireland for making a grant towards the cost of printing.

Dublin
Exaltation of the Cross 1975   PETER J. LUCAS

Postscript. While the book has been at press some new work relating to *Exodus* has appeared. I have attempted to take this work into account up to the end of 1975.

List of Abbreviations

Abbreviated bibliographical references are also to be found in square brackets at the end of the relevant entries in the Select Bibliography.

Names in small capitals refer to previous editors of the poem. For the distinction between IRVING (edition) and Irving (articles supplementing his edition) see Select Bibliography p.151.

AM	*Annuale Mediaevale*
Archiv	*Archiv für das Studium der neueren Sprachen und Literaturen*
AS	Anglo-Saxon
ASC	*The Anglo-Saxon Chronicle*, J. Earl and C. Plummer (eds) (Oxford, 1892–9), cited by MS and date
ASE	*Anglo-Saxon England*
ASPR	The Anglo-Saxon Poetic Records, G. P. Krapp and E. v. K. Dobbie (eds) (New York and London, 1931–53)
BBA	*Bonner Beiträge zur Anglistik*
BT	J. Bosworth and T. N. Toller, *An Anglo-Saxon Dictionary* (Oxford, 1898)
BTS	*Supplement* to Bosworth-Toller's *Dictionary* (Oxford, 1921)
BTSA	*Addenda* to Bosworth-Toller's *Dictionary* and *Supplement*, A. Campbell (ed.) (Oxford, 1972)
Campbell	A. Campbell, *Old English Grammar* (Oxford, 1959)
CCSL	Corpus Christianorum series Latina
EEMF	Early English Manuscripts in Facsimile

EETS	Early English Text Society (Original Series)
EHR	*English Historical Review*
ELN	*English Language Notes*
ES	*English Studies*
ESt	*Englische Studien*
Ex	*Exodus*
Ex.	Exodus
FChristi	*Famulus Christi: Essays in Commemoration of the Thirteenth Centenary of the Birth of the Venerable Bede*, G. Bonner (ed.) (London, 1976)
GCS	Die Griechischen Christlichen Schriftsteller der ersten drei Jahrhunderte
Gen	*Genesis*
Gmc	Germanic
HBS	Henry Bradshaw Society
JBAA	*Journal of the British Archaeological Association*
JEGP	*Journal of English and Germanic Philology*
Jerome, *Hebr. Nom.*	*Hieronymi liber interpretationis hebraicorum nominum*, P. de Lagarde (ed.), in *Onomastica Sacra* (Göttingen, 1887 edn), and in CCSL lxxii
Jordan	R. Jordan, *Handbuch der mittelenglischen Grammatik*, rev. C. Matthes and K. Dietz (Heidelberg, 1968)
JWCI	*Journal of the Warburg and Courtauld Institute*
L	Latin
LGosp.	Lindisfarne Gospels (OE gloss, Northumbrian)
LM	*The Leofric Missal*, F. E. Warren (ed.) (Oxford, 1883)
MA	*Medieval Archaeology*
MÆ	*Medium Ævum*
ME	Middle English
MED	Middle English Dictionary
MGH	Monumenta Germaniae Historica
MLN	*Modern Language Notes*

MP	*Modern Philology*
Napier	A. S. Napier, *Old English Glosses* (Oxford, 1900)
Neophil.	*Neophilologus*
NM	*Neuphilologische Mitteilungen*
North.	Northumbrian
NQ	*Notes and Queries*
ODEE	The Oxford Dictionary of English Etymology
OE	Old English
OED	Oxford English Dictionary
OL	Old Latin
OW	Old Welsh
PBA	*Proceedings of the British Academy*
PBB	H. Paul and W. Braune (eds), *Beiträge zur Geschichte der deutschen Sprache und Literatur*
PG	Patrologia cursus completus, series Graeca
PL	Patrologia cursus completus, series Latina
PMLA	*Publications of the Modern Language Association of America*
PPs	*Paris Psalter* (ASPR, vol. v)
PQ	*Philological Quarterly*
Pr.	Primitive
PRIA	*Proceedings of the Royal Irish Academy*
Ps.	Psalm (cited by Vulgate numbers, with Authorized Version numbers in brackets)
RES	*The Review of English Studies*
RGosp.	Rushworth Gospels (OE gloss, Mercian and Northumbrian)
Rood	*The Dream of the Rood*
SB	E. Sievers, *Altenglische Grammatik*, rev. K. Brunner (Tübingen, 1965 edn)
SC	Sources Chrétiennes
SGG	*Studia Germanica Gandensia*
sim.	similarly
Skeat	W. W. Skeat (ed.), *The Holy Gospels in Anglo-Saxon, Northumbrian, and Old Mercian Versions* (Cambridge, 1871–87)

SN	*Studia Neophilologica*
W	Welsh
WS	West Saxon
WW	T. Wright, *Anglo-Saxon and Old English Vocabularies*, R. P. Wülcker (ed.) (London, 1884, repr. Darmstadt, 1968)
ZfdA	*Zeitschrift für deutsches Altertum*

Introduction

I THE MANUSCRIPT

1 History, Provenance and Origin

Oxford, Bodleian Library MS Junius 11 (SC 5123) is one of the four great codices of OE poetry and contains the unique texts of *Genesis, Exodus, Daniel,* and *Christ and Satan.* Since the edition by JUNIUS (1655) the manuscript has been known as 'the Cædmon manuscript' because its contents partly match the subjects upon which, according to Bede (*Historia Ecclesiastica,* iv, 24), Cædmon composed verses in OE. There is, however, no known connection between the manuscript and Cædmon, nor is it thought that he was the author of the poems contained in it. Indeed the variation in style and treatment between the four poems is so great that they are not thought to be the work even of a single author, and they may not have been composed even at the same time.

The compilation of the manuscript evidently began about the year 1000, the date given to the handwriting of the major part of it (containing *Genesis, Exodus,* and *Daniel*);[1] *Christ and Satan* was added in the first quarter of the eleventh century. Most of the illustrations too must date from this period (c. 1000),[2] although some drawings date from the second half of

---

[1] Ker, *Catalogue of MSS containing AS* (1957) 406–8.

[2] D. T. Rice, *English Art 871–1100* (Oxford, 1952) 203–5. The illustrations were dated 'second quarter of the eleventh century' by C. R. Morey [in Kennedy, *Cædmon Poems* (1916) 191], followed by F. Wormald in *Archaeologia* xci (1945) 121, 134, and in *English Drawings of the Tenth and Eleventh Centuries* (London, 1952) 76, no. 50 (for comment see also pp. 40–1), but for reasons that will appear the illustrations must be contemporary with the handwriting. W. Holmqvist [*Acta Archaeologia* xxii (1951) 47–8], who dates the art in MS Junius 11 to c. 1000, suggested that the later dating of the MS art arose from the fact that it apparently shows Scandinavian influence, a factor which he would discount.

the twelfth century. [1] The principal illustrations, which are
line-drawings (one painted in part, p. 11) by two artists, the
second using coloured inks, belong to the 'Winchester School'
and were formerly thought to have been executed at Canter-
bury. [2] However, new evidence has now come to light on the
basis of which the manuscript may be assigned with some confi-
dence to Malmesbury.

The assignation to Canterbury began with M. R. James who
tentatively identified the 'Genesis anglice depicta' in the early-
fourteenth-century catalogue of Christ Church, Canterbury,
with MS Junius 11. [3] This 'Genesis anglice depicta' could have
been any appropriate manuscript, perhaps even the OE illus-
trated Hexateuch (British Library, Cotton MS Claudius B iv)
later known to have been at St Augustine's, Canterbury. [4] All
subsequent attributions of MS Junius 11 to Canterbury have
been based on unfounded confidence in James's suggestion.

There are three main arguments for assigning MS Junius 11
to the Benedictine Abbey of the Blessed Virgin Mary and St
Aldhelm at Malmesbury (Wilts), the first and third being
straightforward, the second too complex to be presented here
in full.

(1) The second artist is to be identified with the artist of the
Vices and Virtues illustrations in the 'Corpus Prudentius'
(Cambridge, Corpus Christi College MS 23, containing Pru-
dentius's *Psychomachia*), a Malmesbury book. [5] This identifica-

---

[1] Those on p. 31 (lion) and p. 96: Wormald, *English Drawings* 76, Rice,
op. cit. 203; see also Ohlgren, *Speculum* xlvii (1972) 227–33.

[2] On the term 'Winchester School' see F. Wormald, 'Decorated Initials
in English MSS from A.D. 900 to 1100', *Archaeologia* xci (1945) 107–35,
esp. 131–3. On p. 134 Wormald assigns the MS to Christ Church, Canter-
bury, but in *English Drawings* (p. 76) he says of it 'Origin uncertain, but it
probably belonged to Christ Church, Canterbury'.

[3] *The Ancient Libraries of Canterbury and Dover* (Cambridge, 1903) pp. xxv–
xxvi and no. 304 on pp. 51 and 509.

[4] C. R. Dodwell & P. Clemoes (eds), *The OE Illustrated Hexateuch*, EEMF
xviii (Copenhagen, 1974) 15–16.

[5] For the identification of the artists see Pächt & Alexander, *Illum. MSS
in Bodleian* III (1973) 5, and Temple, *AS MSS* (1976) 18, 77; cf. Ker,
Catalogue 407. For a description of CCCC 23 and the attribution to Malmes-
bury based on an inscription containing the name of Abbot Æthelweard II

tion makes it likely that both manuscripts were produced at one place. Since the provenance of the 'Corpus Prudentius' is Malmesbury, and since, in view of (2) and (3) below the likely provenance of MS Junius 11 is Malmesbury, it seems most probable that the two manuscripts were produced there.

(2) There is very close and exclusive correspondence between features of some of the illustrations in MS Junius 11 and features of some of the carved medallions (c. 1170–80) on the voussoirs of the entrance arch of the south porch of Malmesbury Abbey. [1] In particular the inclusion of a figure steering in *Noah's Ark upon the Waters* is found only in the Junius 11 illustration (p. 66) and the Malmesbury carving (Galbraith 44). Also the scene depicting *Eve Spinning and Adam Digging* (with a spade) is implied in the Junius 11 illustration of the *Expulsion* (p. 45) but nowhere else in English pre-Conquest art (Galbraith 41–2), and there is a 'striking' stylistic relationship between the depictions of *Adam and Eve Hiding* in MS Junius 11 (p. 41) and at Malmesbury (Galbraith 47, n. 2). Evidently the carvings at Malmesbury were based on manuscript illustrations, but whether in part directly on MS Junius 11 cannot be determined since the Malmesbury carvings also show affinity with the OE illustrated Hexateuch (Claudius B iv) known to have been at Canterbury. Possibly Malmesbury possessed another illustrated manuscript from which both the artist(s) of MS Junius 11 and the sculptors of the carved medallions worked.

(3) At the bottom of p. 2 of MS Junius 11 there occurs an addition to the manuscript, a medallion portrait entitled 'ælfwine'. [2] This name was quite common among the

---

(c.1033/4–c.1043/4) see M. R. James, *A Descriptive Catalogue of the MSS in . . . CCCC* (Cambridge, 1912) i 44–6. For reproductions of the artist's work in CCCC 23 see R. Stettiner, *Die Illustrierten Prudentius-Handschriften* (Berlin, 1905) pls 49/50 (1–7), 31/32, 51/52 (1–7), 53/54 (1–6), 55/56 (1–7), 57/58 (1–6), 59/60 (1–7), 61/62 (1–6), 63/64 (1–6), 33/34, 65/66 (1–10).

[1] See K. J. Galbraith, 'The Iconography of the Biblical Scenes at Malmesbury Abbey', *JBAA* III xxviii (1965) 39–56. There are also correspondences between some of the illustrations in CCCC 23 and some of the Malmesbury carvings: see Galbraith 54 n. 3.

[2] Temple, *AS MSS* 77, wrongly assigns this medallion to the first artist.

Anglo-Saxons but in view of (1) and (2) above is very likely to be that of the Ælfwine who was abbot of Malmesbury for one and a half years from c. 1043/4 to c. 1045/6. [1]

These three arguments, considered in conjunction with each other, provide strong reason to believe that MS Junius 11 was produced at Malmesbury. There too, no doubt, the manuscript was bound. This binding dates from the first half of the eleventh century. [2] The manuscript is secured to oak boards (covered with whittawed leather) on five bands, headband and tailband of cord, and three horizontal bands of leather thong. Since the use of cord for this purpose was being discontinued in the first half of the eleventh century [3] the covers must have been made and attached before c. 1050. Later there was some re-sewing, probably in the late thirteenth century (c. 1270), the date of the handwriting of some pen trials found on a parchment reinforcing piece used to hold gathering 2 together.

While the book was still in sheets, folded but probably not yet sewn and certainly not covered, it was probably exposed to thick soot-laden smoke, the only likely explanation for the stain running down the inside margin of many leaves, notably pp. 7, 90/91, 116/17, 128/9, 130 (at foot), 143 (at foot), 148/9, 154/5, 170/71, 180/81, 195, 211, 212/13, 226/7 and some others. [4] Presumably there was a fire in the vicinity of the manuscript at some time before c. 1050. This fire was probably that which, according to William of Malmesbury (d. 1143), destroyed 'totum cenobium' at Malmesbury in the time of Edward the Confessor (1042–66); [5] H. Brakspear dated this fire to 1042. [6]

[1] D. Knowles, C. N. L. Brooke, & V. C. M. London, *Heads of Religious Houses* . . . (Cambridge, 1972) 54. Ælfwine succeeded Æthelweard II whose name appears in an inscription in CCCC 23.

[2] Stoddard, *Anglia* x (1888) 158, followed by GOLLANCZ (1927) p.xxxv, and Timmer, *Later Genesis* (1948) 3, was wrong in assigning this binding to 1450–75.

[3] See G. Pollard, 'Some Anglo-Saxon Bookbindings', *The Book Collector* xxiv (1975) 130–59 esp. 136.

[4] *Ex informatione* G. Pollard (private communication).

[5] *Gesta Pontificum*, ed. N.E.S.A. Hamilton, Rolls Series 52 (London, 1870) 363.

[6] *Archaeologia* lxiv (1913) 400. But there seems to be no clear evidence for fixing the date.

Presumably the manuscript remained in the monastery library at Malmesbury until the Dissolution of the Monasteries (1539). After the Dissolution the first information concerning the whereabouts of the manuscript comes from the seventeenth century. Some time before 1651 [1] it was acquired by James Ussher (1581–1656), archbishop of Armagh, who early in the century was collecting books for the library of Trinity College, Dublin. [2] In all probability Ussher got the manuscript from Sir Simonds D'Ewes (1602–50), a member of the Long Parliament (1640–53) and AS antiquarian; [3] certainly it was seen while in D'Ewes's possession by the Dutch scholar Johannes de Laet (1582–1649), probably during de Laet's visit to London in January 1637. [4] Presumably the manuscript passed from D'Ewes to Ussher at some time before D'Ewes's death in 1650, [5] and Ussher gave it to his friend Junius, possibly as a parting gift in 1651.

Franciscus Junius (1589–1677), or François du Jon, was a Dutch scholar much interested in OE philology and AS antiquities. He came to England in 1621 as librarian to the earl of Arundel and tutor to his son, and stayed for thirty years before returning to the Netherlands to live with his sister. Junius, an exemplary student who worked fourteen hours a day, published his edition of the manuscript in 1655. In 1674 he returned to England to take up residence in Oxford and on his death in 1677 it was bequeathed to the university together with his other books and acquired by the Bodleian Library in 1678, where it has remained ever since. It is of course after

[1] We know this because Junius, who got the MS from Ussher, left England for the Netherlands in 1651 and published his edition of it in Amsterdam in 1655. It is hardly likely that the MS changed hands outside England.

[2] See W. O'Sullivan, 'Ussher as a Collector of Manuscripts', *Hermathena* lxxxviii (1956) 34–58.

[3] On whom see A. G. Watson, *The Library of Sir Simonds D'Ewes* (London, 1966), esp. 9–10. D'Ewes may have been the first person to appreciate the importance of MS Junius 11.

[4] GOLLANCZ, p. xv; Timmer, *Later Genesis* 5–8.

[5] Watson, *loc. cit.*, notes that D'Ewes lent Ussher three MSS in 1641 (MSS Harley 208, 213, 556) and bequeathed him another (Dublin, Trinity College MS 186).

Junius that the manuscript is known as 'the Junius manuscript'
of OE poetry.

2 General Description

The manuscript has been fully described by GOLLANCZ and by
Ker (*Catalogue*, pp. 406–8). Here only the salient features are
given together with a full analysis of those that affect *Exodus*.

(i)   Foliation: 116 folios, paginated i, ii, 1–230.

(ii)   Material: parchment.

(iii) Size: (a) Outer edge of leaf, about 321×195 mm.
          (b) Written space, about 225×112–20 mm.

(iv) Ruling: 26 long lines.

(v)   Quiring: 17 gatherings, at least 11 of which origi-
nally had eight leaves.

(vi) Handwriting: pp.1–212 are written in one hand of
about 1000, pp.213–28 in two hands of 1000–1025,
p.229 in another hand probably of the same period.
P.229 ends 'FINIT LIBER .II. AMEN.' and hence
pp.213–29 are known as Book II and pp. i, ii, 1–212 as
Book I.

(vii) Ornamentation and Illustrations: pp.1–71, 143 by one
artist, pp.73–88 by another 'better' artist, p.225 by a
third artist. After p.88 the spaces left for drawings re-
main blank, except for p.99 which contains the begin-
ning of a metalpoint outline drawing of a bird. [1] P.96
contains an unfinished drawing by a twelfth-century
artist.

(viii) Corrections: some spelling-alterations occur on pp.
1–26 (also some changes in punctuation) and in Book
II, possibly by one 'eleventh-century corrector'; [2] it
seems likely that the corrections are 'closely contem-
porary with the manuscript' (KRAPP, p. xiii), probably

[1] For this and other drawings visible with the aid of ultra-violet light
see Ohlgren in *Speculum* xlvii (1972) figs 1–2, 4–6 (after p. 228).

[2] The term used by Ker, *Catalogue* 407. See also Clubb, *Christ and Satan*
(1925), pp. xv and xvi–xvii.

before the book was bound (c. 1050).[1] The same hand probably added accents and hyphens throughout; the fact that the accents and most of the alterations are in red ink on p.23 would suggest as much. Red ink is also used for alterations on p.218. Of these corrections only accents and hyphens occur in the text of *Exodus*, except for a point added (or, rather, misplaced) in verse 21a after *þy*[2] and the guide-letter *h* by line 107 (see Textual note).

Exodus occupies gatherings 12, 13, and the first three pages of 14. *Gathering 12* (pp.143–54) must have originally contained eight leaves, i.e. four folded sheets of parchment, but the central two leaves are lost leaving the present six (see diagram).

The Twelfth Gathering

As a result there is a lacuna in the text between line 141 (the last line on p.148) and line 142 (the first line on p.149). *Gathering 13* (pp.155–68) is also incomplete. Originally it contained eight leaves, but the sixth leaf has been cut out (see diagram); the stub of the excised leaf is clearly visible in the manuscript. Consequently there is a lacuna in the text between

---

[1] On these spelling-alterations see KRAPP, pp. xiii–xvi, and Timmer. *Later Genesis* 39–42. Cf. also E. G. Stanley, 'Spellings of the *Waldend* Group', in E. B. Atwood & A. A. Hill (eds), *Studies in Language, Literature, and Culture of the Middle Ages and Later* (Austin, Texas, 1969) 38–69.

[2] Cf. *Daniel* 543a and 685a where the corrector has probably added a point correctly at the end of the verse.

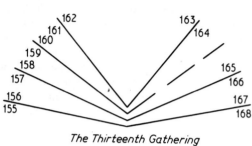

The Thirteenth Gathering

line 446 (the last line on p.163 – p.164 is blank) and line 447
(the first line on p.166 – p.165 is blank). *Gathering 14* (pp.169–
80) presents no problems as far as *Exodus* is concerned: the
poem ends on p.171, p.172 is blank, and *Daniel* begins on p.173.

3 Sectional Divisions

The text of pp.1–212 is divided into sections by Roman nu-
merals entered spasmodically in a continuous series, the first
number 'VII' occurring on p.17 and the last, 'LV', on p.209;
for a complete list of where these divisions occur see KRAPP,
pp. xxxix–xl. The numbers are in the hand and ink of the text.
Of the eight sections in *Exodus* only four are numbered. All the
sectional numbers coincide with the presence of large, some-
times ornamental, initial capital letters and it is assumed that
these large capitals also mark the beginning of a new section.
There are seven such initial capitals (or spaces left for them) in
Exodus; one is lost. Strictly these capital letters marking sec-
tional divisions should be considered as part of the punctuation
(pp.17–24 below) but for the sake of convenience they are dealt
with separately here.

All the sections in *Exodus* begin in gatherings 12 and 13 but
there is a difference in practice between the two. In gathering
12 only the first section is numbered (XLII). This, the begin-
ning of the poem, is also marked by a large zoomorphic initial
capital H by the first artist (responsible for pp.1–71). The be-

ginnings of the other three sections in this gathering are de-
duced from the spaces left blank for initial large capitals. Since
these spaces are not large enough to incorporate the work of
the first artist, it is assumed that the first artist drew the zoo-
morphic H on p.143 before the scribe began writing *Exodus*,
and that when the scribe did begin *Exodus* the first artist was
no longer available. GOLLANCZ (p. xix) suggested that the
spaces left for other capitals in this gathering are of a suitable
size for the work of the second artist. In gathering 13 three
sections are numbered (XLVI, XLVII, and XLVIIII) and
marked at the beginning by rather crude large capitals written
by the scribe; presumably the second artist was no longer
available and no replacement had been found. Evidently the
beginning of section XLVIII and the initial capital that ac-
companied it occurred on the leaf lost from between p.164 and
p.165. This lost leaf must have contained the text of the whole
section.

Section XLIIII (the number is not entered by the scribe)
poses a special problem since the initial capital (marked by a
space with guide-letter *h*) occurs in mid-sentence:

Folc wæs on salum,

Hlud heriges cyrm. (106–7)

Evidently the position of the beginning of this section is wrongly
marked, presumably because a scribe erroneously thought that
a new page coincided with the beginning of a new section. [1]
If this section-division were accepted the preceding section
(XLIII) would be the shortest (44 lines) in the poem and,
indeed, in Book I of the manuscript. The correct position for
the division is probably at line 135, *Ðær*; so it is assumed in this
edition.

In the Table the section numbers in square brackets are not
found in the manuscript and other figures in square brackets
are ones that do not have manuscript authority. As the Table

---

[1] The beginning of section VII is also wrongly marked but GOLLANCZ
explains the error as due to a misunderstanding between the scribe and the
artist (pp. xxx–xxxi).

gathering	section	lines	lines per section
12	XLII	1–62	62
	[XLIII]	63–[134]	[72]
	[XLIIII]	[135]–141+	[7]+
		Lacuna	
	[XLV]	142–251	110
13	XLVI	252–318	67
	XLVII	319–446	128
	[XLVIII]	Lacuna	
	XLVIIII	447–590	144

shows the shortest section which has manuscript authority is
62 lines long (1–62) and the longest 144 lines long (447–590).
Elsewhere in Book I of the manuscript the shortest section is
46 lines long (*Genesis* 872–917) and the longest 180 lines long
(*Daniel* 495–674). In the Exeter Book the variation is 62 (*Christ*
378–439) to 135 (*Christ* 1530–1664), in the Vercelli Book it is
72 (*Elene* 547–618) to 132 (*Andreas* 469–600), in *Beowulf* 43
(456–498) to 142 (2460–2601). In Book II of MS Junius 11
the sections are shorter than usual, ranging from 30 lines long
(*Christ and Satan* 224–53) to 76 (*Christ and Satan* 365–440). The
average length of a section (leaving those of uncertain length
out of account) is: in *Exodus* 102 lines, in *Genesis* 81 lines, in
Daniel 138 lines, in *Christ and Satan* 55 lines, compared with,
for example, 74 lines in *Beowulf*, 88 lines in *Elene*, 112 lines in
Judith. [1]

These sectional divisions have been variously interpreted. [2]

[1] Some of these figures are taken from B. J. Timmer, 'Sectional Divisions
of Poems in Old English Manuscripts', *MLR* xlvii (1952) 319–22, esp. 319,
but the figures he gives for MS Junius 11, Book I, are incorrect because he
fails to take the lacunae into account. If the lines estimated to be lost in the
lacunae are taken into account the average length of a section in *Exodus* was
92 lines: see below, p.15.

[2] According to H. Bradley, 'The Numbered Sections in Old English
Poetical MSS.', *PBA* vii (1915–16) 165–87 (followed by W. A. Craigie,
'Interpolations and Omissions in Anglo-Saxon Poetic Texts', *Philologica* ii

Three facts must be borne in mind in the assessment of them. (1) The divisions occur at line divisions, often, but not always, where there is a shift in subject-matter (e.g. 63, 252, but cf. 319), and normally at the beginning of a sentence, but there are three instances of sections beginning with *oðþæt*: *Genesis* 1248 (XX), also *Beowulf* 1740 (XXV), 2039 (XXVIII). (2) Since the numbers are entered spasmodically they must have existed in or been entered in the exemplar. (3) The numbers continue in a series over the work of four authors (*Genesis A, Genesis B, Exodus, Daniel*). From (3) it follows that even if the divisions were authorial the scribe viewed them in relation to manuscript compilation rather than individual poetic structure. From (2) it follows that at some stage in the transmission of the poems a scribe thought the sections and their numeration sufficiently important to mark them with a continuous series of numbers; if the numbering was originally authorial it would have started at I for each poem. From the irregularities in (1), especially the sections beginning with *oðþæt*, which could introduce an independent statement (Klaeber, *Beowulf*, p. lvii, n. 6), as perhaps in *Genesis* 1248 (cf. Kennedy's translation, p.46) but not in the two *Beowulf* instances, it would appear that the sectional divisions are more likely to be the work of a scribe than the author. These deductions need to be considered in relation to the comparison of the sectional divisions with the amount of text suitable for a single continuous reading in a monastery. This comparison is made in the *Praefatio in librum antiquum lingua Saxonica conscriptum*, printed in Matthias Flacius Illy-

---

(1924) 5–19), the sections represent the contents of the separate sheets of parchment (with the numbers marking the order) in the poet's holograph MS, but this view has been refuted by GOLLANCZ (pp. xxxi–xxxii); see also R. E. Woolf, 'The Lost Opening to the "Judith" ', *MLR* 1 (1955) 168–72, esp. 168–70. For attempts to read literary significance (in terms of structural patterning) into the divisions see E. Carrigan, 'Structure and Thematic Development in *Beowulf*', *PRIA* (C) lxvi (1967) 1–51; D. R. Howlett, 'Form and Genre in *Beowulf*', *SN* xlvi (1974) 309–25, esp. 317–25; E. R. Anderson, 'Cynewulf's *Elene*: Manuscript Divisions and Structural Symmetry', *MP* lxxii (1974) 111–22.

ricus's *Catalogus Testium Veritatis* (1562 edn).[1] The *Praefatio* is
taken to be from a prefatory statement which was probably
attached to a copy of the Old Saxon biblical epic *The Heliand*
sent from Germany to England; this statement apparently
dates from the time of Louis the Pious, holy Roman emperor
(813–40). In the *Praefatio* the following sentence occurs:

> Juxta morem vero illius poematis omne opus per vitteas
> distinxit, quas nos lectiones vel sententias possumus appel-
> lare.

The writer seems to be equating the division of poetry into
fitts (presumably the same as our sectional divisions) with the
division of material suitable for public reading in a monastery
into *lectiones vel sententias*. That it is the nature of the divisions
which are equated is suggested by the tentativeness of *possumus*
and by the inclusion of both *lectiones* and *sententias*, for they are
not identical except possibly in effect – whereas a *lectio* is a
reading-portion a *sententia* is a complete statement on a given
topic. This deduction is supported, if somewhat tenuously,
by the entry in the Erfurt Glossary

ampusatio, una lectio: fiit.[2]

Here the word *ampusatio* (presumably for *amputatio*) can hardly
be incorporated in the sense-equation unless the dominant
notion is 'division'. Thus the comparison made by the writer
of the *Praefatio* may imply that the sectional divisions of OE
poetry are reading-portions but need not necessarily do so.

[1] See F. P. Magoun, 'The *Praefatio* and *Versus* associated with some Old-
Saxon Biblical Poems', in *Medieval Studies in Honor of J. D. M. Ford*, ed.
U. T. Holmes & A. J. Denomy (Cambridge, Mass., 1948) 107–36. The
Praefatio is reprinted in O. Behaghel (ed.), *Heliand und Genesis* (Halle, 1948
edn) 1–2, and the relevant passage is quoted and discussed by GOLLANCZ,
p. xxxii, and Timmer in *MLR* xlvii 320–21 and *Later Genesis* 16–17. Since
the *Praefatio* has not survived in a known medieval manuscript its authen-
ticity is doubtful; cf. T. M. Andersson, 'The Caedmon Fiction in the *Heliand*
Preface', *PMLA* lxxxix (1974) 278–84.

[2] Quoted from H. Sweet, *Oldest English Texts*, EETS 83 (1885) 109, no.
1144; *fiit* is presumably for *fitt*.

4 Lay-out and Lacunae

As it was originally conceived the manuscript was intended to combine text with illustration. Some care was taken by the scribe to leave suitable spaces for the illustrator(s): the words *healf trymt* (p.98) and *healf īmt* (p.100), written by the scribe in the margin by the penultimate (25th) line, were evidently to remind him to leave the top half of p.99 and of p.101 blank (OE *tramet* 'page'). However, since the illustrators never finished their work, what is left as far as *Exodus* is concerned is a combination of text and blank parchment. The Table gives for each page the number of ruled lines (1) with text, and (2) without text. The average number of ruled lines written with text is fractionally over 15, equivalent to 20 verse-lines.

page	*lines with text*	*lines without text*	*remarks*
143	25 at top	1 at bottom	
144	11 at bottom	15 at top	
145	13 at top	13 at bottom	
146	25		top line left blank, beginning of section [XLIII]
147	9 at top	17 at bottom	
148	26		beginning of section [XLIIII] wrongly placed
Lacuna of four pages			
149	17 at top	8 at bottom	top line left blank, beginning of section [XLV]
150		26	
151	25 at top	1 at bottom	
152		26	
153	9 at top	17 at bottom	
154	26		
155	8 at top	18 at bottom	

page	lines with text	lines without text	remarks
156	19 at top	7 at bottom	beginning of section XLVI
157	9 at bottom	17 at top	
158	24 at top	2 at bottom	end of section XLVI
159		26	
160	26		beginning of section XLVII
161	26		
162	26		
163	20 at top	6 at bottom	
164		26	*tribus annis transactis* in later hand
Lacuna of two pages			
165		26	
166	26		beginning of section XLVIIII
167	22 at top	4 at bottom	
168		26	
169	26		
170	26		
171	10 at top	16 at bottom	end of poem

The fact that space was to be left for the illustrations makes it much more difficult to estimate the extent of the lacunae than it would be if all the ruled lines were written with text. There are two lacunae, one of four pages between p.148 and p.149, another of two pages between p.164 and p.165. Of these the second is the more straightforward. Since both p.164 and p.165 are without text it is probable that the relevant space on both sides of the intervening leaf now lost was completely occupied with text.[1] On this assumption 66 verse-lines are lost.

[1] Despite the frequency of illustrations (or spaces left for them) it is quite common for a folio to be completely written with text on both sides. In Book I this phenomenon occurs 14 times: pp. 21–2, 25–6, 29–30, 37–8, 71–2, 79–80, 89–90, 91–2, 93–4, 97–8, 161–2, 169–70, 173–4, 191–2.

This estimate accords well with the evidence from the sectional divisions. It seems likely that section XLVII, the last words of which (line 446) occur on p.163, actually ended there (see also below, p. 20) and that the missing leaf started with the beginning of the missing section XLVIII. This lost leaf must also have contained the end of the missing section since p.165 contains no text and section XLVIIII begins on p.166. In other words the lost leaf contained the lost section, wholly and exclusively. A section of 66 lines is in accord with the known length of sections XLII (62 lines) and XLVI (67 lines).

The first lacuna, of four pages between p.148 and p.149, is more difficult. On the assumption that these four pages, considered as a group, contained the average amount of text per page 80 verse-lines are lost. These 80 lines would have been the remainder of section XLIIII which is assumed to begin at line 135 but which the scribe marked wrongly as beginning at line 107 (see above, p. 9). There could be no objection to a section of 87 lines (135–41 plus the 80 lost lines).

If these estimates of the number of lines lost are accepted *Exodus* was originally 736 lines long and the average length of a section was 92 lines.

5 The Intended Illustrations

Even blank spaces are evidence. They are so because they occur at irregular intervals in the text. In the overall conception of the manuscript which preceded the actual making of it someone, presumably an artist, must have devised a plan of how much space was to be left, where it was to be left, and for what illustrations.[1] Since the illustrations of serial topics such as a biblical book tended to come in cycles which were copied or adapted from one manuscript to another it ought to be possible, by collating known Exodus illustrations with the spaces left in MS Junius 11, to recreate much of what was in

[1] Cf. G. Henderson, *JWCI* xxv (1962) 191, and *Stud. in Mem. D. T. Rice* (1975) 113. For a discussion of this process in relation to one particular case see C. R. Dodwell & P. Clemoes (eds) *The OE Illustrated Hexateuch*, EEMF xviii (Copenhagen, 1974) 53–8.

the deviser's mind. For an attempt at such a recreation I have utilized two manuscripts in facsimile, the seventh-century continental (possibly Spanish) Ashburnham Pentateuch (Paris, Bibliothèque Nationale, MS nouv. acq. lat. 2334) and the OE illustrated Hexateuch (London, British Library, Cotton MS Claudius B iv). [1] It appears, however, that there were to be more illustrations in MS Junius 11 than can be accounted for by reference to these two other manuscripts. [2] Much of the attempted recreation must therefore be regarded as very tentative. In the following list the pages where spaces are left are given with an indication of the extent of the space and this is followed by the possible subject of the illustration had it been provided and a reference where appropriate to the folio in the Ashburnham Pentateuch (P) or OE illustrated Hexateuch (H) (and the description of the folio in the relevant introduction) where such an illustration may be found. Relatively small spaces in the lower parts of pages 149, 156, 163 and 167 have been left out of account.

- p. 144, upper half: The Slaying of the First-born (P 65b item 1).
- p. 145, lower half: The Israelites depart from Egypt (H 90v *above*).
- p. 147, lower half: The Lord leads the Israelites in the Pillar of Cloud by Day (H 90v *centre*).

A Lacuna of four pages probably contained text plus illustrations relating to the Story of Joseph.

- p. 150, whole: The Israelites fearful at the Advance of the Egyptians (cf. P 68a item 1).
- p. 152, whole: The Egyptians in Pursuit of the Israelites (H 91v).

[1] O. von Gebhardt, *The Miniatures of the Ashburnham Pentateuch* (London, 1883); see also E. A. Lowe, *Codices Latini Antiquiores*, V (Oxford, 1950), no. 693a, and (for the suggestion of Spanish origin) C. R. Dodwell, *Painting in Europe* 800–1200 (Harmondsworth, 1971) 114. For the Hexateuch see the preceding note. For a bibliography (unfortunately not complete) of depictions of relevant Exodus scenes in early Christian art see L. Réau, *Iconographie de l'Art Chrétien*, II. i (Paris, 1956) 179 and 191–6.

[2] Cf. Henderson, *loc. cit.* in *JWCI*, and *Stud. in Mem. D. T. Rice* 133–4.

p. 153, lower half: (?) The Pillar of Cloud divides the Israelites and the Egyptians.

p. 155, lower half: (?) The Israelites ready to cross the Red Sea.

p. 157, upper half: Moses divides the Red Sea (H 91v).

p. 159, whole: The Israelites cross the Red Sea (H 92r).

p. 164, whole: Abraham restrained from killing Isaac (H 38r).

A Lacuna of two pages almost certainly completely filled with text.

p. 165, whole: The Immersion of the Egyptians in the Red Sea (P 68a item 2; the lack of such an illustration in H is remarked as 'surprising' by Clemoes, p.55).

p. 168, whole: Moses and the Israelites rejoice (H 92v).

p. 171, lower half: The Israelites collect Booty on the Further Shore (cf. H 92r).

6 Punctuation

Besides the large capitals, which mark sectional divisions, the scribe of MS Junius 11 employed the following means of registering punctuation:[1]

(i) small capitals,

(ii) the end-of-section marker, a point on the line followed by what Isidore of Seville (*Etymologiae* I.xxi) calls a *positura* followed by another point above the line, .7·,

(iii) the continuity marker, a point on the line followed by an accent above the line, .´,

(iv) the single point, (.).

Previous discussion of this punctuation, especially of the use of the small capitals, has unfortunately suffered from the shortcomings of what was then known about medieval punctuation.

---

[1] On the signs available to early medieval punctuators see M. B. Parkes, 'Medieval Punctuation: a Preliminary Survey', *Codicologica*, ed. A. Gruys & J. P. Gumbert, Litterae Textuales, in the press.

GOLLANCZ (p.xx) found the use of small capitals in *Exodus* 'logical so far as employed'. According to KRAPP (p.xx) the small capitals in MS Junius 11 'are not systematically used, but when they appear it is almost always possible to see a definite purpose in their use. . . . Most frequently the small capitals are logical and mark the beginning of a minor division in the narrative, that is, of a paragraph.' These statements require considerable qualification.[1] Judgment as to whether punctuation-markers are used 'systematically' or not necessarily depends on a knowledge of the overall purpose lying behind their use. This purpose can usually only be deduced by comparing the effect of the punctuation with contemporary precepts laid down for the guidance of punctuators.[2] If there is very close and thorough agreement between prescription and practice, and if there is good reason to think the punctuator was influenced by the particular precepts involved, then it would be permissible to speak of punctuation being used 'systematically' (cf. below, pp. 21–2). KRAPP's use of 'purpose' is misleading; it is essential to distinguish between purpose, which can usually only be deduced, and effect, which can be observed and described. Use of the term 'logical', unless qualified by 'in effect', carries with it the danger of pronouncing judgment before weighing the evidence. A modern grammatical function is not necessarily to be assumed for medieval punctuation.

Fundamentally all punctuation indicates the relationship between sense-units.[3] In *Exodus* the manuscript punctuation marks divisions between sense-units or groups of sense-units. To a large extent this punctuation was probably related to the reading or recitation of the text aloud. Thus it will probably

[1] Consideration of them here is confined to *Exodus*.

[2] On late antique usage see R. W. Müller, *Rhetorische und Syntaktische Interpunktion* (Tübingen, 1964). For the later period see C. Thurot, *Notices et Extraits de divers Manuscrits Latins pour servir à l'histoire des doctrines grammaticales au Moyen Âge*, in *Notices et Extraits des Manuscrits de la Bibliothèque Impériale*, vol. xxii, pt 2 (Paris, 1868) esp. 407–17.

[3] For a discussion leading to this definition see Peter J. Lucas, 'Sense-Units and the Use of Punctuation-markers in John Capgrave's *Chronicle*', *Archivum Linguisticum* n.s. ii (1971) 1–24 esp. 2.

give indications for pause; it may also have been 'concerned with indicating inflexion of the voice, so that a person reading aloud could see where the voice was to be raised and where it was to be allowed to drop.'[1]

(i) *Small capitals*

In addition to the large capitals which mark sectional divisions there are a number of small capitals which occur elsewhere in the text of *Exodus*. Some difficulty has been experienced in identifying these small capitals since they are often merely ordinary letters written larger. GOLLANCZ (pp. xix-xx) found twenty such small capitals, but KRAPP (p. xlii) lists twenty-seven; IRVING notes the difficulty (p.44) but does not discuss them. An independent investigation vindicates GOLLANCZ absolutely and the occurrence of these small capitals is listed in the Table.

19 Heah	124 Nymðe	266 Ne	419 Ne
22 Ða	135 Ðær	276 Hof	526 Run
30 Hæfde	164 Wonn	278 Hwæt	549 Swa
93 Him	208 Hæfde	377 Swa	554 Micel
120 Hæfde	259 Ne	415 Ne	563 Gesittað

Nine of the small capitals in *Exodus* mark positions of substantial pause. Four of these occur at the beginning of a speech (259, 278, 419, 554), one where the narrative is resumed after a speech (276), another where the main narrative thread is resumed after a didactic passage (549), and three where there is a break in the narrative such as would be marked by a new paragraph (30, 135,[2] 208). Seven of the small capitals mark positions of pause. Six of these occur at the beginning of sentences containing matter that could be regarded as resumptive (93, 377), summary (22, 120), or emphatic (19, 266), and one occurs at the beginning of a co-ordinate clause 'linked' to its predecessor by asyndetic parataxis (415), a clause containing matter that could perhaps

[1] E. A. Loew, *The Beneventan Script* (Oxford, 1914) 231.
[2] Taken as the correct place for section XLIIII to begin.

be regarded as emphatic. Of the remaining four small capitals three occur, from the grammatical point of view, in mid sentence, one at the beginning of a summatory clause (563), before the second of two parallel noun clauses (object), one at the beginning of a main clause which could be regarded as resumptive since it follows an adverbial clause of condition (526), and one at the beginning of an adverbial clause of concession whose matter could perhaps be regarded as emphatic (124). The other instance (164) occurs in mid clause at the beginning of a phrase parallel with the subject (which occurs before a parenthesis), so the phrase might be regarded as resumptive, but since the text has been incompletely preserved here the treatment of this small capital can only be tentative – possibly it is a mistake induced by starting a new page (p.151).

(ii) *The end-of-section marker*

This mark was usually associated with the marking of final pauses. It occurs only twice in *Exodus*, on both occasions at the end of what may be taken to be, or was taken to be, a sectional division. One instance is at the end of the written text on p.163, after line 446, and may be taken to mark the end of section XLVII (see also above, p. 15). The other instance occurs at the end of the written text on p.147, after line 106, and was presumably intended to mark what the scribe erroneously took to be the end of section XLIIII (see above, pp. 9 and 15).

(iii) *The continuity marker*

This mark occurs three times in *Exodus*, always at the end of the written text on a page. In one of these instances, that on p.167, after line 510, it evidently indicates that the sentence, which, since it is grammatically complete, could have been allowed to end at line 510, in fact continued on p.169, the intervening page (168) being left blank for illustration.[1] The second instance occurs on p.143, after line 29, and

---

[1] Ker, *Catalogue* 408, lists four other instances of this phenomenon, on pp. 28, 30, 32, 50. At the date of MS Junius 11 (c. 1000) the usage is early.

has a similar but not quite identical function. Since the text on
p.143 ends on the penultimate (25th) ruled line the reader's
attention is directed to the continuation of the text on the
sixteenth ruled line of p.144 (the first fifteen lines were left
blank for illustration). This usage occurs regularly in the
manuscript: all eleven instances of the continuity marker in
Daniel, for example, are strictly comparable to that on p.143. [1]
When the resumption of the text begins with a small capital,
as after the instance on p.143 and all the instances from
Daniel except that on p.196, the continuity marker indicates
that the reading of the text should continue after an appropri-
ate pause and the small capital indicates the pause appropriate
for the beginning of a new statement. The third instance of the
continuity marker in *Exodus*, which occurs on p.158, after line
318, is more difficult. Since it comes at the end of section
XLVI it is perhaps a mistake for, or was confused with, the
end-of-section marker; on the other hand perhaps the con-
tinuity marker was used because there is no significant shift
in subject-matter over the sectional division between lines 318
and 319, the only sectional division of which this can justly be
said (cf. above, p.11).

(iv) *The single point*
This mark was usually associated with the marking of minor
medial pauses. In MS Junius 11 the point is sometimes on the
line and sometimes above it but there is no consistency in
placing the point higher or lower in relation to the preceding
letter as might be observable if the scribe had wished to dis-
tinguish medial and final pauses in this way: the point appears
in the most naturally convenient place for it depending on the
last stroke of the preceding letter. The effect of the points
is to separate verses (half-lines) from each other, and hence we
have what has been called 'a metrical punctuation' (KRAPP,
p. xxii). There can be no reasonable doubt that the purpose of
the pointing was metrical. This practice of metrical pointing,

[1] Pp. 178 (line 133), 179 (157), 182 (208), 186 (254a; Farrell 255a),
189 (308), 195 (439), 196 (457), 200 (522), 203 (588), 205 (617), 207 (639).

which has classical antecedents,[1] was probably introduced
into England from the continent by the Benedictines during
the tenth century. It is found also, for example, in *The Battle
of Brunanburh* in the Parker manuscript of the *AS Chronicle*
(Cambridge, Corpus Christi College MS 173); the text of the
poem is in the part of the manuscript written at Winchester
between 950 and 975.[2]

Evidently some considerable care was taken to place the
point correctly. In line 399b a point erroneously placed in the
middle of a word has been almost erased (see Textual Note).
Despite IRVING's over-cautious statements that the scribe was
only 'quite accurate in following the meter' and marked
verses only 'fairly regularly' (p.3) the scribe's margin of error
in this regard in *Exodus* was extremely low, being approxi-
mately two per cent. This figure compares favourably with
the margin of error (over 4%) calculated for the whole of
Book I of MS Junius 11 by Lawrence.[3] The different kinds of
error are listed in the Table.

The Metrical Pointing of Exodus

A	No. of appropriate positions	1175
B	No. of points omitted at the end of an *a*-verse 11	
C	No. of points omitted at the end of a *b*-verse 3	
D	No. of points incorrectly placed for marking the end of an *a*-verse 1	
E	No. of points incorrectly placed for marking the end of a *b*-verse 2	
F	No. of points placed within an *a*-verse as well as at the end 6	
G	No. of points placed within a *b*-verse as well as at the end 2	
H	Total no. of errors 25	
I	Total no. of correct placements (ignoring rows F and G)	1158

---

[1] See E. O. Wingo, *Latin Punctuation in the Classical Age*, Janua Linguarum
ser. pract. 133 (The Hague, 1972) 158–63.

[2] R. Flower & H. Smith (eds), *The Parker Chronicle and Laws* (London,
EETS 208, 1941) ff. 26a–27a.

[3] *Alliterative Verse* (1893) 15–16.

Three of these errors are probably to be discounted. After 160b (row C) there apparently was a point in the manuscript but it has been erased. Similarly after 34a (row B), the last letters of which were written over an erasure by a corrector, the point could have been erased. The last letters of 590b too (row C) were erased and so probably was a point.

Of the remaining twenty-one errors, eighteen can be accounted for in one way or another. The pointing in lines 161–2a (row F) clearly reflects textual corruption (see Textual Note). Similarly it is evident from the misplacing of the point in 145b (row E) that the scribe did not understand the text properly (see Textual Note). In 288a (row B) the fact that there is a word missing from the text may have led to the omission of the point after this verse. Two hypermetric verses have an extra point in mid verse (571a after *feonda*, 573a after *brimu* – row F). Many of the other errors occur in conjunction with light or heavy verses. Thus points are omitted after light verses (64a, 278a, 364a, 376a, 391a, 393a – all row B) and before a light verse in 9b (row C). Extra points are included in heavy verses in 61a (after *hofu* – row F), 448b (after *deaðe* – row G), and 70a (after *forbærned* – row F) which also has anacrusis. The remaining four errors all occur in long verses (5 or 6 words). Thus there is an extra point after *healfa* in 209a (row F), one of only two normal verses consisting of six words in the poem (the other is 189a). Similarly in 143b there is an extra point after *miceles* (row G) the fourth of five words in the verse and the one carrying the alliteration. In 381b (row E) the point is misplaced after the third of five words (*neah*), again the one that carries the alliteration. The alliteration may also be the key to understanding the misplaced point in 56a (after *þy* – row D), though as in 143b the word preceding the point is the fourth of five; possibly the scribe erroneously took *oferfor* to participate in the pattern of alliteration whereas in fact the only word which does so functionally is the last, *folce*, with which *-for* alliterates accidentally.

Thus the errors are to a large extent explicable. Possibly in the eight instances (rows F and G) where a point occurs both within the verse and at the end of it the scribe intended to erase

the unwanted point: he could hardly expunct a point as he
was going along and may have forgotten or not had time to
make the appropriate erasure on revision. However that may
be there are only three errors (omissions of the point after 25a,
341a, and 510a – all row B) which seem to be due to sheer
carelessness. As far as the pointing is concerned the scribe
achieved a remarkably high standard of accuracy.

7 Scribal Error

One of the major difficulties in editing *Exodus* – and most other
OE poetry – is that it survives only in a unique text. According
to Sisam the authority of such a text is suspect, though of the
two examples of 'error' he chose to head his discussion one
(*Genesis B* 328) does not require the proposed emendation.[1]
In these circumstances a modern edition can only reproduce
what is extant with such modifications as can be shown to be
sound.

Before trying to analyse the kinds of error displayed by the
manuscript text it is worth noting that the scribe of that text,
who is probably responsible for many of the errors in it only in
so far as he carried them over from his exemplar, took some
pains to achieve accuracy. First, his pointing is remarkably
accurate – on two occasions (253b, 399b) erroneously placed
points have been erased – and even when it is inaccurate some-
times gives the impression that he was doing his best with a
defective exemplar. For instance at 161–2a the pointing of *on
hwæl . hwreopon . here fugolas .* suggests that the scribe knew
there ought to be three verses (with the alliteration on *h* ex-
tending over two lines) but lacked the necessary words to com-
plete them. Secondly, he corrected himself probably as he was
going along. There are four instances of a letter added for in-
sertion (66, 168, 253, 381) and three of expunction (107), one
with a correction written above (162) and one cancelled (11).
On six occasions letters have been altered from what was writ-

<hr />

[1] Sisam, *Studies* (1953) 29–44; E. G. Stanley, 'A Note on *Genesis B*, 328',
RES n.s. v (1954) 54–8.

ten first (122, 327, 345, 384, 428, 496). In what follows the errors found in the text are related to the scribe's corrections of his own work whenever possible; this should not necessarily be taken to imply that the scribe was the original perpetrator of a particular error.

(i) *Errors due to misunderstanding of the original*
Most of these are straightforward misreadings of letters, *d* for *ð* and *r* for *s* in *dryrmyde* (40), *ð* for *d* (possibly also word confusion) in *sceaðo* (113), *w* for *þ* in *swor* (239), *s* for *f* in *syrd-* (178), *f* for *s* in *ufon* (556), *u* for *a* in *sund* (442), *r* for *n* in *orette* (313) and *leor* (321), probably also *u* for *y* in *ful* (167), *ut* for *id* in *buton* (249), and *i* for *e* in *onsigon* (178). In *benum* (216) *n* for *m* is perhaps an error of omission (of one minim stroke) rather than a misreading like *brun* for *brim-* (499). A special group of errors is occasioned by confusion of *h* and *n*, *h* for *n* in *gehæged* (169) and *hu* (280), *n* for *h* in *ne* (432); *hn* for *h* in *alhn* (392) and *n* for *hn* in *geneoþ* (476) may be due to the fact that the scribe did not recognize any distinction in pronunciation between *hn-* and *n-* (cf. Jordan, §195). The misplaced point in *an twig . ða* (145) clearly indicates that the scribe failed to understand this word.

(ii) *Errors due to conscious 'correction' of the original*
The text shows substitution of words, *god* for *metod* (414), *sæs* for *wæges* (467), of a positive for a negative phrase *he wæs gearu* for *næs he earg* (339), and of a past for a present tense verb *þeahton* for *þeccað* (288). Many errors arise from the alteration of a word to another word whose spelling is not much different, of *feond* to *freond* (45), *-geard* to *weard* (57), *segl(e)* to *swegl(e)* (81, 105), *on* to *ond* and thence its abbreviation 7 (283), *spaw* to *span* (291), *mere-* to *mære* (346), *ecgum* to *eagum* (413), *freode* to *freoðo* (423), *inge-* to *inca-* (444), *wyrde* to *fyrde* (472), *teah* to *ateah* (491), *onfond* to *on feond* (502), *ne mað* to *nemnað* (519). At 471 *basnodon* was probably first miscopied *barnodon* and then 'corrected' to *barenodon*. Sometimes an Anglian word or form seems to have been misunderstood by a WS scribe; hence *ingere* for *ungeare* (33), *ofer clamme* for *on ferclamme* (119), and perhaps *bell* for *bel-*

(121). More difficult to explain is *scealdes* for *-sceldes* (79).[1]
Other instances show erroneous endings which cannot be ac-
counted for by the confusion of endings in 1.OE: *tirfæstne* for
tirfæste (63), *wolcnum* for *wolcne* (350), the latter perhaps in-
fluenced by *þrymmum* (349). Wrong word division occurs in
hand ahofon for *handa hofon* (582) and was probably the first
stage before *flod wearde sloh* was arrived at for *flodweard gesloh*
(494).

(iii) *Errors of omission*

Whole verses have been omitted at 246b, 304b, 411a, and
nearly a whole line at 161. Whole words are missing at 288a,
340a, 432a, 487a, 503a, 514a, 546a, 570a, 574b. In 546a *bið* has
been omitted over a line division so this error is probably at-
tributable to the scribe of the extant text. That he was capable
of omitting a word is shown by *Daniel* 293 where, for *nu we þec*,
he first wrote *nu þec* then added *we* above the line for insertion
in between. Here his eye probably moved from *we* in the
exemplar to his own copy and back to *þec* in the exemplar
('wynn' and 'thorn' having a similar appearance) without his
realizing they were not one and the same word. Such an expla-
nation would account for the omissions at 340, 432, 487, 503
and 570. In an earlier copy *wolde* (412) was presumably omitted
and written above the line for insertion but when this copy
was itself copied *wolde* was reinserted in the wrong place. The
second elements of the compounds *hæðbroga* (118) and *wigheap*
(243) are lacking. Otherwise omissions are of letters. Just as
the scribe first wrote *midum* for *middum* (168) then added a
second *d* above the line so *habað* appears for *habbað* (1). Just as
the scribe first wrote *hof* for *ahof* (253) then added initial *a*
above the line so *ofer holt* appears for *eoferholt* (157). Just as the
scribe first wrote *ætanes* for *Æthanes* (66) and *for* for *feor* (381)
then added the missing letters above the line for insertion in
the appropriate place so *ræwa* appears for *-ræswa* (55), *he* for
hie (151, but cf. note), *eade* for *ealde* (186), *gebad* for *gebead* (191 ;
perhaps also word confusion), *rofa* for *rofra* (226); *cymð* for

[1] See Lucas, *ES* li (1970) 308.

cymeð is an orthographically permissible variant with syncope. Straightforward haplography occurs in *Moyse sægde* for *Moyses sægde* (517); cf. also *beo/hata* over a line division for *beodohata* (253). Letters are omitted finally from *andsacan* (15), *getwæf*de (119), *leod-* (128), *wac*e (233), *þeod*en (277), *man*na (334), *drenc*e- (364), *sceo*don (587), and *mæst* (590) though the erasure of *-st* may not be the work of the scribe. Initially *ge-* is lacking from *gerad* (248). A special group of errors is occasioned by the confusion of *h* and *hw*. On two occasions in *Daniel* the scribe first omitted *w* from the group *hw* (107, 643) and the same omission is found uncorrected at *Exodus* 371, 538. At 176 *hwæl* for *wæl-* suggests that the scribe did not distinguish in pronunciation between *hw-* and *w-* (cf. Jordan §195).[1]

(iv) *Errors of addition*

Straightforward dittography of words occurs at 22 and 146. The redundant word-elements at 313 (*an on orette* for *on onette*) and 373 (*mis micelra* for *missenlicra*) probably arose from dittography in an exemplar; for 373 cf. the scribe's *fr fræge* for *gefræge* (368). In *hwreopon* (162) the *hw* is probably taken from the preceding word-element *hwæl* (161) and similarly *mode* (500) has been influenced by *-yppinge* (499) – cf. *Daniel* 409. In *meoringa* (62) the *o* is probably taken over from *mor* (61). Seven examples of assimilation may also be included here: *hige* for *hie* before a word beginning with *ge-* (307), *gar secges* for *garsecge* before a word ending in *-es* (345), *cyre* for *cyrm* after a word ending in *-re* (466), *æsæled* for *asæled* (471), *huru* for *heoru-* (505), *heoro* for *heora* (510), and *galan* for *golan* (578).

8 Compilation

Whereas the Exeter Book may have 'been written at intervals over a period of years'[2] and thus have grown by accretion, some overall conception of the whole book must have preceded

---

[1] For the suggestion that lack of *w* is not an error see G. L. Brook, 'The Relation between the Textual and the Linguistic Study of Old English', in *The Anglo-Saxons* ed. P. Clemoes (London, 1959) 285(*c*).

[2] A. J. Bliss & T. P. Dunning, *The Wanderer* (1969) 4.

the compilation of MS Junius 11. This statement is valid even though some modification of plan may have occurred while the illustrations were being done.[1] Book II, containing *Christ and Satan*, was probably not part of the original design, but at the time this poem was added the intention must have been to make it an integral part of the manuscript.[2] As far as Book I is concerned its unified conception is implied by the consecutive numbering of the sectional divisions.

MS Junius 11 (Book I) differs from all the other major codices of OE poetry in that it was conceived from the outset as a picture-book, a conception which goes back ultimately to the East[3] but which was well known in England by the year 1000.[4] The illustrations in such a picture book were always based on an exemplar, a fact which explains the degree of foreign influence on English art of this early period. Considerable care was evidently taken at the outset to ensure a satisfactory combination of text and illustration. The relationship between text and illustration, which, since the illustrations were never completed, can be analysed only in relation to the first five-eighths or so of *Genesis*, may provide some clue to the purpose for which the manuscript was compiled. Evidently the drawings are not merely decorative but illustrations relating, or intended by the deviser to relate, to the narrative sequence,[5] though, as GOLLANCZ pointed out (p. xxxiv), the work of the first artist in particular shows the influence of sources other

[1] Cf. G. Henderson, *JBAA* III xxvi (1963) 20, and *Stud. in Mem. D. T. Rice* (1975) 116, 125, 130.

[2] Cf. KRAPP, pp. xi–xii. See now Peter J. Lucas, 'On the Incomplete Ending of *Daniel* and the Addition of *Christ and Satan* to MS Junius 11', *Anglia* xcviii (1978) forthcoming.

[3] See, for example, E. Wellesz, *The Vienna Genesis* (London, 1960), esp. 18–19. On AS contact with the East see Mayr-Harting, *Coming of Christianity* (1972) 124–8.

[4] Cf. O. Pächt, *The Rise of Pictorial Narrative in Twelfth-Century England* (Oxford, 1962) 5.

[5] See Ohlgren, 'The Illustrations of the *Cædmonian Genesis*', *Medievalia et Humanistica* iii (1972) 199–212; the author's unfortunate sub-title 'Literary Criticism through Art' is not an accurate summary of his argument. G. Henderson [*Stud. in Mem. D. T. Rice* (1975) 113–45] points out that the illustration to a particular scene is often dislocated from the text dealing with the same matter, though this was not the intention of the deviser.

than the OE text.[1] In other words the drawings are, or were
intended by the deviser to be, a visual complement to the
written text. As such they presumably had three functions:
(a) to help the reader understand the narrative; (b) to help
the reader perceive, through colour symbolism, the proper
moral interpretation, for the blessed (including the tempter in
disguise) are coloured red (the colour of Christ's blood) and
the damned are coloured brown; (c) to stimulate interest. On
the basis of this evidence the book must have been intended to
give intellectual pleasure and to be educationally instructive.

The punctuation must also be taken into account. One
punctuation-marker, the continuity marker, is used at the end
of a page to indicate the continuity of the text on the next page
containing text despite an intervening space or page for illus-
tration. Clearly the illustrations were not to interfere with the
continuity of the text if it could be avoided. Another punc-
tuation-marker, the single point, marks metrical units. Ap-
parently the punctuation (and possibly the sectional divisions
as well) was designed to help the reading aloud or recitation
of the text (presumably privately since the illustrations could
not be shared with an audience);[2] certainly it could not have
been intended to help a reader construe the text.

On the basis of the available evidence it looks as if MS
Junius 11 was intended for devotional reading in the vernacu-
lar. (In the unlikely event that such reading was regarded as
elementary, because in the vernacular, then the inclusion of
Exodus in the manuscript was ill-considered.) Possibly the book
was intended to have a central theme. J. I. Young, noting
many parallels between *Genesis B* and *Christ and Satan*, has
suggested that the contents of the whole manuscript focus on
the birth of evil and the deliverance of mankind from it.[3] The

[1] This of course is to be expected. Cf. the remarks by F. Wormald in
CHB 318, citing Pächt (p. 28, n. 4).

[2] In view of the Ælfwine medallion perhaps the manuscript was intended
to be 'the abbot's copy'?

[3] In P. Clemoes (ed.), *The Anglo-Saxons* (1959) 204–7. In *Revue de l'His-
toire des Religions* clxv (1964) 13–47 M.-M. Larès has suggested that the
organizing principle of the MS reflects the liturgical usage of the fifth-
century Christian community in Jerusalem, but this suggestion lacks sup-
porting evidence.

theme of Book I could very plausibly be said to be Salvation by Faith and Obedience.

9 The Textual Integrity of *Exodus*

In this edition the whole text of *Exodus* is printed and the lines are given in the order in which they occur in the manuscript. Formerly, however, this textual integrity has been questioned. Suspicion has attached to three passages: (i) lines 362–446, (ii) lines 108–24, (iii) lines 516–48. Since *Exodus* survives in a unique text there is no resorting to other manuscripts to confirm or deny such a suspicion. In so far as they have any basis these suspicions are founded in the theory of textual criticism. Thus the charge against passage (i), that it is an interpolation, rests on analogy with texts (that survive in at least several copies) where an interpolation can be proved.[1] The main charges against the other passages rest similarly: that during the transmission of the text some lines were transposed due to omission and reinsertion (ii), and that a manuscript leaf became detached and was reinserted back to front (iii).[2] None of these suspicions are sufficiently 'controlled by observation'. Even so, considerable argument has arisen in relation to each passage.

(i) Lines 362–446 comprise a brief, allusive account of the story of Noah and the Ark and a longer treatment of the story of Abraham and Isaac. Since the passage does not concern the exodus it has been thought to be an interpolation, labelled *Exodus B*[3] and even *Isaaks Opferung*[4] and *Noah und andere Patriarchen*.[5] Craigie thought the passage to be an interpolation

---

[1] See P. Maas, *Textual Criticism*, tr. B. Flower (Oxford, 1958) 14–15, 34–5.

[2] For both these processes see J. Willis, *Latin Textual Criticism* (Urbana, 1972) 148–50.

[3] By Balg, *Dichter Cædmon* (1882) and Ziegler, *Poetische Sprachgebrauch* (1883).

[4] By G. Binz, *Anglia Beiblatt* xiv (1903) 357.

[5] By A. Brandl in H. Paul (ed.), *Grundriss der germanischen Philologie* (Strasbourg, 1908 edn), Bd 2¹, p. 1029.

inserted to fill a lacuna. [1] This view, however, has not prevailed. GOLLANCZ (pp. lxxii–lxxiii) favours retention of the passage, though he adduces no argument except to note that the statement in lines 377–9 that Abraham's father was ninth in line from Noah seems to be linked with the reference to genealogists in 359–61. BLACKBURN retains the passage, but his argument too is weak (p. xxiv). KRAPP, who also retains the passage, argues that the story of the Flood goes naturally with the drowning of the Egyptians but fails to give any convincing reason for the inclusion of the story of Abraham and Isaac. Despite these scholar's efforts to justify the inclusion of the passage, no justification ought to be required. The passage is there in the unique manuscript and the onus of proof must lie with those who argue for its omission. Clearly no such proof is possible on the available evidence, for, as IRVING rightly saw (p.29), the passage is an integral part of the poem when viewed from a literary standpoint. As I shall try to show below the theme of *Exodus* is Salvation by Faith and Obedience: in the exodus God saves his people – providing they are faithful and obedient (124). The Abraham and Isaac episode illustrates that obedience is required even when one of the strongest human bonds (kinship) runs contrary to it. This episode thus emphasises the historicity of the covenant between God and the Israelites (and Christians in general). In the Noah episode God saves his faithful followers through the Ark, the vessel of salvation, a motif which links with the nautical imagery found elsewhere in the poem (see note to 80b–84). Similarly in *Beowulf* the so-called 'digressions' are relevant to the main theme of the poem. The treatment of the passage is an example in miniature of how textual study can founder without literary insight.

(ii) Lines 108–24 describe the fire-pillar. Because it was thought inappropriate that both the cloud-pillar and the fire-pillar should be mentioned together (*seglas* 89, *beamas twegen* 94) before each had been described individually Napier suggested that lines 108–24 had been misplaced in an earlier (lost) manuscript of the text.[1] He advocated placing them after 85. But his suggestion is ill-founded since it depends on the validity of an untenable theory concerning the textual transmission of the poem (Bradley's view that the numbered sections represent the contents of the separate sheets of parchment in the poet's holograph manuscript).[2] Less easily dismissed is GOLLANCZ's proposal (p. lxx) that the lines belong after 92. He thought 93–107 and 108–24 to be reversed from their proper order. Here as with (i) the burden of proof must lie with those who wish to alter the manuscript order. In fact GOLLANCZ's proposal does not even surmount the initial difficulty for it places 108–24 *between* the two references to the pillars together (89 and 94). And the initial difficulty itself is imaginary as there is no reason to suppose that the author would have found the more logical order of presentation attributed to him either necessary or desirable.

(iii) Lines 516–48 begin with a statement that Moses gave the Israelites divinely inspired advice and continue with a didactic passage pointing out that the events of the exodus are to be understood figurally and allegorically and that the general moral significance of the events should be remembered too. The relevance of most of these lines (523–48) was first questioned by Craigie who thought them to be an interpolation, 'the concluding portion of a moralizing poem which has no connexion with the theme of the *Exodus*.'[3] This view was challenged by GOLLANCZ (p. lxxv) who held that lines 523–48 are 'integral' to the poem, though he conceded that the last lines of the poem were copied in the wrong order. GOLLANCZ's proposed order was 515, 580–90, 549–79, 516–48. This rearrangement was criticized by KRAPP (pp. xxx–xxxi) who thought that, far from making the poem 'an organic whole', it tended to make it 'less a whole than the present arrangement' (as in the manuscript). Nevertheless the idea was revived by the poem's most recent editor, IRVING, who printed lines 516–48 at the

[1] *MLR* vi (1911) 165–8.
[2] See above, p. 10, n. 2.
[3] *Philologica* ii (1924) 9.

end of the poem (i.e. 515, 549–90, 516–48), justifying this decision on the grounds that the manuscript order is illogical – the poet 'generalizes on the significance of the scriptures and the meaning of a Christian life and *then* goes on to finish his story' (p.11). IRVING's attribution to the poet of a modern sense of logical narrative progression was rightly queried by Wrenn.[1] Others have shown on literary grounds that the sequence of statements as recorded in the manuscript is in fact preferable to the rearrangement. The didactic passage concerns the figural/allegorical interpretation of the exodus, as the reading *Dægweorc ne mað* (519) makes clear. In the words of Isaacs,

'the Red Sea crossing, with the Egyptians swallowed up and the Hebrews led through to the Promised Land, is a *type* of judgment day when the damned will be swallowed up to hell and the blessed led to heaven. ... The passage which IRVING shifts (549–590) ... would make good sense after l. 515, but it makes better sense where the manuscript has it because the intervening passage has established explicitly the relationship between the exodus and judgment day.'[2]

These arguments have subsequently been accepted by Irving who 'would now put the MS back the way it was' (note to 516–90).

10 The Corrector's Accents

These are 'acute' in form and appear in a lighter shade of ink than the text. They are attributed, in Ker's phrase, to the 'eleventh-century corrector' but were probably entered before about 1050 (see above, pp. 6–7). The list given by Krapp in ASPR II lxx–lxxiv is accurate except for the following corrections:

[1] *RES* n.s. vi (1955) 184. Similarly G. T. Shepherd in *MLR* xlix (1954) 269.

[2] *Structural Principles in OE Poetry* (1968) 155–6. For a similar view see also Earl in *NM* lxxi (1970) esp. 555.

328 *For* únfórhte *read* únforhte; *the mark over the* o *is not an
     accent*
346 *For* gewat *read* gewát
For 368 (*1st*) *read* 365
381 *For* éac *read* eác (*cf. 446*)
410 *Add* þónne
507 *For* léan *read* leán
515 *For* agéat *read* ageát
519 *For* déop *read* deóp

According to my hand-count there are 439 accents in *Exodus*,
on average less than one per line. Whatever they were intended
to mark they must have marked it only sporadically and there-
fore inconsistently. Consequently 'conclusions can more safely
be drawn from their presence than from their absence'.[1] The
real possibility must be faced that the corrector was not too
sure of what he was doing. In line 313 the redundant word *án*
receives an accent, and BLACKBURN (pp. xvi–xvii) noted that
accents were 'freely used' in defective verses, almost as if extra
accents could make up for lost syllables.

What little is known about accents in manuscripts contain-
ing OE is summarized by Ker in his *Catalogue* (1957), p. xxxv.[2]
The accents in *Exodus* seem to fit into the general pattern in
the eleventh century of marking stress rather than vowel
length. Presumably they had something to do with the at-
tempted reading aloud or recitation of the text. BLACKBURN was
substantially correct when he argued (pp. xv–xviii) that the
accents 'mark the position of metrical stress', as, for example,
in 431a, *gársecges gín.* Such a theory accounts for 75% of the
accents. A further 12.5% mark metrical secondary stress, as,
for example, in *lígfýr adránc* (77b), where both full stresses and
the secondary stress are marked. There are still, however, 55
accents not accounted for. Ten of these occur in proper names
and Thornley has noted the correspondence between the
placing of these accents and the traditional Hebrew accen-

---

[1] Sisam, *Studies* (1953) 186.

[2] See also D. G. Scragg, 'Accent Marks in the Old English Vercelli
Book', *NM* lxxii (1971) 699–710.

tuation of the names.[1] It is more likely, however, that the accents correspond to the contemporary Latin accentuation of the names (itself based on the traditional Hebrew accentuation), as, for example, in *Faraónes* (32, 156), *Simeónes* (341), *Cananéa* (556). Since the corrector was presumably a monk who may well have been more familiar with eleventh-century Latin than with classical OE verse these accents on proper names are probably not a reliable guide to the general use of all the accents. Some of the accents seem to be expository in function, as, for instance those that mark a conjunction at the beginning of a new clause (*ác* 243, 416, 443, 457, 489, 513; *hú* 89, 244; *nú* 531; *þónne* 410). Clearly these accents too could have aided the reading aloud of the text. Others could be mistaken attempts to mark metrical secondary stress (*onwíst* 18, *ingére* 33, *ántwíg* 145 (2nd), *ánmód* 203 (2nd), *únrím* 261 (2nd), *sǽcír* 291 (2nd), *wealhstód* 523) or even full stress (*únforhte* 180, 328). Others again (some 5% of the total) have no apparent explanation: the frequent marking of the unstressed prefix *ā-* is particularly baffling (*árísan* 217 (1st), *árǽrde* 295, *ádrenced* 459, *ástah* 468) though it occurs elsewhere too.[2]

II LANGUAGE

The present manuscript text of *Exodus* was probably written at Malmesbury about the year 1000. As is to be expected the language of the text is predominantly late West Saxon, but there is also an admixture of forms usually considered to be Anglian. In what follows the principal features of the language of the poem are illustrated and discussed. No attempt is made to discuss general WS features. References to forms which are the result of alterations to the manuscript spelling are given in italics.

Only one feature characteristic of early WS is discernible, *ie* for later *ȳ* [Campbell §301] in *onnied* 149 beside *nȳde* 116, *nȳd-* 208, 475, *genȳddon* 68.

[1] *TPS* (1954) esp. 179–82.
[2] Scragg 701 notes 77 instances in the Vercelli Book.

There are a number of features characteristic of late WS:

(1) $\breve{\bar{y}}$ for earlier $\breve{\iota}e$ [Campbell §301]: *hȳrde* (p.t.) 124, 410, *gȳt* 235, *stȳran* 417, *gyfan* 263, *scyldas* 125, *fyrd* 54, 88, 135 etc., *yldra* 141, *yrre* 506, *gyst-* 535, *syndon* 283, 297.

(2) *i* for earlier *ie* before palatal consonants [Campbell §301]: *cīgean* 219, *līge* 110, 122, 400, *līgfȳr* 77, *lixan* 157, *lixton* 125, 175.

(3) Unrounding of *y* to *i* [Campbell §317]: *cista* 229, 230, *herecyste* 177, 257 beside *herecyste* 301 and *guðcyste* 343, *hild* 569 (cf. *gehyld* 382).

(4) Rounding of *i* to *y* [Campbell §318]: *fyrst(e)* 208, 267, 304, 189, *hwylc* 439, *gehwylces* 538 beside *gehwilc(-)* 187, 230, 374, 521.

(5) *y* for *e* in the group *sel-* [Campbell §325]: *sylf-* 9, 27, 280, 434, 542, *syllic* 109, *gesyllan* 400.

(6) *u* for *eo* in the group *weor-* [Campbell §321]: *wurðmyndum* 258, *gewurðien* 270, *gewurðodne* 31 beside *geweorðod(e)* 581, 86.

(7) Instability in the vowels of unaccented syllables, especially in inflexional endings:[1] *-um* for *-an* (dat. sg. wk.) in *magoræswum* 17, *-an/-on* for *-um* (dat. pl.) in *eagan* 171, *wenan* 165, *cǣgon* 525, *sweoton* 127 [Campbell §378]; *-an* for *-on* (p.t. pl.) in *beodan* 166 (perhaps mistaken for an infinitive), *fōran* 93 (beside *fōron* 106), *golan* 578 [Campbell §377]; *-a* for *-u* (simplex or nom. sg.) in *heora-* 181, *þraca* 326 [Campbell §377]; *-as* for *-es* (gen. sg.) in *forðwegas* 248, *wērbēamas* 487, *-es* for *-as* (nom. pl.) in *wælslihtes* 328 [Campbell §379]; *-en* for *-an* (acc. pl. wk.) in *ginfæsten* 525 [Campbell §379]; *-eð* for *-að* (pr. 3 pl.) in *healdeð* 535; *-a* for *-e* (acc. sg. f.) in *antwigða* 145, *treowa* 366, *-e* for *-a* (gen. pl.) in *werode* 8, also in *ungeāre 33*, *-e* for *-u* (nom. pl. n.) in *blodige* 329, 573 [SB §293 Anm. 3] (cf. *dēore* 186 and Campbell §646). Similarly to be explained are isolated instances of the past tense singular and past participle of weak verbs II in *-ade*, *-ad*, *mōdgade* 331 (beside *mōdgode* 459), *swiðrade*

---

[1] See K. Malone, 'When did Middle English Begin?', *Curme Volume of Linguistic Studies* [Language Monographs 7 (1930)] 110–17; G. L. Brook, 'The Relation between the Textual and the Linguistic Study of Old English', in *The Anglo-Saxons* ed. P. Clemoes (London, 1959) 280–91 esp. 284 (*a*).

242 (beside *swiðrode* 309, 466), *genīwad* 35 [cf. Campbell §757] ; this interpretation would also account for *-yde* in *ðrysmyde 40*.

(8) *rð* for earlier *rhð* [Campbell §477 (6); Brook, *op. cit.* 284 (c)] : *wideferð* 51 beside *ferhð(e)* 119, 355, *ferhð-* 267, 399.

There are also many features, mostly sporadic, which are usually taken to be non-WS:

(1) Pr. Gmc *ǣ* appears as *ē* (not WS *ǣ*[1]) in *bēlegsan 121*, *gefēgon 570*, *fērclamme 119*, *mēce* 414, 495 (the usual form of this poetical word), *onsēgon 178* (cf. *gesāwon* 103, 126, 155, 387, 572, 583), *wērbeamas* 487 beside *wǣre* 140, 147, 387, 422 [Campbell §128]. The *ē* in *forgēfe* 153, *forgēton* 144, *ongēton* 90, 453, 552 may be due to late WS smoothing [Campbell §312].

(2) Pr. OE *æ* before supported *l* appears as *a* (not WS *ea*) in *alde* 495 (in the fossilized phrase *alde mēce*, beside *eald-* elsewhere), *aldor* 12, 31, 270 (beside *ealdor-* 317, 335), *alh 392*, *Alwalda* 11, *alwihta* 421, *bald* 253, *hals-* 582, *nalles* 307, *Waldend* 16, 422, 433, and also in *hildecalla* 252, *sincalda* 473 [Campbell §143].[1] Such forms are common in poetry.

(3) Earlier *e* after an initial palatal consonant remains in *dægsceldes 79* (beside *scyldas* 125), probably a Mercian feature [Campbell §183].

(4) Earlier *ēa* subject to *i*-mutation appears as *ē* (not WS *īe, ȳ*) in *bēmum 216* (beside *bȳme* 182, *bȳman* 159, 222, *-bȳman* 99), *bestēmed* 449 (the usual form of this poetical word), *ēðfynde* 580 [Campbell §200.5].

(5) Earlier *ea* (by breaking before *r*) subject to *i*-mutation appears as *e* (subsequently lengthened) in *ealdwērige 50* (and note; cf. *awyrged* 533) [Campbell §200.2].

(6) Earlier *æ* undergoes back mutation to *ea* in *beadumægnes 329*, *beadosearo* 573, *beodohāta* (with *eo* for *ea*) *253*, *eaferan* 412, *heaðorincas* 241, *heaðowylmas* 148, but such forms of these words are common in poetry [Campbell §207].

---

[1] On these spellings see E. G. Stanley, 'Spellings of the *Waldend* Group', in *Studies in Language, Literature, and Culture of the Middle Ages and Later*, ed. E. B. Atwood & A. A. Hill (Austin, Texas, 1969) 38–69.

(7) Earlier *i* undergoes back mutation and is written *eo* in *beodan*[1] (WS *bidon*) 166, *freoðowǣre* 306, and also in *burhhleoðu* 70 (and note) beside *beorhhliðu* 449, *sǣleoda* 374 [Campbell §212].

(8) Anglian smoothing is shown in *hergas* 'shrines' 46 (WS *heargas*) [Campbell §§222–3] and in *cinberge* (WS *-beorge*) [Campbell §227].

(9) Normal *ēa* appears as *ēo* in *gehnēop 476*, *rēodan* 413 (common in this word) beside *rēadan* 134, *rēade* 296, *ea* as *eo* in *beodohāta 253*, and *ēo* as *ēa* in *hēald* 61 [Campbell §278]; this interchange of *ea* and *eo* is usually considered to be Northumbrian.

(10) Uncontracted forms of the third person singular present indicative, *dēmeð* 543, *lǣdeð* 544, 555, *wyrceð* 282, and *cymeð 540* (required by the metre), formerly considered Anglian, are regular in all but the very latest poetry (Sisam, *Studies* 123–6]. The form *hafað*, pr. 3 sg. of *habban*, is usual in 'Anglian' poetry [SB §417 Anm. 1c] and is also the usual form in the West Mercian Vespasian Psalter gloss [Campbell §762].

(11) An Anglian form of the present participle (*forhtende* rather than *forhtigende*) is indicated by the metre in line 453 [Campbell §757].

Some other morphological features may be Anglian: lack of contraction in *ne willað* 266 [Campbell p. 347 n. 5; SB §428 Anm. 4]; zero-inflexion in the accusative singular of feminine *ō*-stem nouns [SB §252 Anm. 2], *mearc* 160, *þēod* 160; according to Campbell §751(2) *bēton* 131 for normal *bētton* is Northumbrian.

Besides these phonological and morphological features some vocabulary elements are probably Anglian:[2] *cīgean* 'summon' 219, *gefēgon 570* p.t. of *gefēon*, *ungeāre 33*, *nymðe* 124, 439.

It is exceedingly difficult to draw any firm conclusions from this linguistic information. One of the chief difficulties arises from the possibility that there was a general OE poetic *koiné* of a mixed dialect character and that poems were written or

---

[1] Even if this word was mistaken for an infinitive the mistake is likely to have arisen from a form such as *beodon*.

[2] See R. Vleeskruyer, *The Life of St. Chad* (Amsterdam, 1953) 23–37.

transmitted in this 'literary dialect'.[1] Nevertheless, the language of the text, when considered in conjunction with the newly discovered information about the probable origin of MS Junius 11, may yield sufficient hints to permit some tentative suggestions concerning the earlier history of the text.

Since there is virtually nothing to indicate that the present text passed through an Alfredian recension (early WS) that possibility can presumably be eliminated. On the other hand a few linguistic features, together with those that are generally Anglian, suggest the possibility that the poem may have passed through a West Mercian recension: notably non-WS (7) above, especially *beodan*, also non-WS (3), though the form *-sceldes* unfortunately rests on an emendation, and possibly *hafað* under non-WS (10). In view of the geographical position of Malmesbury it is plausible to suppose that the poem came there via a West Mercian centre such as Worcester or Lichfield. Again a few other linguistic features, together with those that are generally Anglian, suggest the possibility that the poem may have been composed in a Northumbrian dialect: notably non-WS (11) above, also non-WS (9). But the evidence for these suggestions is thin.

III METRE

Exodus exemplifies classical OE alliterative metre written according to a high standard. As such it bears comparison with *Beowulf*. Three sub-types not found in *Beowulf* occur in *Exodus*: d4a *on folcgetæl* (229a), *in randgebeorh* (296b), *On feorhgebeorh* (369a);

1A*1b(ii) *wician ofer weredum* (117a);

2A3a(iii) *wrætlicu wægfaru* (298a).

A feature of *Exodus* is the avoidance of most of the 'long' sub-types found in *Beowulf*. These sub-types are listed with the number of examples found in *Beowulf* given in brackets: a2e

---

[1] This view was cogently proposed by Sisam in his paper 'Dialect Origins of the Earlier Old English Verse', *Studies* (1953) 119–39.

(6), a2f (1), a2g (1), d3d (9), d3e (2), d4c (4), d4d (1), d5d (2), 1A1c (4), 1A*1c (3), 1D*6 (1), 2B1e (1), 2B2c (2), 2B2d (1), 2C1d (6), 2C1e (1), 2C2e (1), 2E2b (5), 3B1d (21), 3B1e (1), 3B2c (1), 3B*1e (7). While the absence from *Exodus* of sub-types that occur only once in *Beowulf* is not surprising (since *Beowulf* is more than five times as long as *Exodus*) the lack of these 'long' sub-types considered together must be the result of strict discipline in compositional technique. The only apparent instance of a failure to conform to Kuhn's 'Law of Particles' (Bliss §20) is easily removed by a transposition of word order (see note to 411–2).

In alliteration all instances of the following types have double alliteration in the *a*-verse, as in *Beowulf:* 1A2, 1A*2–3, 1D2–6, 2A2, 2A3a, 2A4. The proportion of Types 1A1 (96%) and 1A*1 (88%) showing double alliteration in the *a*-verse is almost the same as in *Beowulf* (95% and 92% respectively), but there is one example of Type 1D*1 (*ðēoda ǣnigre* 326) and one instance of Type 2E2 (*frumcnēow gehwǣs* 371) showing single alliteration in the *a*-verse where double alliteration is 'compulsory' in *Beowulf* (Bliss §§64, 66). With regard to distribution of verses, as in *Beowulf* the following types occur only in the *a*-verse: a, e, 1A2, 1A*2–3, 1D3–6, 1D*, 2A2, 2A4. *Beowulf* has two examples of Type 1D2 in the *b*-verse but there are none in *Exodus*. As in *Beowulf* the metre sometimes requires that words (or elements of compounds) ending in vocalic *r, l, n* should be treated as monosyllabic:[1] *wuldọrfæst* 390a, *mēagọllice* 528a, *wealfæstẹn* 283a, the emended *þeodẹn* 277a, also probably *þēodmægẹn* 342a. Again as in *Beowulf* dissyllabic forms are called for where the spelling indicates a contraction:[2] *Frēā* 196, *nêar* 308b, *slêan* 412a, *gǣð* 526b, also probably *Liffrêan* 271a.

In two relatively minor respects *Exodus* differs from *Beowulf*: (1) As Bliss argues (§§46–7) there are no instances in *Beowulf* of anacrusis when the caesura is in position (i). There is one clear exception to this 'rule' in *Exodus*, *ālȳfed lāðsið* 44a, which scans as Type 2A2. Another possible exception is *forbærned burhhleoðu* 70a, if it is assumed to have resolution of *hleoðu* with

[1] Klaeber, *Beowulf*, 276, item 3.
[2] Klaeber, *Beowulf*, 274–5 §1.

the 'short' vocalic ending, but alternatively it could be scanned as Type 1D*3 (with the caesura in position (iii)) in which case it would be another exception under (2) below. However, if the original reading was *-hliðu* (cf. Bliss §37) the verse would scan as 1D*2 and show no irregularities.

(2) In *Beowulf* when there is resolution of a secondary stress 'long' vocalic or consonantal endings are avoided (Bliss §37). There is one exception to this 'rule' in *Exodus*, *gylpplegan gāres* 240a, against five regular examples (137a, 325b, 329a, 298a, 61a) and another instance, *beorselas beorna* 564a, which probably was regular with the older *i*-stem plural *beorsele*. Conversely in the sequence of syllables $\smile \acute{\ } \grave{\ } $x (Type 1D3) the ending is regularly a 'long' vocalic or consonantal one in *Beowulf*. In *Exodus* there is an exception to this rule, *beran beorht searo* 219a, also possibly 70a (see (1) above), against ten regular examples (14a, 40a, 125a, 248a, 282a, 327a, 354a, 399a, 475a, 515a).

Some interesting facts emerge from a comparison of the proportions of the different types of verse as between *Exodus* and *Beowulf*. Both poems are in the epic manner with so-called 'digressions' built in to their structure and it might be expected that both poems would show similar proportions of the different verse-types. This possible expectation is not fulfilled. The proportions in *Exodus* differ from those in *Beowulf* in three major ways (1–3) and five minor ways (4–8).

(1) Type C: there are less than half as many verses of Type 2C (the only verse of Type C) – 4.1% in *Exodus* against 8.6% in *Beowulf*.

(2) Type B: there are less than two thirds as many of these verses (9.9% against 15%), Type 2B being particularly infrequent comparatively (only one third as many) and Type 3B being notably infrequent comparatively in the *b*-verse.

(3) Type E: there are more than half as many again of these verses (13.6% as against 8.6%); Type 2E occurs more than twice as frequently in the *b*-verse.

(4) Types 1*A*, 1A, 1A* occur less frequently in the *a*-verse and Type 1A more frequently in the *b*-verse.

(5) Type 2A is a little more frequent, especially in the *b*-verse where there are half as many again.

(6) Type d occurs a little more frequently, especially in the *a*-verse.

(7) Type 1D* occurs a little more frequently.

(8) Type 1D: the proportion of this type in the *a*-verse is much higher.

These differences imply that the control of the verse medium by both poets was such that they could and did select proportionately from the available metrical variations according to what they felt to be appropriate.

This conclusion is confirmed by a comparison of certain passages within *Exodus* with each other. An attempt at such a contrast was made by C. Wall,[1] but unfortunately her findings as regards metre are vitiated by erroneous scansion. Nevertheless she was right to make the attempt and her threefold distinction between passages of 'narration', 'description' and 'direct speech' can be sustained on other metrical evidence, though the distinction between 'narration' and 'description' is to some extent arbitrary. If the proportion of the various types of verses in the whole poem is taken as a norm against which to measure it can be seen that direct speech differs from this norm in one way, that passages of description differ from it in another way, and that these two modes of difference are more or less opposed. For direct speech I have taken all the speeches in the poem (259–75, 278–98, 419–46, 554–64), a total of 77 lines. Only 31 of these lines (40%) have double alliteration in the *a*-verse against a norm of 48.5%. There are more verses of Type C (7.8% as against 4.1%), Type B (13.6% as against 9.9%) and Type a (7.8% as against 4.9%) and fewer of Types E (7.1% as against 13.6%) and D (8.5% as against 11.4%). For description the outstanding passage is undoubtedly lines 447–87. Of these 41 lines 32 show double alliteration in the *a*-verse (78% as against 48.5%). There are many more verses of Types D (18.3% as against 11.4%) and E (19.5% as

[1] 'Stylistic Variation in the OE *Exodus*', *ELN* vi (1968) 79–84, esp. 83.

against 13.6%), no verses at all of Type a (though 488a is one) and very few of Type d (3.6% as against 12%). The passage is clearly a *tour de force* of alliterative pyrotechnics. Another descriptive passage (98–134) shows the same trend to a lesser extent. Double alliteration in the *a*-verse is at 70.3%, again there are no verses of Type a and more of Types D and E (against, in this passage, fewer of Types C and B). Between these two extremes come passages of narration, as an illustration of which I have taken lines 208–58. Here the proportions of the different types of verses and of lines with double alliteration in the *a*-verse are much the same as the averages for the whole poem. The contrast between these three different kinds of passage reveals a remarkable ability to mould words into a complex verse form: there can be no doubting the superb craftmanship shown by the poem.

While alliteration functions as part of the structure of OE verse rhyme was occasionally used as an ornamental addition.[1] *Exodus* contains one outstanding example of internal rhyme, *flōd blōd gewōd* 463, and two examples of 'grammatical' rhyme, *lāð æfter lāðum* 195, *cynn æfter cynne* 351; there is almost a rhyme in the preceding verse, *folc æfter wolcne* 350. Possibly there is deliberate rhyming of *gehnēop/hwēop/swēop* 476/478/481.

IV STYLE

Exodus is one of three outstanding poems in OE. Whereas *Beowulf* is remarkable for its allusive juxtapositions and *The Dream of the Rood* for its dream condensation, *Exodus* stands out by virtue of the sheer brilliance of its writing. Various aspects of the style of the poem have often been the subject of passing comment or brief mention.[2] For instance, Greenfield considers

[1] See E. Sievers, 'Old Germanic Metrics and OE Metrics' in *Essential Articles for the Study of OE Poetry* ed. J. B. Bessinger & S. J. Kahrl (Hamden, Connecticut, 1968) 267–88 esp. 287–8.

[2] The only previous extended discussions of the poem's style are those by Schücking, *Untersuchungen zur Bedeutungslehre der angelsächs. Dichtersprache* (1915) 12–18 (mainly diction), and IRVING 31–4. See also Brodeur in *Nordica et Anglica* (1968) 109–13.

Exodus 'one of the most stirring and exciting of Old English poems . . . [which] exhibits an epic tone and quality'.[1] Earlier, Kennedy thought the style of *Exodus* 'highly sophisticated in a conscious striving for effect. Details of description are massed and elaborated; there are many images, some vigorous and unusual, others derived from tradition and cliché.'[2] According to C. L. Wrenn the poem 'shows a unique use of metaphor' and 'is extremely individual in vocabulary',[3] and B. Mitchell notes its 'dramatic power, descriptive ability, bold imagery, and daring use of words'.[4] But the importance of the poem's style has probably never been fully appreciated, mainly because only comparatively recently has the meaning of the poem begun to be properly understood.

Perhaps the most obvious overall feature of the poem's style is its variety; evidently *Exodus* was not intended to be stylistically homogeneous. As has already been shown (pp. 42–3) the poem exhibits a proportional variation in the use of metrical patterns according to their suitability in a given passage, be it one of 'narration', 'description' or 'direct speech'. The validity of this mode of differentiating between various parts of the poem is further borne out by an analysis of the basic syntactic structures in the same passages.[5] There are two main indicators of difference: (i) the average length of a syntactic unit containing an independent clause;[6] and (ii) the percentage of such units which are co-extensive with a verse or half-line (see Table). Again the most marked distinction is between

[1] *Crit. Hist. OE Lit.* (1966) 155–8.

[2] *Earliest English Poetry* (1943) 180ff.

[3] *A Study of OE Lit.* (London, 1967) 98.

[4] In *The Battle of Maldon and Other OE Poems*, tr. K. Crossley-Holland (London, 1965) 9.

[5] As was noted by Wall, *ELN* vi (1968) 79–84 esp. 81–3.

[6] I have deliberately eschewed the term 'sentence' since it may mean different things to different people: for a discussion of some problems relating to the definition of a sentence in a medieval English text see Peter J. Lucas, 'Sense-Units and the Use of Punctuation-Markers in John Capgrave's *Chronicle*' *Archivum Linguisticum* n.s. ii (1971) 1–24 esp. 12–13. Within the term 'syntactic unit containing an independent clause' I have included units where the force of the verb 'to be' is carried over from the previous clause, e.g. 107a, 451a.

	Direct Speech	*Narration*	*Description*	
	259—75, 278—98, 419—46, 554—64	208—58	98—134	447—87
No. of verses	154	102	74	82
No. of units	26	25	25	42
Average length per unit (verses)	5.9	4.1	2.96	1.95
No. of units co-estensive with verse	4(15%)	7(28%)	11(44%)	24(57%)

the passages of direct speech and a passage of description (447–87). In direct speech the average length of a syntactic unit containing an independent clause is three times as long as the average such unit in the descriptive passage. The proportion of units co-extensive with a verse is almost four times as many in the descriptive passage as in direct speech. As can be seen from the Table the other descriptive passage (98–134) exhibits the same trend as lines 447–87 to a lesser extent. The figures for the narrative passage come in between those for the passages of direct speech and description. Evidently *Exodus* reflects its author's ability to select syntactic structures which alter the tempo of the poem according to the appropriateness of the content in a given passage. In direct speech the tempo is relatively relaxed and shows greater variation than is usual elsewhere (units vary in length from one to twenty-two verses [432–42]). In a descriptive *tour de force* such as lines 447–87 the tempo is increased to produce a breathless staccato-like effect. Indeed the control of tempo through the selection of syntactic structures is evident in the opening lines of the poem where an unusually complex type of parallelism is employed to indicate that the poem requires to be responded to at more than just the literal level, that hints of a deeper meaning will also be suggested (note to 1–7).

Besides control of tempo the poem also exhibits remarkable control of point of view. In the descriptive passage already mentioned (447ff.) there is control of both temporal and visual focus. From the temporal standpoint the three main elements in the scene – the sea threatening, the Egyptians fearful, and the sea finally destroying them – seem to recur chronologically disordered, a feature which enhances the chaotic impression created by the scene. From the visual standpoint the four main elements in the scene – the wall of water (468–9a), the Egyptian army trapped in death (469b–71a), the sands awaiting the resurgence of the sea (471b–6), the sky darkened (477) – are all described separately, then brought together in a brief resumptive passage (482–3).[1] Again in the passage where the Israelites, encamped by the Red Sea, fearfully watch the Egyptians approach (154–207) focus shifts back and forth from the exultant Egyptians to the cringing Israelites (note especially the inclusion of lines 178b–9 in a passage otherwise concerned with the Egyptians). Yet another aspect of the control of point of view displayed by the poem is the description of one event in terms that suggest another. Notable instances are the description of the death of the Egyptian first-born in terms appropriate for the departure of the Israelites (41ff.), the description of the Israelite entry into the Red Sea in terms appropriate to the approach of the Christian catechumen to baptism (310ff.), and the description of the drowning of the Egyptians in terms strongly suggestive of the Last Judgment (447ff.). Indeed throughout the poem there are hints that the exodus itself is being described in terms appropriate to the journey of all Christians through this life to the heavenly home.

Hints of an allegorical dimension to the poem are to be perceived at the level of style. Quite frequently words are used in unusual collocations. In lines 88b–90a the 'sails' (a metaphor for the pillars of cloud and fire) are called *lyftwundor leoht* 'bright miracles of the air', a phrase more appropriate to the pillar in another metaphorical guise, as the Cross. Similarly the verb in this passage, *hlifedon* 'towered', would be more appropriate applied to the pillar as Cross.[2] Thus the allegorical interpreta-

[1] As noted by P. A. M. Clemoes in *Techniques Narratives au Moyen Âge* ed. A. Crépin, Actes du Colloque l'Association des Médiévistes Anglicistes de l'Enseignement Supérieur (Amiens, 1974) 5–21 esp. 10–12.

[2] See Lucas in *FChristi* (1976) 198–9.

tion of the Israelites following the pillar as Christians (cf. *eorðbuende* 84) following the Cross is implied. This allegorical interpretation is specifically linked, as the mention of 'sails' has already suggested, to nautical imagery. In lines 80b–87a the Israelites, elsewhere called 'sea-men' (105 and note), are seen as on board a ship, with mast, cross-bar and rigging, a clear allusion to the patristic commonplace (though not from the exegesis of the exodus) of the Ship of the Church together with the Mast of the Cross. The rigging of the ship merges into a tent (85), an allusion to the Tabernacle of the Tent of the Presence of the Lord where God manifested his presence to the Israelites (86–7a). Juxtaposition of these two concepts 'Ship' and 'Tent', is possible because in allegorical exegesis both represented the Church, the family of all Christians.[1] Thus the style of the poem provides collocational juxtapositions which are explicable only by reference to an allegorical dimension in the poem's interpretation.

Evidently some passages in *Exodus* show an allusive condensation of meaning. Two methods in particular were used to augment this effect. One was to use a word in contexts where its meaning is more than one of its references. Thus the word *beam* (94, 111) refers to the pillar but also to the Cross which is the fulfilment of the pillar as a symbol of salvation. Another method was to use a word in contexts where it carries more than one sense. A clear example is *segl* (81). Apart from its primary meaning 'sail' in this context, the word could also mean 'veil', 'curtain', a sense which harmonizes with the notion 'Tabernacle' (which had a central beam [*bælc* 73] hung with a curtain), and 'banner', a sense which harmonizes with the conception of the pillar as Cross (which when viewed as a victory trophy was hung with a kind of streamer).[2] This use of words in more than one sense (*ambiguum*) is a device of rhetorical word-play.[3]

Once it is established that some passages in *Exodus* show an

[1] See further *ibid*. 201–2.

[2] See further *ibid*. 202–3.

[3] On which see R. Frank, *Wordplay in OE Poetry* (unpubl. thesis, 1969). Cf. also her article 'Some Uses of Paronomasia in Old English Scriptural Verse', *Speculum* xlvii (1972) 207–26 esp. 208 n.7.

allusive condensation of meaning it becomes apparent that the whole poem must be read with close attention to verbal nuance. There are a few statements so cryptic that, although they make sense straightforwardly interpreted, they seem to be pregnant with meaning in addition to the literal. Thus the statement *Folc wæs on lande* (567 and note) seems to signify more than that the Israelites have successfully crossed the Red Sea; their whole journey has been described as a sea-journey (*flodweg* 106) and they have now reached the heavenly port, the allegorical equivalent of the Promised Land. Again the statement *Sið wæs gedæled* (207 and note) seems to imply more than that the Egyptians are cut off from the Israelites by the Lord's cloud lowered between them; from now on the paths of the two peoples are separate, ultimately taking the Israelites and Christians to heaven and the Egyptians and evil-doers to hell. Occasionally there is almost obscurity, as in the apparent allusion to Adam contained in *ferhðbana* 'soul-slayer' (399 and note).

Another way of exploiting the full semantic richness of the vocabulary used is the repeated use of a word or its derivative in different contexts. In line 480 *Metod . . . mod gerymde* means that God 'manifested his will'. An important aspect of this passage is the syntactical running together of God and the *flod*, (note to 480b), a notion already suggested by the phrase *mere modgode* 'the sea raged' (459 and note), where it is implied that the sea is animate, and by the use of the adjective *modig* for the sea (469). What is implicit in lines 459 and 469 becomes clearer in lines 479ff. where the action of the sea is the manifestation of God's will. The image of God's *mod* being represented in terms of the physical phenomenon of the *flod* is crystallized in lines 488–9: that *merestreames mod* means God's will manifested in the rejoining of the sea-waters becomes explicit through the use of *He* which must almost certainly refer to God himself. Later the association between God and the *flod* is condensed into a single compound, *modwæg* (500).

The facility of the OE language for making compounds is amply illustrated in our poem. Indeed, according to the figures given by Carr, *Exodus* shows the highest proportion of different

compounds per line (2 : 3.8) of any of the longer OE poems. [1]
In many instances (those prefixed by an asterisk in the glossary)
the single occurrence in *Exodus* is the only one recorded in OE.
Such *hapax legomena* may well be coinages. Specially notable
compounds are those where the semantic relationship between
the two elements is ambiguous, e.g. *flodblac* 498, or where it is
one of abstract association, e.g. *heorawulfas* 181. Sometimes a
compound is so richly allusive that it would appear to be spe-
cially made for its context, e.g. *gyrdwite* 15. Some are striking
because, although the relationship between the two elements
is strictly denotative, the combination is applied to a concept
for which the second element would not ordinarily be used on
its own, e.g. *nydboda* of the sea returning to engulf the Egyptians
(475). Others stand out because they are used of concepts to
which they would not ordinarily apply, e.g. *beorhhliðu* 449 and
randgebeorh 296 of the 'walls' of water mounted up on either
side of the path through the Red Sea, *heofonbeacen* (usually a
designation of the sun) of the fire-pillar 107. A feature of the
poem is its use of compounds linked by common or similar
second elements but contrasted by their first elements to pre-
sent opposed concepts. For instance the cloud-pillar is called
a *dægsceld* 79 whereas the fire-pillar is called a *nihtweard* 116:
the second elements *-sceld* and *-weard* are similar in that both
suggest protection while the first elements *dæg-* and *niht-* pro-
vide the contrast between the two mutually exclusive concepts,
a cloud-pillar that appears only by day and a fire-pillar that
appears only by night, each replacing the other alternately.
This principle of linked contrast is used thematically to dif-
ferentiate the Israelites who are called *sæmen* (105, 479) from
the Egyptians who are called *landmenn* (179). (The Israelites
are sea-men because, allegorically, they are aboard the Ship
of the Church and because, literally, they succeed in crossing
the Red Sea, whereas by contrast the Egyptians are neither
aboard the Ship of the Church nor do they succeed in crossing
the Red Sea.)

Exodus, however, reveals a poet who was capable of more

---

[1] *Nominal Compounds in Germanic* (1939) 414.

than the clever employment of stylistic devices. He was a man of imaginative power and poetic resource who used language in a way that occasionally brings to mind Langland or Shakespeare. The poem's vivid metaphors have often been remarked. What is involved in phrases such as *ecg grymetode* 'the blade roared' 408 or *meredeað geswealh* 'sea-death swallowed' 513 is the use of verbs normally associated with animate subjects to describe the action of inanimate ones. In phrases such as *wære fræton* '[the Egyptians] ate the covenant' 147 or *ageat gylp wera* '[God] poured forth men's vows' 515 verbs normally used of concrete objects describe the actions applied to abstract concepts; a similar process is shown when the Egyptians are called *teonhete* 'malicious hate' 224. Thus the animate and the inanimate, the concrete and the abstract, are fused. This ability to fuse distinct concepts is a rare poetic gift. *Exodus* displays this quality also in the treatment of the literal and the figural. A notable example is the term *heofoncandel* (115 and note) applied to the fire-pillar, but almost certainly suggesting, through its second element, the Paschal Candle carried in procession as part of the liturgy for Holy Saturday; in the *Exultet* from the Paschal Vigil the Latin word *columna* was used for both the Paschal Candle and the fire-pillar, the word thus fusing the two concepts. The relevance of the Holy Saturday liturgy here and the identification of the fire-pillar with the Paschal Candle through the term *heofoncandel* is confirmed by a probable allusion to the wording of the *Exultet* in verses 113b–5a (see note). *Heofoncandel* displays remarkable verbal economy because lexically it is more appropriate to the figural meaning (Paschal Candle) than to the literal (fire-pillar). But perhaps the most remarkably poetic passage in the poem is lines 71–97, where several distinct concepts are fused.[1] The pillar of cloud and fire is viewed metaphorically as a sail-yard (with sail) which stood as a symbol for the Cross (with banner). The Tent (*feldhusa mæst* 85) is referred to after concentrated nautical imagery (80b–84). The division (76b) perhaps appropriate to the veil of the Tent (Holy: Holy of Holies) is accorded to the

[1] See Lucas in *FChristi* 193–209.

cloud (*wederwolcen* 75). Terms applicable to the Cross (*leoht* 90, *hlifedon* 89) are used where the pillar is apparently being viewed as a sail (89b). Mention of the Holy Spirit (96 and note), appropriate as a signification for the sail, follows the use of the word *beam* (94), which confirms the identification of the pillar with the Cross (especially its transverse bar). Evidently the various notions were intended to fuse poetically, to form a tapestry of ideas embroidered as on a back-cloth in a coherently unified pattern.

Despite the poem's manifest qualities previous writers have also allegedly found 'some evidence of a limited vocabulary' (IRVING 33).[1] While it is indisputably true that some words occur very frequently, for instance, *werod* twenty-one times and once as the second element of a compound, *folc* sixteen times and three times as the second element of a compound, it is unclear whether blame should be attributed to the poet for this practice. It seems inherently unlikely that a poet who was capable of the stylistic devices and imaginative power already mentioned would have repeated such words other than deliberately.[2] After all the poem is about people, whether or not they shall experience salvation. If there is any fault (which seems doubtful) it is more likely to have been one of aesthetic tact (deliberately using some words too frequently) than one of ignorance (lacking the skill to avoid repetition of diction).

V SOURCES

The main narrative thread in *Exodus* concerns the departure of the Israelites from Egypt, the trek to the Red Sea, the crossing of the Red Sea by the Israelites, and the drowning of the pursuing Egyptian host. Thus the immediate and primary source of the poem is the relevant parts of the book of Exodus

[1] But cf. Carr, *Nominal Compounds* 415, also J. R. Hulbert, *JEGP* xxxi (1932) 506–7.

[2] IRVING 33 also criticizes the use 'a dozen times' of phrases with *mæst*, e.g. *drihtfolca mæst*, pointing out that such phrases occur only eight times in the much longer *Beowulf*. But it may be misleading to regard *Beowulf* in this respect as a standard or norm against which to judge other OE poetry.

in the Bible, especially Ex. 13.20–14.31. Selected events pre-
ceding the exodus are dealt with succinctly (8–29), and of the
ten plagues only the last, the death of the Egyptian first-born,
is specifically mentioned (34–5). The poem ends with the
Israelites distributing the Egyptian treasure washed up on the
further shore of the Red Sea. Outside Ex. 13.20–14.31 the
poem draws on the rest of Exodus as appropriate, notably
Ex. 15.1–21, the Song of Moses, and the later chapters which
describe the Tabernacle of the Tent of the Presence of the Lord
(*feldhusa mæst* 85). The stories of Noah (362–79), Abraham and
Isaac (380–446), and Joseph (140–41 and lacuna, 142–7, 588)
are based on the relevant parts of Genesis, and the allusion to
the building of the Temple at Jerusalem (389–96) implies
familiarity with the relevant parts of Kings and Chronicles.

For an early medieval poem the statement 'the immediate
and primary source of the poem is the relevant parts of the
book of Exodus in the Bible' is not as straightforward as may
appear, since it is impossible to be sure what text or texts of
the Bible were used by the author. Differences in wording be-
tween the Old Latin version(s) and the Vulgate can be sub-
stantial enough to show that an author used one rather than,
or as well as, the other. For his commentaries on the Acts Bede
(d. 735), writing in Northumbria, used versions of the *Vetus
Latina* as well as the Vulgate.[1] Ælfric (d.*c*.1012), writing in
Wessex, translated from a version of Genesis closer to the OL
versions of the Bible than to the best manuscript tradition of
St Jerome's Vulgate.[2] At the time 'questions as to the nature
of the biblical text did not very much matter'; St Gregory the
Great (d. 604) 'interspersed many Old Latin variants among
the Vulgate so as to obtain a text which might easily lend itself
to moral or ascetic interpretation'.[3] Perhaps the author of

[1] M. L. W. Laistner, 'The Latin versions of Acts known to the Venerable
Bede', *Harvard Theological Review* xxx (1937) 37–50, repr. in *The Intellectual
Heritage of the Early Middle Ages*, ed. C. G. Starr (New York, 1957) 150–64.

[2] A. E. Nichols, '*Awendan* : a Note on Ælfric's Vocabulary', *JEGP* lxiii
(1964) 7–13.

[3] H. H. Glunz, *History of the Vulgate in England* ... (Cambridge, 1933)
11–12, 17.

Exodus selected variants that suited his purposes. Unfortunately the edition of the OL Bible by Sabatier (1751) is neither complete nor entirely trustworthy, and the new edition being prepared at Beuron under the directorship of B. Fischer o.s.b. does not yet include Exodus (though Genesis is available). Nevertheless a few details, one inferred from the Septuagint (note to 289b, *suðwind*), two from that part of the text relating to Genesis (notes to 384–6, and 442 *sæbeorga sand*) suggest that the author of *Exodus* knew an OL version certainly of Genesis and probably of Exodus.[1] Future scholars may be in a position to confirm this statement by adducing further correspondences of detail.

There is no reason to believe that the organization of the poem, the selection, disposition and treatment of events, and the inclusion of many non-scriptural features, is other than that of the Anglo-Saxon author. The poem has no known single literary source. In the last century it was thought that *Exodus* owed much to a Latin poem, *De Transitu Maris Rubri*, by Avitus, bishop of Vienne (d.518),[2] but this view was demolished by Moore, who cited parallels from other texts for all the features supposed to be uniquely common to Avitus's poem and *Exodus*.[3] Even details in the poem can hardly ever be pinned down to specific sources. As D. Whitelock has said, 'Any set of persons in Anglo-Saxon times that is well-informed on the Old Testament can be assumed to be cognizant of the Christian faith as a whole'.[4] The real 'source' of *Exodus* is the Christian tradition in which the poem must have been written. It is here that we must search for influences on the poem and for the origin of particular details, for the poet's creative impulse was no doubt fed by memory of what had been inculcated within him. Three elements in this Christian tradition may be

[1] Cf. also notes to 389–96, 555a.

[2] Ed. R. Peiper in MGH auctores antiquissimi VI.ii (Berlin, 1883) 254–74, also in PL lix 355–68. The first to suggest the *Exodus*-poet's acquaintance with Avitus's work was Groth, *Composition und Alter der . . . Exodus* (1883) 17–18, but his cautious approach was pushed much further by Mürkens, *BBA* ii (1899) 68–77.

[3] *MP* ix (1911) 83–108.

[4] *The Audience of Beowulf* (Oxford, 1951) 7.

singled out, the Bible, scriptural commentary, and the liturgy.
Although they will be dealt with separately it should be re-
membered that they were all part of one whole, inescapably
linked with each other like the corners of a triangle. At the
head of the triangle was the Bible, by far the most important
and the most studied book in the Middle Ages, the ultimate
source of all spiritual knowledge. At the two lower corners of
the triangle were the liturgy, which 'provided an excellent
initiation into the Bible', as the Bible did into the liturgy, and
scriptural commentary, which was founded in the Bible, as the
Bible was explained by it, and which 'was an integral part of
divine worship'.[1]

The Bible

Predictably *Exodus* reflects an intimate familiarity with the
Bible, especially, Exodus and Genesis apart, those portions
which refer to the events of the poem. The Book of Numbers
corroborates Exodus concerning the number of the Israelites
(224–32), details of their route (63a, 66, 67b, 133b–4) and the
tradition of the destruction of the Egyptian idols (46–7), and
it provides authority for the lowering of the cloud to mark out
camps (91–2, 128). Two notions, the fire-pillar as a means of
coercion (121b–3), and the exclusion of the young and the old
from the chosen band of warriors (233–46), are found in both
Numbers and the Psalms. The importance of the Psalter in
relation to the poem is somewhat overstated by Irving 206–7.
Only two specific details of any significance in the poem prob-
ably derive from the Psalter, the protective cloud as a tent
(71b–97) and the image of God's mighty hand (275). On the
other hand the Book of Wisdom probably provides authority
for several details in the poem: the corpses of the first-born in
heaps (41a), possibly the 'unknown way' to the Red Sea (58),
the cloud-cover as a protection from the heat (72, 74), the
Egyptians forgetfulness of their indebtedness to Joseph (144),
the green path through the sea (312a), God striking with
a sword (495b), the acquisition by the Israelites of the drowned

[1] Quotations from Leclercq, *CHB* 194.

Egyptians' treasure (582–9a). But it will be clear from what follows and from the Commentary that the poem reflects a close knowledge of the Bible as a whole.

Patristic exegesis

In lines 523–6 interpretation according to the Spirit as well as the Letter is evidently called for. Undoubtedly the poem reflects a knowledge of biblical exegesis though the extent to which it does so is a matter of disagreement among scholars and depends largely on how the poem is interpreted. Since the exodus was 'the greatest of Old Testament events' (Childs 238), the Fathers of the Church (*boceras* 531) wrote a good deal about it, and it will be convenient to indicate here the principal traits and sources of the exegetical tradition without any necessary implication that any particular exegetical notion or commentary is reflected in the poem. In illustrating general points, however, it will be convenient to select details that may be helpful for the interpretation of the OE poem rather than try to give a full representative account of the exegetical tradition.

For ancient Israel the exodus was the founding event, when the nation came into being. In the New Testament this event was seen as being 'fulfilled' in the life of Christ, 'I called my son out of Egypt' (Matt. 2.15, referring to Hos. 11.1). As 'the true redeemer of Israel' Jesus 'ushers in the messianic age which the original exodus from Egypt only foreshadowed' (Childs 233). This kind of interpretation, which was second nature to any informed Christian living under the early or medieval Church, and which is still legitimate, is called typology. The basis of typology is that a connection is established between two events fixed in historical time, 'the first of which signifies not only itself but also the second [which it foreshadows], while the second encompasses or fulfils the first'. [1] Thus the drowning of the Egyptians was seen as a type for the Last Judgment and the exodus itself was seen as being fulfilled by the redemption – just as the Israelites were saved by the exodus so later all Christians were saved by the redemption. Similarly a connec-

[1] E. Auerbach, ' "Figura" ', in *Scenes from . . . European Lit.* (1959) 53.

tion could be made between persons (Moses as a type of Christ).

But in the most extended reference to the exodus in the New Testament (1 Cor. 10.1ff.) the event is interpreted according to a different method:

> ... our ancestors were all under the pillar of cloud, and all of them passed through the Red Sea; and so they all received baptism into the fellowship of Moses in cloud and sea. ... All these things that happened to them were symbolic ... (1 Cor. 10.1–2, 11).

Paul's interpretation here is explicitly allegorical. Essentially allegorical interpretation equates something historical or terrestrial with something extra-historical or extra-terrestrial, an event with some concept outside historical time, a person with some personal concept outside the confines of man alone, a place with some situational concept within a scheme that looks beyond the earth, something concrete with something abstract. Thus Egypt was seen as the World, Pharaoh as the Devil, the Crossing of the Red Sea as Baptism, the trek through the wilderness as the journey of exile through this life, the pillar of cloud and fire as the Holy Spirit which guides Christians eventually to the Promised Land of heaven.[1]

Both typology and allegory are terms used in relation to the biblical exegesis of the Fathers of the Church and it is important to distinguish between them.

> The distinction generally made is that typology is based on historical correspondences and thus related to the Bible's own historical emphasis; while, judged by that same emphasis, allegory is non-historical and anti-historical.[2]

---

[1] The best account of patristic interpretation of the exodus is that by Daniélou, *Shadows to Reality* (1960) bk iv. For the Crossing of the Red Sea interpreted as signifying Baptism see also idem, *Bible and Liturgy* (1956) ch. v.

[2] J. Barr, *Old and New in Interpretation* (London, 1966) 104, where there is a useful discussion of the meaning given to these terms by modern biblical and patristic scholars. Cf. also H. de Lubac ' "Typologie" et "allégorisme" ', *Recherches de science religieuse* xxxiv (1947) 180–226.

In 1 Cor. 10.11 the Latin term which corresponds to 'symbolic' in the English version is *figura* but it is convenient to reserve this term for the literary descendant of biblical typology. Thus 'figural' is a literary term, as also is 'allegorical', and these terms are to be distinguished in much the same way as biblical typology and allegory.

> Since in figural interpretation one thing stands for another, since one thing represents and signifies the other, figural interpretation is 'allegorical' in the widest sense. But it differs from most of the allegorical forms known to us by the historicity both of the sign and what it signifies.[1]

Since the exodus was such an important event comment on it is to be found almost everywhere in the writings of the Church Fathers. In this respect the area of search for possible influences on the OE poem is almost immeasurable. Here only commentaries that relate specifically to Exodus can be mentioned. One of the earliest and most influential commentators was Origen, the great third century exegete who belonged to the 'allegorical' school of Alexandria (as opposed to the school of Antioch which favoured emphasis on the literal sense). Unlike most of the Greek Fathers Origen's work became widely known in the West in Latin translation; indeed his *In Exodum Homiliae* are known only in the Latin version by Rufinus. The importance of Origen's influence in determining the character of biblical exegesis in the West during the Middle Ages has been emphasized by Leclercq.

> 'The more . . . the thought of the early middle ages is studied, the more the conclusion of modern scholars is confirmed that Origen was the most important source of all. . . . Most of the allegories, symbols, images and even the actual phraseology come from Origen, either directly through the numerous transcripts of his own writings, or through inter-

[1] Auerbach 54. Auerbach's essay may be regarded as the definitive study of the figural literary mode.

mediaries like Isidore, Rabanus Maurus and especially Gregory the Great.'[1]

It is possible that Origen's work on Exodus was known in Northern England at the time of Bede (d.735).[2] Of the Latin Fathers who wrote before the time of *Exodus* both Augustine (d.430) and Isidore of Seville (d.636) composed a series of *Quaestiones* on Exodus. There are also *Quaestiones* formerly attributed to Bede,[3] but the date of these may or may not be earlier than the OE poem. Similarly the *Commentaria in Exodum* of Rabanus Maurus (d.856) may or may not have preceded *Exodus* depending on the date of the OE poem (see Intro. §VII). Later commentators may reflect ideas which were current earlier but from the point of view of establishing possible influences on *Exodus* it is safer to rely on sources that antedate or, at the latest, were probably contemporary with the OE poem.

A number of non-scriptural features in the poem reflect ideas which probably derived from patristic exegesis. Through the word *lifweg* (104) the exodus is clearly equated with the journey of Christians (*eðellease* 534) through life. On this journey, which is seen as a sea-voyage (*flodweg* 106, implied also at 118b) Christians travel aboard the Ship of the Church (implied 80b–84) with its mast and sailyard which was the Cross (83). As well as a Ship the Church is represented as a Tent (85). The pillar of cloud and fire is equated with the Holy Spirit (96, 104a), and the fire-pillar is connected with nocturnal terror (121b–3). That the Crossing of the Red Sea is to be identified with Baptism is clearly implied in lines 310–46, just as the Drowning of the Egyptians, so it is implied, is to be taken as foreshadowing the Day of Judgment for the wicked (447–515). Pharaoh is cast as the devil (15, 45b), Moses as a type of Christ (implied at 323–6, 519–48). Other details which probably reflect patristic exegesis are: an unhistorical Christ caus-

---

[1] *CHB* 194–5.

[2] Cf. Bonner, *ASE* ii (1973) 74.

[3] For the attribution to pseudo-Bede see Stegmüller, *Repertorium* (1950–55) ii 186 no. 1648.

ing the Egyptian idols to be destroyed when He descended to free the Israelites (alluded to at 46b); the Israelites caught between Pharaoh and the Red Sea (209–10); the identification of the place where Isaac was offered with the site of Solomon's Temple (389–96); the intended sacrifice of Isaac as a foreshadowing of the Crucifixion (implied at 402). There are also at least four onomastic allusions (*mansceaðan* 37, *eorþ werod* 194, *ða þe gedrecte* 501 of the Egyptians, *onriht Godes* 358 of the Israelites), which show that the author was familiar with patristic name-etymology.[1]

There is also the possibility that some non-scriptural features in the poem may be explained by reference to the *Antiquitates Judaicae*, a historical work by Josephus (d.*c.*100) which drew on the Bible.[2] But none of the details so far adduced provides convincing evidence that the poet of *Exodus* drew directly or even indirectly on Josephus.[3] In every instance other sources or explanations are available.

The Liturgy

Over sixty years ago Bright suggested the liturgy for Holy Saturday (Easter Eve), 'the most important service of the whole year', at which new converts were baptized, as a 'source' for *Exodus*,[4] but his proposal has not received much attention, and, when it has, it has not been greatly favoured.[5] Although Bright probably overstated his case (as, for example, when he claimed *Exodus* to be a *carmen paschale*) there can be little doubt

[1] Of which the most convenient source is P. de Lagarde (ed.), *Onomastica Sacra* (Göttingen, 1887 edn). Jerome's *Hebr. nom.* is also to be found in CCSL lxxii (1959) 57–161. On the influence of patristic onomastics on OE writers see F. C. Robinson, 'The Significance of Names in OE Literature', *Anglia* lxxxvi (1968) 14–58.

[2] For the Latin version see F. Blatt (ed.), *The Latin Josephus* (Copenhagen, 1958).

[3] Cf. Robinson, *Anglia* lxxx (1962) 363–4 and 376–7, and Irving 208 and 222 note 26. The strongest claim they make is for lines 27b–29 (see Irving's note) but the content of these verses is adequately explained by Ex. 6.3.

[4] 'The Relation of . . . *Exodus* to the Liturgy', *MLN* xxvii (1912) 97–103. The quotation is from Tyrer, *Holy Week* (1932) 147.

[5] IRVING 14–16. See further Irving 205–6.

that the poem reflects a knowledge of the liturgy. Lines 113b–15a (see note) correspond closely to the wording of a statement in the *Exultet* of the Paschal Vigil and the treatment of the fire-pillar, especially the reference to it as *heofoncandel* (115 and note), probably reflects the use of the word *columna* with dual meaning (fire-pillar: Paschal Candle) in the Holy Saturday service. Other details in the poem can probably be accounted for by reference to some of the readings for the service, for instance both the conception of the cloud-pillar as a protection which merged into a tent (71b–85) and the rough-sea weather (118b) on the exodus may well come from 1sa. 4.5–6, but it is impossible to be sure here that the source of inspiration was the liturgy rather than the Bible.[1]

Bright's argument was mainly concerned with the organizing principle of the poem. He thought that the grouping together within one poem of the stories of the exodus and crossing of the Red Sea, the Deluge, and the Offering of Isaac derived from the Paschal Vigil, the readings for which usually included the relevant passages from Genesis and Exodus.[2] He also sought, in effect, to transfer to the poem the same unifying principle as that of the Paschal Vigil – baptism. But Bright's theory falls far short of proof. All we can say is that, especially as the poem reflects a knowledge of the wording of the *Exultet* from the liturgy for Holy Saturday, the grouping of the readings in relation to the theme of the service may have provided a source of inspiration for the poem. The Paschal Vigil is a 'source' for the organization of the poem only in the sense that it may well have influenced the creative process that lies behind the poem's composition. Some investigators have tried to find a source for the poem in a specific form of the liturgy or parts of it,[3] but these attempts too fall far short of proof.

---

[1] Such a distinction would probably not have been made by the poet and his contemporaries. See further above, pp.53–4.

[2] See Tyrer, *Holy Week* 156–60.

[3] Notably McLoughlin, 'OE *Exodus* and the *Antiphonary of Bangor*', *NM* lxx (1969) 658–67. Cf. also Larès, 'Échos d'un rite hiérosolymitain . . .', cited above p.29, n.3.

VI THEME

As a mere narrative *Exodus* is so inadequate that earlier scholars thought that some sections were interpolations.[1] But OE poetry is not primarily narrative. The Aristotelian desire for unity of time, place and action is the result of the introduction of these ideas into England in the Renaissance. To criticize the poem on such grounds is to impose upon it the norms of another age. From what has been said under Style and Sources *Exodus* evidently has an allegorical dimension. At this level insights arise from a series of hints which are unmistakable because they arise from 'unrealistic' situations or from words being used in unusual collocations.[2] But the poem is not a consistent allegory, not even predominantly allegorical or figural. Considered separately, neither of these two levels, the narrative or the allegorical, is fully coherent. Moreover, an uneasy tension seems to exist between the two: a shift in the narrative from one episode to another does nothing (indeed, could hardly be expected) to illuminate a possible allegorical interpretation; and allegorical hints, even though they may form a 'chain of associated notions',[3] and even though such poetry need not be expected to present time as an unbroken horizontal process, are (because merely 'associated') not sufficient to provide a satisfying organic 'structure' which incorporates the non-sequential treatment of biblical-historical events.[4]

It is at the thematic level that the most powerful unifying factor in the poem is to be found. The central theme is Salvation by Faith and Obedience. In return for complete faith in God and obedience to his commands the Israelites are pro-

[1] See above, pp.30–33.

[2] On this aspect of the poem see Cross & Tucker, *Neophil.* xliv (1960) 122–7; Earl, *NM* lxxi (1970) 541–70; and Lucas in *FChristi* (1976) 193–209. Cf. also Huppé, *Doctrine and Poetry* (1959) 217–23, and Lee, *Guest-hall of Eden* (1972) 41–8. Earl, following Huppé, sees the allegorical element in the poem as dominant.

[3] This phrase was used by G. V. Smithers in 'The Meaning of *The Seafarer* and *The Wanderer*', *MÆ* xxvi (1957) 149.

[4] Cf. Earl, *NM* lxxi 563–5.

vided by Him with salvation.[1] For Noah salvation meant escaping in the Ark from the effects of the Flood, for the people with Moses being provided by God with the means of escape from the Egyptians, whom He destroys, and with access to the promised *eðel*. In the allegorical dimension salvation means, for Christians, avoiding the devil and arriving safely at the heavenly home. Complete faith is demonstrated by Abraham who is willing to sacrifice his own son at God's behest; Isaac is saved by the Lord's intervention. This arrangement, the provision of salvation in return for faith and obedience is the result of a mutual agreement, the abiding *haligu heahtreow* (388), between God and the Israelites. When Noah helped save mankind from the Flood,

> Hæfde him on hreðre   halige treowa.   (366)

The covenant was confirmed by Abraham and Isaac – *Wære hie þær funden* (387) – for Abraham demonstrated his faith by his willingness to sacrifice his son – *wære heolde* (422),

> Hu þearf mannes sunu   maran treowe?   (426)

In entering the Red Sea the Israelite host firmly *freoðowære heold* (306). By contrast the Egyptians break their covenant with the Israelites – *Wære ne gymdon* (140, sim. 147, 149–50) – and for this unethical action the Egyptians are severely pun-

---

[1] Farrell [*RES* n.s. xx (1969) 401–17] thinks the poem exemplifies the theme of the Help of God, a theme 'of great popularity from the earliest Christian times' (404), but, while it may be relevant, this theme is hardly an adequate summation of the predominant emphasis in the poem. There is more emphasis on God's controlling power, His direction of events, than on His assistance to the Israelites: God is not so much a helper as a leader. And there is emphasis on the reciprocal nature of the relationship between God and the Israelites: the Lord uses his power in response to a people's attitude towards Him, whether of faith in the case of the Israelites or disregard in the case of the Egyptians. Rather than try to fit the poem to an externally documented motif, however common, it is sounder critical procedure to allow the poem to state its own theme. Farrell himself admits the theme of the Help of God can only be 'a partial basis' for an interpretation (406).

ished by God, who thus simultaneously fulfils His covenant with the Israelites.

This contrast is further brought out by the difference in God's treatment of the two peoples. In His attitude to both His power is the crucial factor: He withholds it against the Israelites (cf. 121-4) and unleashes it upon the Egyptians. The Egyptians suffer as a result of God's manifestation of His will in the sea which destroys them. In connection with His attitude towards the Israelites the metaphorical description of the cloud-cover as a sail (81) is important. The metaphor shows that God's attitude towards the Israelites is one of benign masterfulness: He, so to speak, puts the wind in the Israelites' sail. Of the two partners bound by the covenant, He is the controlling one. While the physical phenomenon of the cloud gives symbolic shape to God's presence and guiding power, the 'sail'-metaphor reinforces the symbolic value of the cloud because the ground of the metaphor is God's control of the exodus seen as a sea-journey. God's control of the exodus is also the ground of the 'tent'-metaphor (85; cf. 133, 223). In an admirably imaginative yet concrete way the metaphoric expression of the tent, together with that of the net (74), conveys the idea that the Israelites are herded together in a confined and enclosed space. Cowed into submissiveness, they are driven forward, as the 'sail'-metaphor implies, by the inexorable will of God. The merging of the nautical metaphor into the 'tent'-metaphor serves to indicate that God's power was infused amongst the Israelites, not merely an external force.

There is little individual characterization in *Exodus*. In so far as the poem has a human hero it must be Moses, but most of what we know about him is contained in lines 13-14, that he was *freom folctoga, horsc ond hreðergleaw* . Moses is very much God's agent (and mouthpiece) on earth. Even though the path through the Red Sea is created *þurh Moyses hand* (480) we are reminded that really it was God who struck *mid halige hand* (485-6). [1] For the true 'hero' of the poem is God. He is the

---

[1] Similarly 262/275. Cf. Ex. 6.6 'I [the Lord] will redeem you with an outstretched arm'.

chief distributor of reward, giving *handlean* to Moses (19),
dædlean to the Egyptians (263). For being foremost in entering
the Red Sea passage He gives the tribe of Judah *deop lean* (315),
and, ironically, He gives a different form of *deop lean* to the
Egyptians when they are engulfed in the sea (507). God is
really present with the Israelites on the exodus (86, 91–2) and
it is to Him that, in the manner of the Germanic *comitatus*, they
are *þeodenholde* (87). Abraham acts *Haliges hæsum* (385). The
Egyptians are doomed because *hie wið God wunnon* (515). The
Lord's will is manifested through the sea returning to engulf
the Egyptians; indeed He Himself destroys them (489) and
strikes the sea with a sword (495), a remarkably physical de-
scription of spiritual judgment. In no other OE poem is God's
power so dynamically presented.

As well as having a central 'hero', God, *Exodus* displays other
features of Germanic heroic poetry.[1] The Israelite host is con-
stantly seen as an army on the march; they act bravely – *hie
hit frecne geneðdon* (571). We are told how both the Israelites
and the Egyptians selected the best warriors (227–46, 183–9).
There is an elaborate build-up towards a battle that is only
prevented by the lowering of the cloud between the antagonists
(154–207). Even the overthrow of the Egyptians in the sea is
described in terms of defeat in battle (447–515), and their
treasure is looted afterwards (585–90). Their defeat is the more
spectacular in view of their earlier martial vigour.

That *Exodus* is very much a poem in the Germanic tradition
is shown also by the stress on kinship. In AS society loyalty to
one's kin was a bond surpassed only by loyalty to one's liege-
lord. Both the Egyptians and the Israelites are united against
each other by kinship. While the Egyptians are *Faraones cyn* (14),
Egypta cyn (145), the Israelites are a *sibgedriht* (214), *Moyses
magas* (52), *mægwine* (146, 314), *cneowmagas* (318), they march
through the Red Sea passage *cynn æfter cynne* (351) and recog-
nize *mægburga riht* (352). The poem exploits the Germanic con-
cept of lineage, *frumcyn feora* (361), to show that the Israelites
are historically united. After Noah had saved the *frumcneow* of

[1] Irving 209–20 sees this aspect of the poem as dominant.

every species (371) Abraham *cende cneowsibbe* (356). In such a group-conscious organization there could be little room for the individual.[1] The nation's founder, Abraham, could, however, be singled out, since by doing so, as in *Him wæs an fæder* (353) – *an* being the alliterative stave – the unity of the group is emphasized. The Israelites are *freobearn fæder* (446), an ambiguous phrase since *fæder* could refer to either Abraham or God.

Within this conception of kinship the most important link for the maintenance of the pedigree was the *frumbearn*. Thus when Abraham was told to kill his *frumbearn*, Isaac, it was the hardest test of obedience God could have set, though in accordance with ideal Germanic custom Abraham puts loyalty to his Lord before loyalty to his son, a variation of the common AS theme of *comitatus* before kinship. And when the Egyptian first-born are killed by the Passover Angel the blow was the hardest they could receive. As is clear from the Bible God's action in slaying the Egyptian first-born was in retaliation for Pharaoh's treatment of the nation of Israel, whom the Lord considered as His first-born son (Ex. 4.22–3), 'a metaphor which expresses the unique relation between God and his people' (Childs 102). It is thus not only according to a well-established trait of Germanic heroic society but also in the spirit of the biblical narrative that the Egyptians' motive in pursuing the Israelites should be their desire to avenge their kinsmen (199), a detail that is added in the poem to the scriptural account. As Shippey has noted the poem reflects here a 'concern for human motivation on a realistic level'.[2]

Shippey also remarks that such a concern 'is markedly alien to the type of commentary most practised by Augustine and his followers', and he finds *Exodus* 'marked in several places by interest, not in symbolic or doctrinal commentary, but in other events of Bible story [which are] related ... to those being described not as mystic analogues, but as simple, factual motives or results'. He concludes that *Exodus*, like *Genesis* and *Daniel*, is 'resistant to allegorical or figural readings'.[3] While

[1] Cf. above pp.63–4.
[2] *OE Verse* (1972) 141.
[3] *Ibid.* 140–41, 153. By 'resistant' I take it he means 'not susceptible'.

Shippey's scepticism in accepting *Exodus* as a 'figural narrative' is salutary and justified his argument is to some extent misdirected. There is no reason to expect *Exodus*, a poem, even if it did employ figural narrative, to be *like* exegesis. Again, while there are indeed passages in *Exodus* which reveal an interest in 'factual motives or results' there are other passages which reflect an interest in scriptural commentary;[1] the implication that the presence of one kind of passage excludes the other is unfounded. The allegorical dimension to the poem is as much a fact as the presence of the episodes about Noah and Abraham, or, as the poem itself tells us, the significance of the exodus has been no more hidden than the Ten Commandments (519–22).

This sentiment is expressed in the one passage in the poem (516–48) entirely concerned with the allegorical dimension. Interpretation according to the Spirit as well as the Letter is evidently called for.

> Gif onlucan wile   lifes wealhstod . . .
> ginfæsten god   Gastes cægon,
> run biŏ gerecenod.   (523–6)

The keys of the Spirit, by which the mystery will be explained, are typological and allegorical exegesis as expounded by the Fathers of the Church,

> nu us boceras   beteran secgaŏ
> lengran lyftwynna.   (531–2)

Exodus never offers an explicit explanation of the *significatio* of the events of the exodus in the manner of exegesis, and the lines just quoted should not be regarded as a licence to read into the poem any convenient ideas found in patristic commentary relating to the exodus. Allusions to allegorical and figural interpretations are to be admitted only when they are manifestly supported by the text. That the text does sometimes require such interpretation is revealed as early in the poem as the open-

---

[1] Cf. *ibid.* 143 and n. 17.

ing lines, where *wordriht* (3), presumably the Pentateuch, con-
veys *bote lifes* (5) only in so far as the exodus of the Israelites
is interpreted as the salvation of mankind. Later this equation
is made explicit as the journey of the Israelites to the Promised
Land is seen as the journey taken by Christians (*we* 529, *us*
530–31) through this life (*lifweg* 104) to the heavenly home.
Just as the Israelites are *eðellease* (139, also 383b) because they
have not yet reached the Promised Land, so Christians
(*eorðbuende* 84) are homeless exiles (*eðellease* 534, *wreccum* 533)
because they have not yet reached heaven. For the Israelite
nation stands allegorically for another nation, the Christians,
who, just as the Israelites struggled with Pharaoh, were locked
in confrontation with the devil, Pharaoh's allegorical equiva-
lent (45, 503). A vital step to be taken by anyone desiring
Salvation was to undergo Baptism, an interpretation given to
the Crossing of the Red Sea (310–46) and to the escape from
the Deluge. In the teaching of the Church Fathers Baptism is
rather more than just 'a beginning',[1] for in Baptism 'man is
set free' and led 'from the world into the Kingdom of God'.[2]
Thus the Crossing of the Red Sea 'in itself represents the
journey of the Christian soul as it moves toward salvation'.[3]
(For those who did not seek Salvation through Baptism the
ultimate result would be the torment of the Last Judgment,
as foreshadowed in the poem by the destruction of the Egyp-
tians (447–515).) A Christian then must be a sailor, and in
harmony with this notion the Israelites are so described in the
poem (105, 133, 223, 331, 333, 479). The journey through life
is seen as a sea-voyage (*flodweg* 106), a notion taken from pa-
tristic exegesis though not that relating to Exodus. Buffeted by
life's storms (*holmegum wederum* 118) Christians travel over the
sea of this life to their ultimate home in the heavenly port of
eternal salvation. The vessel of salvation was the Ship of the
Church, an interpretation also given for Noah's Ark, with its
sailyard which stood for the Cross (83). Christians aboard the

[1] Cross & Tucker's phrase, *Neophil.* xliv 123.

[2] Daniélou, *Shadows to Reality* (1960) 178.

[3] Earl, *NM* lxxi 545, citing Zeno (d.*c.*375), Cassiodorus (d.*c.*580), and
others.

Ship of the Church were propelled by the Sail of the Holy Spirit (81, 105) which was attached to the Sailyard of the Cross. When the ship arrived, *folc wæs on lande* (567) and Salvation was at hand (*bote gesawon* 583).

This allegorical dimension becomes apparent from time to time throughout the poem but is never more than momentarily predominant. A good example of how the poem tends towards but does not become allegory is the passage describing the pillar of cloud. Through mention of the sail (81), sailyard (83) and rigging (82) the way is prepared for the introduction of the concept of the Ship of the Church but instead the poem passes on to *feldhusa mæst* (85), a term which by association suggests an allegorical meaning (the Tent of the Church) while at the same time relating at the literal level to the nomadic existence of the Israelites on the exodus (cf. 133, 223). Again in the same passage the cloud-cover (*wederwolcen* 75) is described as a sail (81) then the sails (*seglas* 89) merge into the pillars of cloud and fire (*beamas twegen* 94): while the equation of the cloud and the sail through the nautical metaphor 'is of the nature of allegory, . . . [such a phenomenon] is not usually given that name unless it goes on for some time'.[1] Here the passage has turned away from the momentary 'allegory' back on itself. In this way the allegorical dimension remains a chain of associated notions rather than a fully developed structural element.

This allegorical dimension is also carefully integrated into the poem. It always relates to the theme, which is enhanced by it. It is sometimes suggested by a detail appropriate to the poem's heroic idiom, as, for instance, when Baptism is brought to mind because the Israelites enter the Red Sea fighting.[2] The nautical imagery for the journey of life relates to the crossing of the Red Sea, albeit on dry land. The Sailyard of the Cross is associated metaphorically with the pillar in both its forms (*beamas twegen* 94). The sail and the pillar-Cross are linked not only because each represented the Holy Spirit but also because

---

[1] W. Empson, *The Structure of Complex Words* (London, 1952) 345.

[2] Cf. Lee, *Guest-hall of Eden* (1972) 48, who remarks on 'the poem's extraordinary fusion of heroic diction and biblical symbol'.

each is presented as a banner or standard (among other aspects). The image of the Tent is appropriate to the Israelites pitching camp on their journey across the desert.

Dame Helen Gardner has said that 'Propitious ages [for the writing of religious poetry] are those in which the poet can rely on his readers doing much of his work for him'.[1] *Exodus* is the product of such a propitious age. As the poem progresses there occur periodically passages, intellectually absorbing and imaginatively resourceful passages, which reveal or hint at allegorical or figural interpretations. These hints, however, are subordinate to, though not discordant with, the overriding theme of the poem. As a whole the poem is spiritually uplifting not so much because it makes use of ideas culled from scriptural commentary but rather because of the insistence with which it concentrates on a central, structurally unifying, religious theme.

VII DATE AND ORIGIN

The dating of Old English poetical texts is notoriously difficult; not only do all draw upon a single strong poetical tradition but all have survived in late West Saxon manuscripts.[2]

Exodus has traditionally been considered one of the earliest English poems, possibly earlier than *Beowulf*, which is usually assigned to the eighth century. This view is found, for example,[3] in the note to lines 1409–11 of C. L. Wrenn's edition of *Beowulf* (1953 and later edns):—

... it seems likely that the *Beowulf*-poet has in mind the O.E. poem *Exodus*: for 1410 is a verbal repetition of *Exodus* 58. ... It is, however, not entirely certain, though it seems more likely, that *Exodus* is older than *Beowulf*. ... A notice-

[1] *Religion and Literature* (London 1971) 137.

[2] Bliss & Dunning, *The Wanderer* (1969) 102.

[3] Following Marquardt, *Anglia* lxiv (1940) 152–8.

able parallel has been shown between 1409ff. and *Æneid* XI,
522ff.: it could be thought that the *Beowulf*-poet was echoing
Virgil rather than the O.E. *Exodus*. But the verbal repetition
cited above, and the strong probability that the original
O.E. *Exodus* is older than *Beowulf*, make the idea of a Vir-
gilian echo seem the lesser likelihood.

The line *enge anpaðas, uncuð gelad* is the only one which *Exodus*
(58) and *Beowulf* (1410) have in common,[1] and has been the
subject of controversy. Schücking proposed that the *Beowulf*-
poet may have borrowed the line from *Exodus*,[2] a suggestion
taken up by Klaeber who examined this and other parallels in
wording between the two poems[3] and concluded that 'the
balance of probability inclines at least slightly in favour of the
priority of *Exodus*'.[4] But when Imelmann pointed out the
similarity of the line to *Aeneid* xi 524–5[5] Klaeber changed his
mind and returned to the older view that 'the poet of *Exodus*
must have known our *Beowulf*'.[6] Schücking, however, re-
mained unrepentant, considering in Klaeber's *festschrift* that
even if the *Beowulf*-poet did have the lines from the *Aeneid* in
mind he borrowed the phrasing of his imitation from *Exodus*.[7]
In the light of this controversy Wrenn's statement quoted
above probably puts the case for the priority of *Exodus* as
strongly as possible. By contrast Irving's recent view (note to
line 58) that 'the oral-formulaic theory ... would surely ex-
plain the coincidence [of *Exodus* 58 and *Beowulf* 1410] as acci-
dent rather than as evidence of borrowing either way, thus

[1] Brodeur [*Nordica et Anglica* (1968) 109 n.10 and 112 n.15] also de-
scribes *Ex* 214 as identical with *Beowulf* 387 and 729, but the lines are only
very alike.

[2] *Untersuchungen* (1915) 38ff.

[3] According to Brodeur, *loc. cit.*, '*Exodus* has in common with *Beowulf* 146
substantival and adjectival compounds, [and] 58 verses' besides the lines
mentioned above, but of the 58 verses probably not all are absolutely
identical.

[4] *MLN* xxxiii (1918) 224.

[5] *Forschungen zur altenglischen Poesie* (1920) 419.

[6] *Anglia* l (1926) 203.

[7] *Studies in Eng. Philology*, ed. Malone & Ruud (1929) 213–6.

writing *finis* to an ancient controversy' seems over-emphatically trenchant. In any event the controversy has at least focussed attention on the fact that 'in proportion to its length, *Exodus* contains a much greater number of poetic compounds, and of verses, in common with *Beowulf* than does any other poem'.[1] It is probable that the two poems were first composed in the same general period.

What internal evidence there is points towards an early date for *Exodus*. There are a number of instances of the contracted forms characteristic of early poetry[2] (p. 40) and of monosyllabic words ending in a vocalic liquid or nasal (p. 40). The poem lacks formulae of the type *eallra þrymma þrym*, with *eall* in the dip, which are characteristic of the later Christian poetry.[3] There is no evidence of Old Norse influence.[4] Individually these details may carry little weight but taken together they do suggest an early date.

The *terminus a quo* for the original composition of the poem is probably about 700. If Christian poetry in the Germanic heroic style may be presumed to have begun with Cædmon, whose *Hymn*, according to Bede, was composed during the abbacy of St Hild (657–80), then some time must be allowed for the evolution of the new kind of poetry and its establishment as a convention. The *terminus ad quem* is probably about 800 since sufficient time must be allowed between the early poetry and the later, probably ninth-century poetry of Cynewulf and his group, which is often imitative of *Beowulf* and *Exodus*. Thus *Exodus* was probably composed in the eighth century at some time between the time of Bede and the time of Alcuin. But the possibility that the poem was first composed after 800 cannot, on the available evidence, be eliminated.

[1] Brodeur, *Nordica et Anglica* 109.

[2] In *Gloria I*, a late poem, a dissyllabic form is required by the metre at line 27a, *þone heahan dæg*, but the form *heahan* may be due to an analogical re-formation (so SB §295 Anm. 1). Cf. C. & K. Sisam, *The Salisbury Psalter*, EETS 242 (1959), 25 n.2.

[3] L. Fakundiny, *RES* n.s. xxi (1970) 133.

[4] But even in late North. OE there is little evidence of ON influence: for some exceptions see A. S. C. Ross, 'Four Examples of Norse Influence in the Old English Gloss to the Lindisfarne Gospels', *TPS* (1940) 39–52. Cf. note to *hildecalla* 252.

The question of date is closely connected with the question of origin. There is much to suggest that *Exodus* was composed in a monastery. The familiarity with the Bible which the poem reflects (pp.54–5) could easily have been instilled by the monastic *lectio divina*. Reading was done aloud, with the lips, and the process of reading and meditating on the divine word has been described as 'rumination', for it 'means assimilating the content of a text by means of a kind of mastication which releases its full flavour'.[1] Scriptural commentary too (pp.55–9) is likely to have been assimilated in a monastery and the supposition that *Exodus* is a monastic poem is confirmed by the use made of the liturgy for Holy Saturday (pp.59–60). The theme of the poem, Salvation by Faith and Obedience, could appropriately have been featured by someone devoted to the monastic vocation, in which the only value was eternal life, the only evil sin.[2]

On the basis of linguistic evidence it was tentatively suggested that *Exodus* may have been composed in a Northumbrian dialect and transmitted to Malmesbury via a West Mercian centre such as Worcester or Lichfield (p.39). If so then the poem originated in a Northumbrian monastery. Such a supposition would be consonant with the kind of biblical exegesis reflected by the poem for it seems to show greater affinity with the allegorical school of Alexandria, whose influence reached Northumbria via Ireland,[3] than with the literal school of Antioch, whose teaching was introduced into southern England by Theodore, archbishop of Canterbury (668–90). If the poem did originate in a Northumbrian monastery then its assignation to the eighth century would tend to be confirmed since it is likely to have been composed and transmitted before the Viking attacks on the monasteries became widespread.

---

[1] Leclercq, *Love of Learning* (1961) 78.

[2] *Ibid.* 31.

[3] Cf. 'the possibility that OE. *Exodus* originated in a centre influenced by this Insular church' mentioned by Farrell, *RES* n.s. xx (1969) 405.

The Text

EDITORIAL PROCEDURE

The text has been edited from MS Junius 11. The spelling of the manuscript has been followed except for the correction of apparent errors. Emendations and additions are noticed in the Textual Notes (below the text), which give the forms in the manuscript and the names of those who proposed the principal emendations or additions that have been adopted. In three lines (246, 304, and 411) a whole verse has been supplied and in line 161 all except the first word. Wherever a reconstruction is offered it is intended to be uncontroversial, that is, to contain nothing that is metrically, semantically or syntactically unusual in OE poetry.

Abbreviations, which are not numerous, have been expanded without notice. The word 'and' in this poem is always written with the Tironian sign *7*, and this has been expanded as *ond* because this form is the only full spelling of the word that occurs in the manuscript (cf. also note to 283). The same abbreviation is also used for the prefix in *andsaca* (503) where it has been expanded in accordance with the only full spelling of the word (15). The abbreviation *þ* is always used for *þæt* and always means *þæt* (but cf. note to 185). Final *m* is sometimes indicated by a nasal titulus over the preceding vowel, as in *dreã* (532), *þã* (543), *sũ* (279, 345, 357), *heofonũ* (376, 493) and other dative plural forms in *-um*. The word *ponne* is contracted as *poñ* only in line 544. In line 232 the Roman numeral *x.* has been treated as an abbreviation for *tyn* and so expanded.

Word-division has been regularized, and departures from the word-division of the manuscript are not usually included in the Textual Notes. Modern punctuation has been supplied, and the division into paragraphs is also editorial, though it sometimes coincides with the presence of capitals in the manuscript (see Introduction, p.19). Section numbers are given on the left of the page; those in square brackets are not entered in the manuscript but, unless in italics (135), the beginning of the section is indicated by a large capital (or space left for it) – the large capital at 107 has been ignored (see Intro. p.9). An extra space with asterisks between lines indicates that a portion of the text is lacking in the manuscript (between lines 141 and 142 and between 446 and 447).

Exodus

XLII· Hwæt, we feor ond neah   gefrigen habbað   [p.143
ofer middangeard   Moyses domas,
wræclico wordriht,   wera cneorissum –
in uprodor   eadigra gehwam
5 æfter bealusiðe   bote lifes,
lifigendra gehwam   langsumne ræd –
hæleðum secgan.   Gehyre se þe wille!

TEXTUAL NOTES

1 habbað *Grein*] habað

COMMENTARY

1] *Hwæt* is an interjection conventionally used to introduce some OE poems; so also begin *Andreas*, *Beowulf*, and *Juliana*.

1–7] 'a peculiarly elaborate example' of 'the complex type of parallelism' favoured in some OE poems [Gradon, *Form and Style in Early Eng. Lit.* (1971) 157]: *domas*, *wordriht*, *bote*, and *ræd* are all acc. after *secgan*, but *bote* and *ræd* represent distinct aspects of *domas/wordriht*. Presumably *domas* and *wordriht* refer to the Pentateuch, which does indeed contain *langsumne ræd*. It also conveys *bote lifes*, but only in so far as the exodus of the Israelites is interpreted as the salvation of mankind. Evidently *bealusiðe* has a double reference, as SEDGEFIELD suggested, (1) to the journey of the Israelites through the wilderness to the Promised Land, and (2) to the journey of man through life to the heavenly home. Thus the stylistic device is used to indicate to the audience the kind of response required for the understanding of the poem as a whole. Trahern [*AS Poetry* (1975) 292–3] adduces Ecclus. 45.6 but the OE words do not match those of the Vulgate as closely as he suggests.

1b] MS *habað* is purely scribal; the grammatical form has been restored to avoid the appearance of metrical difficulty.

3] *wordriht* occurs only here and in *Beowulf* 2631 where it probably means 'formal (unwritten) obligation'. Here the reference is to written law. Irving, referring to C. Donahue [*Traditio* vii (1949–51) 263–77 esp. 268 and n.29; see also idem, *Traditio* xxi (1965) 55–116 esp. 69–71], seeks to relate the word to Irish *recht litre* 'law of the letter', i.e. ecclesiastical law derived from Scripture, but this is speculation.

6b] *langsumne ræd*: cf. *ece rædas* 516 and note.

6b–7] IRVING compares *Meters of Boethius* 'Proem' 9–10.

7b] Irving 211 compares the biblical admonition 'He that hath ears to hear, let him hear' (Mark 4.9).

Þone on westenne   werode Drihten,
soðfæst Cyning,   mid His sylfes miht
10 gewyrðode,   ond him wundra fela
ece Alwalda   in æht forgeaf.
He wæs leof Gode,   leoda aldor,
horsc ond hreðergleaw,   herges wisa,
freom folctoga.   Faraones cyn,
15 Godes andsacan,   gyrdwite band,
þær him gesealde   sigora Waldend

11 forgeaf] a *expuncted and surmounted by point (to cancel expunction)*
15 andsacan *Thorpe*] andsaca

8–29] This passage refers primarily to God's appearance in the burn-
ing bush to Moses on Mt Horeb (Ex. 3), their first meeting (22b), but other
material is also incorporated.

8a] *Þone*: Moses.

8b] *werode* is gen. pl. for regular *weroda*.

10] *wundra fela*: specifically the miraculous 'signs' designed to influence
Pharaoh, the rod turning into a snake (Ex. 4.3–4) and the diseased hand
(4.6–7).

12–14] Moses is described in terms of a Germanic chieftain with the
emphasis (esp. in 13a) on his mental rather than his military qualities; cf.
Tacitus, *Germania*, ch. xi, 'it is . . . their [chiefs'] prestige as counsellors . . .
that tells'.

14b–15] In OE poetry the phrase *Godes andsaca*, used of Pharaoh in line
503, usually refers to the devil (*Gen B* 442, *Christ and Satan* 190) and *Godes
andsacan* to the fallen angels (*Christ* III 1593, *Christ and Satan* 268, 279, 339).
Thus the way is open for Pharaoh and his followers to be identified with the
devil and his followers, an identification which is conventional in allegorical
exegesis, e.g. Isidore, 'Pharao figuram habuit diaboli' (PL lxxxiii 108). Simi-
larly *bindan* is frequently used of the binding of the devil (e.g. *Gen B* 379), a
notion ultimately derived from Rev. 20.1–3, also Matt. 12.29, Mark 3.27.
Thus the strife in the poem – principally between God and Pharaoh – can
be seen as the strife between God and the devil. The reference in 15b is to
the drowning of the Egyptians (cf. 470) brought about by Moses extending
his rod over the Red Sea (Ex. 14.16) thereby causing the waters to close
over them. Later in the poem the drowning of the Egyptians is described in
terms strongly suggestive of the Last Judgment (note to 447–515). Prior to
the Last Judgment the Second Coming is to be announced by means of
'The Sign of the Son of Man in Heaven' (Matt. 24.30), which was con-
ventionally interpreted as the Cross [Reijners, *Terminology of the Cross* (1965)
122–3]. It is probably no coincidence that Moses's rod (*gyrd-*) was also con-
ventionally interpreted as the Cross [Reijners 107–18, also Caesarius of
Arles (d. 542), CCSL ciii 463].

modgum magoræswum   his maga feorh,
onwist eðles   Abrahames sunum.
Heah wæs þæt handlean   ond him hold Frea,
20 gesealde wæpna geweald   wið wraðra gryre;
ofercom mid þy campe   cneomaga fela,
feonda folcriht.   Ða wæs forma sið
þæt hine weroda God   wordum nægde:
þær He him gesægde   soðwundra fela,
25 hu þas woruld worhte   witig Drihten,

22 feonda] *written twice*

17] *magoræswum* is dat. sg. for regular *magoræswan*.

19] *handlean* 'reward' probably refers to what Moses is able to achieve
through the power of his hand (with which he holds his rod). The divine
power communicated through Moses's hand (and rod) is clearly indicated
at 262–3 (where it is also associated with 'reward'), 280 and 480 (cf. 486),
and is based on Ex. 14.16, 21, also Deut. 34.12 and Isa. 63.12. Cf. 275 and
note.

19–20] A comma is necessary after *Frea*. If the clause were *ond him hold
Frea gesealde wæpna geweald*, by Kuhn's Law of Sentence Particles (a finite
verb is a sentence particle and must either occupy a position of stress [or
secondary stress] or be placed in the first metrical dip of the verse-clause)
gesealde would have to be stressed; if it is stressed it must alliterate – but it
does not.

20–22] A reference forward in time to the Israelites' wars against vari-
ous peoples (Ex. 17.8–13, 23.20–33 etc.). Vickrey [*Traditio* xxviii (1972)
129–30] refers these verses to the battle which he believes takes place be-
tween the Israelites and the Egyptians face to face in the Red Sea, but the
text lacks adequate evidence for the occurrence of such a battle.

22] *folcriht*: fixing the sense of this word here and in *Beowulf* 2608 has
proved difficult. In OE prose it means 'legal rights in the people's common
land' and by extension 'law of the people'. Accordingly Farrell [*NM* lxvii
(1966) 364–5] takes it here as 'the customary law of the Egyptian people
which is being conquered', though, as Irving points out, the reference is
more probably to the Canaanites. Another suggestion, supported by BTSA,
is that *folcriht* means 'property', but, again as Irving points out, this in-
terpretation involves taking *ofercom* to mean 'subdued' when construed with
cneomaga fela and 'obtained' when construed with *folcriht*. All these problems
disappear if we interpret *folcriht* in poetry as 'legitimate power over people',
'authority', and the same sense would be appropriate for *leodriht* in *Andreas*
679 (cf. Brooks's note).

25–7] This incident, where Moses is told by God the story of the cre-
ation, is an addition to the biblical narrative. IRVING notes that according

eorðan ymbhwyrft   ond uprodor,
gesette sigerice,   ond His sylfes naman,
ðone yldo bearn   ær ne cuðon,
frod fædera cyn,   þeah hie fela wiston.
30   Hæfde He þa geswiðed   soðum cræftum   [p.144
ond gewurðodne   werodes aldor,
Faraones feond,   on forðwegas.
Þa wæs ungeare   ealdum witum

33 ungeare *Klaeber*] ingere

---

to *The OE . . . Heptateuch* ed. S. J. Crawford, EETS 160 (1922) 21, the story of the Pentateuch was dictated to Moses by God on Mt Sinai; Horeb and Sinai are not clearly distinguished (see, e.g., Ex. 17.6, Deut. 5.2).

27b–29] *His sylfes naman*: 'Yahweh', though the name does not occur in the Vulgate Ex. 3.13–15, and Ex. 6.2–3 has 'Adonai'. The reference to the Israelites' previous ignorance of the name (28–9) is certainly to Ex. 6.2–3 but these verses clearly refer back to 3.13–15. On the text of Ex. at this point see Hyatt 75–81, Childs 60–70.

28] *yldo* is gen. pl. for regular *ylda*. Inflexional vowel-substitution with a marked preference for -*o*, is more common in this word than in any other (also in 437), and this irregularity may be due to the word being somehow associated in meaning with *yldo* 'age': cf. Klaeber's note to *Beowulf* 70.

30] *Hæfde . . . geswiðed*: probably 'strengthened'.

30–32] Since these lines to some extent recapitulate what precedes they are best taken as an independent unit.

32] *on forðwegas*: Moses's exile in Midian.

33a] *ungeare*: Klaeber [*Archiv* cxiii (1904) 146] was the first to propose a form of *ungeāra* for MS *ingere*; a WS scribe may well have misunderstood the original word since *geāra* 'is certainly Anglian' [R. Vleeskruyer, *Life of St Chad* (1953) 28]. As Vickrey notes [*Archiv* ccx (1973) 42–3], *ungeare* may be interpreted to mean 'soon'. The affliction of the Egyptians followed shortly after the strengthening of Moses, both events being in the past for the narrator.

33b] *ealdum witum*. The appropriate torments suffered by the Egyptians. are the ten plagues. Since *deaðe* and *hordwearda hryre* refer to the tenth plague, the death of the first-born, *witum* would appear to refer to the first nine plagues – *geniwad* probably implies as much. Irving notes that *wite* is the usual rendering of L *plaga* in *The OE Heptateuch*. As J. R. R. Tolkien suggested the plagues are *eald* in the sense that they are 'famous in history', unless the predominant reference is to the figural level at which *eald wite* are the torments of hell.

> deaðe gedrecced   drihtfolca mæst,
> 35 hordwearda hryre   (heaf wæs geniwad):
> swæfon seledreamas   since berofene.
> Hæfde mansceaðan   æt middere niht
> frecne gefylled,   frumbearna fela,

34 gedrecced *Cosijn*] gedrenced *with* renced *in later hand over erasure*

34] The pp. *gedrecced* is by analogy with the regular formation for a w.v. 1b (cf. Campbell §751.2) and has been preferred on the grounds that a later hand is likely to have written something similar to what the MS originally had but not identical with it. The verb is probably ironic since in patristic onomastics the name *Aegyptus* was explained etymologically to mean *affligens* 'afflicting', a usage clearly alluded to in lines 37 and 501. The reading *gedrenced* could possibly be accepted as a metaphorical usage which looks forward to the drowning of the Egyptians.

35] *hordwearda hryre* must belong with 33–4 and be taken as parallel with *deaðe*. If *hordwearda* were taken to begin a new sentence, *Horwearda hryre heaf wæs geniwad*, by Kuhn's Law of Sentence Particles (see note to 19–20) *wæs* would have to be stressed, but this produces unacceptable metre. Phrases like *heaf wæs geniwad* usually stand on their own and are often parenthetic, e.g. *Wanderer* 50, 55.

36] At first sight the phrase *swæfon seledreamas* seems to constitute an unusual use of the verb *swefan* 'sleep', 'die while asleep' but in fact it is the use of *seledreamas* that is unusual. Like *hordwearda* (35) *seledreamas* denotes the Egyptian first-born, here described as 'hall-joys'. The description of them as being deprived of their treasure is an allusion to the spoiling of the Egyptians by the Israelites on the night before their exodus (Ex. 12.36), a notion incorporated into the liturgy for Holy Saturday, 'nox, quae expoliauit aegyptos' (*LM* 97); cf. Childs 175–7. *Since berofene* is a variant of a metrically formulaic phrase (cf. *Beowulf* 2457, 2931, *Andreas* 1084, *Christ* III 1525, *Riddle 13* 7), but it is not, as IRVING claimed, 'syntactically homeless'.

37] The subject of *Hæfde* is God (the logical subject of the intervening sentences in the passive) carried over from 30. *Mansceaðan* refers to the Egyptian first-born, an onomastic allusion, as Robinson points out [*NM* lxix (1968) 166–7]. In patristic name-etymology *Aegyptus* was interpreted to mean *persequens*, *affligens*, *tribulans* (see further note to 501), for which '*mānsceaðan* is a fairly exact OE counterpart'.

38] As noted by D. Slay [*TPS* (1952) 4 n.2] this line has double alliteration in the *b*-verse, a dubious feature which may be accidental (since the second stress in the *b*-verse does not normally alliterate). Alternatively the original may have had *frumbearna gehwylc* (J. R. R. Tolkien; cf. *PPs* 77/51); scribal interference with the pattern of alliteration occurs at 339, 414, 467.

abrocene burhweardas.   Bana wide scrað,
40 að leodhata,   land ðrysmyde
   deadra hræwum –   dugoð forð gewat.
   Wop wæs wide,   worulddreama lyt,
   wæron hleahtorsmiðum   handa belocene,
   alyfed laðsið   leode gretan,

---

40 ðrysmyde *Wrenn*] dryr/myde *over line division*

39] The pp. *abrocene* is in agreement with the object *burhweardas*. Since *abrecan* with a personal object is not recorded elsewhere, Cosijn's proposed emendation to *abrotene* 'slain' [*PBB* xix (1894) 458] is plausible semantically as well as palaeographically (confusion of *c* and *t*). However, Vickrey avoids the difficulty [*Archiv* ccx (1973) 44] by taking *burhweardas* to mean the Egyptian idols (called *deofolgyld* in line 47) who were destroyed together with the first-born (Ex. 12.12).

39b–40] The *bana* is the Passover Angel seen as hateful (*að*) from the Egyptian point of view.

40] MS *dryrmyde* is not a known word and clearly requires emendation. The usual emendation to *drysmyde* provides a word which also occurs in *Beowulf* 1375 where its meaning is uncertain. Wrenn's suggestion (*RES* N.S. vi (1955) 186–7) that both are from *þrysmian*, a verb formed on *þrosm* 'smoke', is extremely plausible palaeographically and provides both passages with a known word of appropriate sense. Normally *þrysmian* means 'stifle' but in the *Beowulf* passage 'become choked' seems more likely, as Wrenn suggests. Here either is possible but 'stifle' is preferable as the more certainly attested.

41a] *deadra hræwum*: for the implication that the corpses of the first-born lay together in large numbers cf. Wisd. 18.12 (IRVING) and esp. 18.23 (Irving).

41b] *dugoð forð gewat* refers euphemistically to the death of the Egyptian first-born in terms appropriate for the departure of the Israelites (cf. *dugoð* 91) [Ziegler, *Poetische Sprachgebrauch* (1883) 121–2 compared *Gen* 1068, 1178, 1601, 1742, to which IRVING adds 1192]. Editors and others have disagreed as to whether this verse, lines 44–5a and verse 48b refer to the first-born or to the Israelites. There is almost certainly a dual reference, a device which probably derived from scriptural commentary; Vickrey [*Archiv* ccx (1973) 45–6] cites passages from Origen, Rabanus and Bede (*recte* pseudo-Bede) which imply that 'the journey of the Egyptians to death *is*, on a figural level, the journey of the Israelites to life'.

43] Since the destruction of the first-born is described in terms that in another context might be applicable to an attack on the hall of a Germanic chief it is appropriate in the ensuing disaster-ridden atmosphere that the Egyptian 'scops' (*hleahtorsmiðum*) should be silent, unable to use their hands *gomenwudu gretan* 'to play the harp'.

44–5a] Translate: 'the people, the travelling host, were allowed to

45 folc ferende –   feond wæs bereafod.   [p.145
   Hergas on helle   (heofon þider becom)

45 feond *Thorpe*] freond

---

undertake a hateful journey'. Like *dugoð forð gewat* (see note to 41b) these verses have a dual reference, (1) to the metaphorical journey of the first-born to death, a journey that is described in terms of (2) the departure of the Israelites. Both journeys are hateful to the Egyptians. In *Resignation* 53 *laðne sið* refers to the journey of the soul from the body.

45b] All previous editors, including Irving (at the second attempt) read *feond*. The *feond* is Pharaoh, who is, allegorically, the devil (see note to 14b–15). He is doubly deprived (1) of the Egyptian first-born, and (2) of his Israelite work-force. By providing a change of viewpoint – from that of the Egyptians (contained in *laðsið*) to that of the Israelites – thus indicating that two viewpoints are possible, the emended reading harmonizes with the dual reference indicated for 41b, 44–5a and 48b. If MS *freond* were retained it could represent either Pharaoh, who as earthly lord is deprived of his retainers the first-born, or any Egyptian who lost a son at the Passover. Because it lacks precision (*freond* would not *necessarily* refer to Pharaoh) the MS reading would not accord with the dual reference evident in this passage. Vickrey's suggestion [*ASE* i (1972) 163–4] that *freond wæs bereafod* refers simultaneously both to Pharaoh's loss of treasure and to the devil's loss of *his* treasure (humankind) involves an equation not adequately founded in the text of the poem [so J. E. Cross, *NQ* ccxix (1974) 187].

46–7] The well-known tradition of the destruction of the Egyptian idols on the night of the Passover probably derives from Ex. 12.12 and Num. 33.4, 'quos [primogenitos] percusserat Dominus (nam et in diis eorum exercuerat ultionem)'.

46a] *Hergas on helle* 'hellish shrines'; cf. *Beowulf* 3072. *Hergas* is best taken as for WS *heargas* and shows Anglian smoothing (see Intro. 38), though previous editors have taken it as acc. pl. of *here* 'army' in apposition with *folc* (45). K. Malone would probably have rendered *on helle* as 'in hell on earth' (i.e. Egypt) – cf. his remarks on *feond on helle* (of Grendel, *Beowulf* 101) in *Britannica* (H. M. Flasdieck *Festschrift*) ed. W. Iser & H. Schabram (Heidelberg, 1960) 193, and his 'Grendel and his Abode' in *Studia Philologica et Litteraria in hon. L. Spitzer* (Bern, 1958) esp. 298–9 – but such a rendering would obscure the dual reference to Egypt *and* hell. For the pairing of *hergas* and *deofolgyld* see Kock, PPP 6.

46b] On the basis of Ex. 12.12 IRVING suggested that *heofon* 'stands for God himself' – 'startlingly' as it seemed to Wrenn [*RES* n.s. vi (1955) 187]. For those who agree with Wrenn the best emendation available is *hēof* 'mourning', but it is quite unnecessary. *Heofon* in the sense 'divine power' is attested by BTS *heofon* VI and OED *Heaven* sb. 6, and the phrase no doubt contains an allusion to the well-known belief that an unhistorical Christ caused the idols to be destroyed while descending to free the Israelites: 'Haec [Pascha] quoque templa idolorum destructa significat, adventum

47 druron deofolgyld.   Dæg wæs mære
    ofer middangeard   þa seo mengeo for.
    Swa þæs fæsten dreah   fela missera

Christum [*sic*: ? Christi] in Aegyptum, quo simulacra Aegypti destructa
sunt' (pseudo-Bede, *In Exodum* (12.15), PL xci 307). *Heofon* probably denotes
the divine power which descended into Egypt to free the Israelites, thus
typifying Christ's descent to liberate the patriarchs from hell. The asso-
ciation between the delivery from Egypt and the harrowing of hell, for
which the former event is a type, is suggested by the antithesis *helle/heofon*.
Another explanation of the phrase, proposed by Robinson [*Anglia* lxxx
(1962) 365], is that it refers to the physical lowering of the heavens suggested
by *inclinavit caelos et descendit* (2 Sam. 22.10 and Ps. 17.10 [18.9]). Trahern
[*AS Poetry* (1975) 294–5] adduces Wisd. 18.14–16, but this reference, which
is specifically to the first-born, would only be appropriate if *hergas* were
taken as 'the armies [of the Egyptian first-born]'.

47b–48] Like lines 41b and 44–5a these verses have a dual reference,
for they describe the death of the first-born in terms applicable to the de-
parture of the Israelites. *Dæg wæs mære* suggests the latter reference particu-
larly strongly since as Bright noted [*MLN* xxvii (1912) 14] the phrase is
reminiscent of Ex. 12.42 and 13.3, also 12.14 (IRVING).

48–9] Since *seo mengeo* refers to the first-born, and since the natural
subject of *dreah* is *ealdwerige Egypta folc* (50), *swa* (49) must begin a new
sentence. This argument overrules my earlier suggestion [*NQ* cciv (1969)
365] that *swa* means 'because'.

49] What happened to the Egyptians is described here in terms appro-
priate to the Israelites (who were held captive in Egypt), just as the death-
journey of the Egyptian first-born is described in terms appropriate for the
Israelite departure (see notes to 41b, 44–5a, 47b–48). The Egyptians (seen
allegorically as the followers of the devil – see note to 14b–15) endured
confinement in hell (a concept denoted by *fæsten* in *Whale* 70); presumably
the reference is to their doing so after being drowned in the Red Sea. *Fela
missera* is no doubt *litotes* for 'for ever'; Vickrey [*Archiv* ccx (1973) 47] suggests
an allusion to the binding of the devil *per annos mille* (Rev. 20.2).

49b] *missera*: a difficult word etymologically, which occurs only in the
gen. and dat. pl. Most authorities link it with ON *misseri*, which, according
to J. de Vries, *Altnordisches Etymologisches Wörterbuch* (Leiden, 1961) s.v.
missari, is probably a loan from OE. The OE nominative is usually recon-
structed as **missere* and the word was probably a compound on *miss-* 'divers',
'split in two' and *-(g)ēre* 'year' [so K. M. in *ZfdA* xiii (1867) 576], though
almost certainly not recognized as such in OE (since it occurs in *b*-verses of
Type 1D). Apparently the compound joined the *ja*-stem noun-class. In the
ON word the vowel of the second syllable shortened [A. Noreen, *Altnordische
Grammatik* (Alabama/Tübingen, 1970) §151.6].

50] *ealdwerige* corresponds to WS nom. sg. m. **ealdwīerig* and shows
non-WS *i*-mutation in the second element. The adj. **wīerig* is formed on
the noun *wearh* 'villain' by addition of the Pr.OE suffix *-īg*, which caused
i-mutation, and the stem vowel became long by compensatory lengthening

50 ealdwerige Egypta folc,
    þæs þe hie wideferð wyrnan þohton
    Moyses magum, gif hie Metod lete,
    on langne lust leofes siðes.
        Fyrd wæs gefysed, from se ðe lædde,
55 modig magoræswa, mægburh heora.
    Oferfor he mid þy folce fæstena worn,

55 magoræswa *Thorpe*] mago ræwa

---

following the loss of *h* (Campbell §241). As was presumably realized by
H. Sweet, who gives the word as *wīerig* in his *Student's Dict. of AS*, this for-
mation giving a long stem vowel is necessary to explain *wērig* in *Fortunes of
Men* 42b and probably *Christ* II 802b. It is a variant of the older formation
giving *werge* with a short stem vowel [M. Trautmann, *BBA* xxiii (1907)
155–6], a formation which is necessary to explain *wergra* and *wyrigra* in *PPs*
90/7, 63/2. *Ealdwerige* is an eminently suitable adj. to apply to the Egyptians
in view of their devilish affinities (see note to 14b); cf. also the standard
patristic name-etymology of *Aegyptus* as *persequens* (see notes to 37 and 501).
The Egyptians are accursed because of their malice towards the Israelites
just as of old the devil (*hostis antiquus*) is accursed because of his malice
towards man. The compound is similar to nouns used of persons with
devilish attributes, e.g. *ealdgewinna* of Grendel (*Beowulf* 1776), *ealdfiend*,
ealdhettende, *ealdgeniðlan* of the Assyrians (*Judith* 315, 320, 228), and *ealdfiend*
(again) of the Babylonians (*Daniel* 57, 453). There is a slight metrical diffi-
culty. The verse may be scanned as Type 1*D*, but, since 'syncopation is the
rule in OE metre' (Campbell §358), difficulty arises from the necessity of
taking the 'syncopated' vowel *i* as syllabic. However, this phenomenon
probably occurs at *Daniel* 94, where the *e* in *hæðena* must be syllabic if the
b-verse is to be hypermetric [ale(3El) rather than d5b] like the *a*-verse, and
therefore cannot be ruled out as a possible metrical licence; it follows that
there are insufficient grounds for emendation *metri causa* (cf. Bliss §8). If
there were, the best emendation would be Sievers's *ealdwerigra* [*PBB* x (1885)
461]. IRVING's suggestion of *ealdorwērige*, which he glosses as 'fatally weary?'
does not make good sense since the Egyptians do not die on account of being
tired; on the contrary, they are killed because they pursue the Israelites so
energetically.

53] *on langne lust* qualifies *leofes*. Translate: 'the journey cherished with
long-lasting eagerness'. There is an evident contrast between *leofes siðes* and
laðsið (44); cf. *Daniel* 249/51.

54–62] These lines are framed in an 'envelope pattern' (*Fyrd . . . lædde*:
fyrde gelædde). Vickrey [*Traditio* xxviii (1972) 132–8] sees here 'the readiness
of the Israelites to fight' and finds the presence of this motif sufficient grounds
for linking the lines with the battle which he thinks takes place between the
Israelites and the Egyptians face to face in the Red Sea.

56ff.] The emphasis (*guðmyrce* 59, *mearchofu* 61, *meringa* 62, *mearclandum*

57 land ond leodgeard   laðra manna,
    enge anpaðas,   uncuð gelad,
    oðþæt hie on guðmyrce   gearwe bæron:

57 leodgeard *Grein*] leod weard

---

67) on borderlands and those who dwelt in them has caused puzzlement: IRVING thought the passage to be based on 'some strange conception of lands and people', and certainly it does not seem adequate to think of these borderlands simply as the dwelling-places of those expelled from society like Ishmael [Gen. 16.12; cf. *ASE* ii (1973) 73]. Apparently the Israelites travelled along border-roads which followed the courses of territorial boundaries, a notion that may be Celtic in origin [see P. Ó Riain, 'Boundary Association in Early Irish Society', *Studia Celtica* vii (1972) 12–29]. In Celtic border-areas trading-posts were established which later grew into towns and such a conception may lie behind the description of Etham as a *burh* (66). Naturally defensive strongholds (*fæstena worn*) were established in border-areas. Cf. Ex. 13.17–18.

57] Emendation to *leodgeard* is preferable as giving excellent sense, whereas MS *leodweard* offers considerable difficulty. The phrase *land ond leodgeard* occurs in *Gen* 229 and 1773. As well as here *land ond leodweard* occurs in *Gen* 1180 and 1196, but, as recommended by BTSA *leodweard*, all three instances should be emended to *leodgeard*. If the word were *leodweard* the second element would have to be *weard* m. 'one who keeps'; if it were *weard* f. 'protection' the accusative *wearde* would be required. Hence *leodweard* would mean 'guardian of the people', not an appropriate meaning in the context. Farrell's rendering [*NM* lxvii (1966) 367] 'that which the people keeps' lacks support. E. v. K. Dobbie [*JEGP* liii (1954) 230] finds analogous support for *leodweard* in *eorðweard* (*Beowulf* 2334) acc. sg. m., a *hapax legomenon*, but, unless this word denotes a person, it too would be better emended – to *eorðgeard*.

58] This line is identical with *Beowulf* 1410; see Intro. 69–71. Helder [*AM* xvi (1975) 16] notes that *uncuð gelad* may reflect *ignota via* in Wisd. 18.3. This would tend to confirm the identification of *lyfthelm* (60 and note) with the cloud-pillar.

59] *guðmyrce* 'warlike border-dwellers': cf. *ælmyrce* 'foreign borderers' in *Andreas* (ed. Brooks) 432 and note. The element *-myrce* is a derivative of *mearc* 'border'. The older view that *-myrce* is the adj. MURK 'dark' is revived by Vickrey [*Traditio* xxviii (1972) 135–6 and n.68] who, comparing *eorp werod* (194 and note), thinks *guðmyrce* 'war-blacks' refers by way of an onomastic allusion to the Egyptians, a very forced reading.

60] IRVING's rejection of BLACKBURN's identification of *lyfthelm* as the pillar of cloud on the grounds that it 'has not yet appeared' begs the question. *Lyfthelm* rather denotes the cloud-cover (*dægsceld* 79) which is later revealed to be the same thing as the cloud-pillar (see note to 71b–97). This cloud accompanies the Israelites through all the lands that they traverse

60 wæron land heora   lyfthelme beþeaht.
    Mearchofu mor heald –   Moyses ofer þa,
    fela meringa,   fyrde gelædde.

62 meringa *Irving*] meoringa

---

from the time they leave Egypt. See also note to 58. In both *lyfthelm* and *dægsceld* the second element is from the language of protective armour.

61a] The present reading follows THORPE 181 and Bright [*MLN* xxvii (1912) 14]; *heald* is for *hēold* (p.t. sg. ot *healdan*) with North. confusion of the diphthongs *ēa* and *ēo* (Campbell §278). Translate: 'the wilderness contained borderland dwellings'. For the expression cf. *Beowulf* 161–2. *Pace* Farrell [*NM* lxvii (1966) 368] the verse is stylistically no more 'oblique and cryptic' than, e.g., 463b or 483a. Objective description of external phenomena, without stating the reaction to them of the people concerned, is a characteristic feature of the poem's style. The verse may be scanned as 2A4 (cf. *Beowulf* 330a) and the metrical objections raised by Farrell are imaginary. GOLLANCZ p. lxxxi saw here a reference to the second camp on the exodus, Succoth, a word which in Hebrew meant 'tents' (Gen. 33.17), and Farrell tries to find support for this suggestion in Ex. 13.20, but the crucial phrase *in extremis finibus solitudinis* relates to Etham, not, as Farrell thinks, to Succoth, as is clear from Num. 33.6. Most editors read *mearchofu morheald* taking *morheald* as a compound adj. (otherwise unrecorded) formed on *heald* 'inclined', and possible translations might be 'the borderland dwellings in the undulating wilderness' or 'the borderland dwellings sloping towards the moor', but this reading seems strained and does not make very good sense.

62] Even if it were intelligible MS *meoringa* can hardly stand. The most favoured reading, *meorringa* 'hindrances', first proposed by Mürkens [*BBA* ii (1899) 88–9, 113] adducing Gothic *marzjan*, would be from *mearring [MARRING], a vbl. n. formed on *mearrian*, with North. *eo* for *ea* (Campbell §278). Against this reading is the fact that the expected North. form would be *marrung* with retraction instead of breaking (Campbell §144) and with the usual *-ung* of verbal nouns formed on class 2 weak verbs (Campbell §383); also the sense 'hindrances' is not entirely suitable as a parallel to *mearchofu*. The present reading assumes a vbl. n. formed on *(ge)mǣran* 'fix limits', with *ē* for WS *ǣ*[1], and with much the same meaning as the related *(ge)mǣre* 'boundary' [cf. R. E. Zachrisson, *SN* vi (1933–34) 30–31, who derives the place-name Meering (Notts) from such a vbl. n.]; in sense it provides an excellent parallel to *mearchofu*. D. Slay [*TPS* (1952) 4] notes that *fela* does not usually carry the alliteration in such a phrase; J. R. R. Tolkien's reading *felamodigra* '(the army) of very brave men', recorded by BTSA *meoring*, avoids this difficulty but only at the cost of a drastic emendation.

[·XLIII·] Heht þa ymb twa niht   tirfæste hæleð,   [p.146
           siððan hie feondum   oðfaren hæfdon,
    65 ymbwicigean   werodes bearhtme
        mid ælfere   Æthanes byrig,
        mægnes mæste,   mearclandum on.
        Nearwe genyddon   on norðwegas;

    63 Heht *Thorpe*] eht *with space for large initial capital;*
        tirfæste *Bouterwek*] tirfæstne
    66 Æthanes] h *suprascript with caret to mark place of insertion*

63a] *ymb twa niht*: the Israelites spent the first night at Rameses (Ex.
12.37, Num. 33.3) and the second night at Succoth (Ex. 12.37, 13.20, Num.
33.5–6). The verse scans as Type a2, and Type a is what we should expect
when the phrase *Heht þa* is immediately followed by an unstressed syllable,
as here. But, so far as I have discovered, the occurrence of two words instead
of a compound in this type (a2) is unparalleled. There is, however, quite a
close parallel in *Beowulf* 736a where *þa niht* occurs in place of the compound
usual in this type (1A*2). The relatively simple emendation to *nihte*, which
would enable the verse to be scanned unexceptionably as Type 2C1c, is
therefore unnecessary.

63b] Emendation to *tirfæste* (pl.), the propriety of which is suggested
by *hie* (64), is required because Moses must be the subject of the sentence.
If MS *tirfæstne hæleð* were to stand it would have to denote Moses and it
would be necessary to understand God as the subject of *Heht* even though
Moses is the subject of the previous sentences.

65] *werodes bearhtme*: see note to 99.

66] Etham (Ex. 13.20, Num. 33.6) is the third camp (87) after Rameses
and Succoth (note to 63). In the Bible it is not stated to be a *burh* (cf. note
to 56ff.) nor do the Israelites besiege it. Helder [*AM* xvi (1975) 6–7],
quoting Augustine, takes Etham as the stronghold of the devil (also the city
of God) but there is insufficient textual support for this identification in
Ex. IRVING connected the nautical imagery in 81ff. with one of the patristic
name-etymologies for Etham, 'consummatus siue suscipiens nauigationem',
but man's journey through life, which the exodus represents allegorically,
was commonly seen as a sea-voyage aboard the Ship of the Church. The
patristic name-etymology merely reflects the common tradition and should
not be seen as a specific influence on the poem.

67a] *mægnes mæste*: i.e. the most powerful armed force. Irving's sugges-
tion that the phrase is an onomastic allusion to the common patristic name-
etymology of Etham as 'fortis' is unhappy since to 'go with *Æthanes byrig*',
dat. after *ymbwicigean*, the form *mæstre* would be required.

67b] *mearclandum on*: this phrase may be based on Ex. 13.20 (also Num.
33.6) 'in extremis finibus solitudinis'. See note to 56ff.

68] This line has been read in two ways. (1) After Napier [*MLR* vi

wiston him be suðan   Sigelwara land,
70 forbærned burhhleoðu,   brune leode,
hatum heofoncolum.   Þær halig God

(1911) 168] *nearwe* is taken as a noun: the difficulties of the situation (the heat, the terrain, and the presence of enemies) forced them onto northerly tracks. This reading is preferable and, so read, the text is probably based on Ex. 14.2–3, though Irving compares *OE Heptateuch*, Ex. 12.33. If accepted the nom. pl. form *nearwe* probably indicates that *nearu* is a fem. *wō*-stem rather than a neut. *wa*-stem. (2) After Grein [*Germania* x (1865) 418] *nearwe* is taken as an adv. meaning 'with difficulty', a sense otherwise unrecorded. The verb *genyddon* is then taken to mean 'pressed on', but this sense is not otherwise recorded unless in Vercelli *Soul and Body I* 117 *Se* [*wyrm*] *genydde to . . . on þam eorðscræfe* where the reading of Exeter *Soul and Body II*, *Se geneþeð to . . .*, is much superior. Emendation of *genyddon* to *geneddon* 'ventured' [cf. Dietrich, *ZfdA* x (1856) 340] is a possibility but the sense of *nearwe* is still a problem.

69] *Sigelwara land*. The land of the Ethiopians is not mentioned in Ex. nor anywhere else in connection with the exodus so far as is known. Its introduction here is probably largely a matter of literary convenience since it provides exactly the right kind of exotic setting in which to describe the cloud-cover which merges into the cloud-pillar. It also creates a mental association appropriate for the later introduction of Moses's Ethiopian wife (see note to 580). *Sigelware*, lit. 'sun-dwellers', is probably the result of popular etymology since traditions about the intense heat of Ethiopia were well-known. The older name was *Sigelhearwan*, on which see J. R. R. Tolkien, *MÆ* i (1932) 183–96, iii (1934) 95–111.

70a] *burhhleoðu*: the same word as *beorhhliðu* (449) where it is used of the walls of water. AS scribes sometimes associated or confused *beorh*(-) and *burh*(-). Other examples are *burgum* 'hills' (222) and, in other texts, *burghleoþum* 'hillsides' (*Riddle 27* 2), *beorhleodum* 'citizens' (WW i 178/41), *beorhleod* (Napier 7/293), *beorleodum* (Napier 8/358). Cf. also E. A. Kock, *Anglia* xlv (1921) 124–5. On the metre of this verse see Intro. 40–41.

70b–71a] The tradition that the Ethiopians were brown because of the heat of the sun was well known and one of the standard patristic name-etymologies for them was *tenebrae* (Jerome, *Hebr. Nom.* 2, 16). There is no hint here of the allegorical interpretation which regarded the Ethiopians as darkened through sin, unless, as Irving 206–7 thinks, 71a is an allusion to God's use of burning coals to punish sinners (Ps. 10.7 [11.6], 139.11 [140.10]).

71b–97] This passage, remarkable for its use of metaphor and imagery, is primarily concerned with the cloud-pillar, which, as is evident from a collation of Ex. 40.36 and 13.21 (see also Isa. 4.5–6), was fused with the cloud-cover (*wederwolcen* 75) which surmounted the Tabernacle of the Tent of the Presence of the Lord (Ex. 25–6, 35–6, 38–40). From 88b the cloud is paired with the fire-pillar (seen as a separate entity – cf. Ex. 13.21, 14.20).

wið færbryne   folc gescylde,
bælce oferbrædde   byrnendne heofon,
halgan nette,   hatwendne lyft.
75 Hæfde wederwolcen   widum fæðmum
eorðan ond uprodor   efne gedæled,

Central to the passage is the notion of the cloud as equivalent to a tent (*feldhus* 85), specifically the Tabernacle. This description probably derives from the variant reading of Ps. 104 (105).39 found, e.g., in the Codex Amiatinus, 'Expandit nubem in tentorium' (cf. note to 72) but could easily have been suggested by, e.g., Ex. 40.32, 'operuit nubes tabernaculum testimonii; et gloria Domini implevit illud'. What the poet evidently had in mind was an overhead screen of cloud, like the roof of a tent, for which he uses a variety of names, nearly all of which can be linked with the Tabernacle. For more detailed discussion see the following notes and Lucas, *ES* li (1970) 297–311 and in *FChristi* 193–209.

72] The notion that the cloud protected the Israelites from the heat of the sun probably derived from the Bible, though it is not in Ex. Moore (*MP* ix (1911) 89) adds Wisd. 19.7, 'nubes castra eorum obumbrabat' to Bright's earlier citation [*MLN* xvii (1902) 212] of Ps. 104.39, 'Expandit nubem in protectionem eorum', and Isa. 4.5–6. Moore also cites several commentators on Ps. 104.39, notably Cassiodorus (d.c. 580), 'Nubes data est, ut solis temperaret ardorem' (PL lxx 751; CCSL xcviii 954). See also note to 74 and cf. Ps. 120 (121).6 and *Daniel* 457.

73] *bælce* refers to the central beam in the roof of the Tabernacle (Ex. 36.33), or, by extension, the ceiling of the Tabernacle, and is used here as a metaphor of the cloud-pillar or cloud-cover over the Tabernacle. OE *bælc* descends from Gmc **balkuz* 'partition' (related to **bal(u)kōn* 'beam' giving OE *balca*) which developed in OE as a *u*-noun but became assimilated to the *a*-declension (Campbell §614). The spelling with *æ* is unusual (cf. *utagecælcad* in LGosp., Mt. 23.27), but lack of Breaking/Retraction before supported *l* is explained by the fact that final *lk* after a front vowel would have had a palatal quality (Campbell §428 and n. 2), whereas Breaking/Retraction occurred only before 'dark' or velarized supported *l*. See further Lucas, *ES* li (1970) 303–5.

74] By *nett* is probably meant an overhead curtain such as was attached to the cross-beams of the Tabernacle; see also note to 81. The image could easily have been suggested by the use of the L word *velamentum* 'covering', 'curtain' for the cloud-cover in Wisd. 10.17 (cited by Irving 207).

76] The notion of division by a curtain or 'veil' (*nett* 74, *segl* 81) suggests the *velum* which divided the holy place before the altar from the holy of holies behind it (Ex. 26.33). Implicit in this division is a scale of values (earth/heaven; holy/holiest), and it follows that progression from one to the other is desirable. Such a journey, through life on earth to heaven, is the allegorical equivalent of the Israelite exodus.

lædde leodwerod,   ligfyr adranc
hate heofontorht.   Hæleð wafedon,
drihta gedrymost.   Dægsceldes hleo
80 wand ofer wolcnum;   hæfde witig God
sunnan siðfæt   segle ofertolden,
swa þa mæstrapas   men ne cuðon,

---

79 dægsceldes *Cosijn*] dæg/scealdes *over line division*
81 segle *Thorpe*] swegle

79] *dægsceldes hleo* 'the protective covering (in the form) of the day-shield'; cf. 72. The cloud-cover is here identified with the cloud-pillar, which is a day-time phenomenon only – hence *dæg-*; the corresponding word for the fire-pillar is *nihtweard* (116). The second element *sceld*, without diphthongization after the initial palatal consonant (WS **scield*), is the usual Mercian form and is recorded elsewhere in WS (Campbell §185). Irving notes that the shield occurs as an image for protection afforded by God to the faithful in Ps. 90 (91).4–6 and Eph. 6.16. An alternative reading is *dægsceades*, but *scead* 'shadow' does not seem to be used of an object providing protection (as opposed to the shelter provided *by* such an object). See further Lucas, *ES* li (1970) 307–8.

80] *ofer wolcnum*: 'over the sky' as opposed to *under wolcnum* 'on earth', as KRAPP points out. IRVING's desire to take *ofer wolcnum* literally is unnecessary.

80b–84] In these lines the nautical imagery (which recurs at 89, 105–6, 118, 133, 223, 331, 333, 479) implies that the Israelites are viewed as on board a ship, even though they are to cross the Red Sea on dry land. This mode of presentation is a clear indication that the Israelite exodus is to be understood allegorically as the journey of all *eorðbuende* over the sea of this life towards the heavenly port. The vessel of salvation was the Ship of the Church and its sailyard (the cross-bar of the mast) represented the Cross; both conceptions are patristic commonplaces, though not from the exegesis of Ex.; see further Intro. 58 and 67–9.

81] *segl* functions with two senses here, 'veil' and 'sail'; both are used as metaphors for the cloud. The sense 'veil' relates to the *velum* for the Ark of the Covenant in the Tabernacle (Ex. 26.31, 36.35), while the sense 'sail' relates to the nautical imagery. The sail is the means by which, with the breath of the Holy Spirit (see note to 96), God propels the Ship of the Church.

ofertolden: although this word is a *hapax legomenon* it is hard to exclude the possibility that it carries connotations of the noun *(ge)teld* 'tent' which was formed from the simplex *teldan*.

ne ða seglrode   geseon meahton
eorðbuende   ealle cræfte,
85 hu afæstnod wæs   feldhusa mæst,
siððan He mid wuldre   geweorðode
þeodenholde.   Þa wæs þridda wic
folce to frofre.   Fyrd eall geseah
hu þær hlifedon   halige seglas,
90 lyftwundor leoht;   leode ongeton,

83] *seglrod* is an otherwise unrecorded compound on ROOD and implies the allegorical equation of the sailyard with the Cross, a further metaphor for the cloud-pillar. Thus the nautical imagery (a sail fastened to a sailyard on a mast) is fused with the figural evocation of the Cross, probably as a victory trophy adorned with a banner (OE *segl* is used to gloss L *labarum* 'banner', 'battle-standard', Napier 1/2130, WW i 435/14, 476/19). At first men could not recognize the Cross in the rigging but its presence is later made explicit by the word *beam* (see notes to 88–90 and 94).

85] *feldhusa mæst*: the Tabernacle. Tents are appropriate for the Israelites on their journey (cf. 133, 223). The Tabernacle is mentioned explicitly here at the end of the lines where most of the nautical imagery is concentrated, probably because allegorically it denoted the same concept as the Ship, namely the Church (Lucas, *FChristi* 202). The change of image, from the Ship (of the Church) to the Tent (of the Church), forces the reader/listener to recognize what the two images have in common – their allegorical interpretation. At the same time the return to the tent-image is a return to the exodus itself. In this way the allegorical level of meaning becomes only momentarily predominant; the concept 'ship', though clearly implied, is never actually spelled out.

86–7] An allusion to the Shekinah, the dwelling of God in the Tabernacle.

87b] *þridda wic*: Etham (see note to 66). *Þridda* nom. sg. n. is for regular *þridde*.

88–90] Now the people saw what they could not see before (83): the Cross. For the words used of the sails would apply more appropriately to the Cross. (The plurality of *seglas*, which, like *beamas* 94, denotes the pillars of cloud and fire, need cause no difficulty since only one pillar appeared at a time.) Brodeur [*Nordica et Anglica* (1968) 112] complained that *leoht* 'is not a proper epithet for the pillar of cloud', but *leoht* is appropriate for the Cross, e.g., in *Christ* III 1089, in which passage (1081ff.) the Cross supplants the sun in men's view (1101–2; cf. also *Guthlac* 1313b and note to 107b–11a); the same conception may well be implied here since the natural inference from *lyfthelm* (60) and *dægsceld* (79) is that of a dark object against a bright sky. Similarly *hlifian* would be used more appropriately of the Cross, as in *Rood* 85, than a sail. See further note to 94.

    dugoð Israhela, þæt þær Drihten cwom,
    weroda Drihten,   wicsteal metan.
    Him beforan foran   fyr ond wolcen
    in beorhtrodor,   beamas twegen,
95 þara æghwæðer   efngedælde
    heahþegnunga   Haliges Gastes   [p.147
    deormodra sið   dagum ond nihtum.
     Þa ic on morgen gefrægn   modes rofan

91–2] Like 86–7 these lines refer to the real presence of God in the Tabernacle suffused with the cloud. Num. 9.15–23 explains how the appropriate stopping-places were indicated to the Israelites by the cloud.

92a] Since the MS reading is unexceptionable in sense and metre it must be allowed to stand. Yet it seems unlikely that the repetition of *Drihten* from 91 was intended in the original and there is a strong temptation to read *weroda Waldend*.

93–7] The pillar of cloud and fire is described in Ex. 13.21–2, from which it appears that there was one pillar which took the form of a cloud by day and of a fire by night, but the text is by no means clear and could easily have been understood to indicate two pillars. Here there are clearly two pillars, one a day-time phenomenon (*dægsceld* 79), one a night-time phenomenon (*nihtweard* 116), thus never more than one at a time. There is no need to follow Moore [*MP* ix (1911) 87, 102] in thinking the difference between the one pillar of the Bible (properly understood) and the two pillars of the OE poem constitutes an 'addition' by the OE poet; as Moore himself points out the notion of two pillars occurs in other writers, e.g. Bede (*recte* pseudo-Bede) in PL xci 310. Cf. note to 121.

94b] The range of meaning carried by the word *beam* is well illustrated by *Riddle 30*. Here, as well as meaning 'pillars', *beamas* must imply the notion 'Cross' (esp. its transverse bar), which is a metaphor for the pillar. This inference is later confirmed by the description of the pillar as *wuldres beam* (568), a phrase used of the Cross in *Rood* 97 and *Elene* 217; see also 249a and note. The metaphoric association of the pillar and the Cross is the literary descendant of the typological identification of the exodus with the redemption: the pillar signifies not only itself but also the Cross (esp. its transverse bar), while the Cross is the fulfilment of the pillar as a symbol of salvation.

96] Evidently an allusion to the allegorical equation of the pillar(s) of cloud and fire with the Holy Spirit [Daniélou, *Shadows to Reality* (1960) 181–2]; the sail of the Ship of the Church was also equated with the Holy Spirit [Rahner, *Greek Myths* (1963) 347]. The word *heahþegnunga* implies that the pillars are viewed as the thanes of the Holy Spirit.

98–100a] Owing to morphological ambiguity these verses can be read in more than one way. Presumably *rofan* is acc. after *gefrægn* and 'subject'

hebban herebyman   hludan stefnum,
100 wuldres woman.   Werod eall aras,
modigra mægen,   swa him Moyses bebead,
mære magoræswa,   Metodes folce,
fus fyrdgetrum.   Forð gesawon
lifes latþeow   lifweg metan;
105 segl siðe weold,   sæmen æfter

105 segl *Bouterwek*] swegl

---

of *hebban* (though Cosijn [*PBB* xx (1895) 98] took it as gen. sg. referring to
Moses). On this basis *herebyman* is taken as obj. of *hebban* and *woman* as
parallel to either *rofan* or *herebyman* despite the apparent syllepsis. Alterna-
tively *woman* may be obj. of *hebban* and *herebyman* gen. sg. qualifying *hludan
stefnum*.

99] *herebyman*. For the use of trumpets as ordained by God for the
Israelites in the Bible IRVING refers to Num. 10.1–10. In *Ex* the sound of
trumpets signals establishing camp (132), moving on (as here; Num. 10.2,
5–6), the calling of an assembly to hear a speech (216; Num. 10.3, 7), and
celebration (566; Num. 10.10). As is evident from the slightly wider range
of functions accorded to the trumpet in *Ex* (Num. 10.1–10 makes no pro-
vision for the use of the trumpet to indicate the establishment of a camp)
the noise of the instrument is used as one of the traditional trappings of epic
poetry; cf. *werodes bearhtme* 65.

100] *wuldres woman*. Etymologically *woma* means 'noise', in OE especially
of battle (cf. 202, *Elene* 19, *Juliana* 576, and the compound *hildewoma* in
Juliana 136, 663) but overtones of the sense 'herald' are suggested by the
compounds *dægwoma* 'dawn, break of day' (344, also *Guthlac* 1218 and Ælfric,
Colloquy, ed. Garmonsway, p. 20, line 23 where it renders *diluculum* 'dawn')
and *dægredwoma* 'rising sun' (*Andreas* 125, *Guthlac* 1292) and by the related
verb *wēman* 'proclaim' (*Andreas* 1480). Cf. Schücking, *Untersuchungen zur
Bedeutungslehre der angelsächs. Dichtersprache* (1915) 91–8.

103] *fyrdgetrum* is parallel with *werod* (100) and *mægen* (101).

103b–106a] For discussion of these verses see the following notes and
Lucas in *FChristi* 195.

104a] *lifes latþeow*: the cloud-pillar, and, by implication, the Cross. The
phrase implies God's presence (it is used of God in *Elene* 520, 898); hence
it reinforces the identification of the cloud-pillar (and the sail) with the
Holy Spirit.

104b] *lifweg*: perhaps literally 'the road to safety', but the word un-
doubtedly conveys allegorical meaning as well: that the Israelite exodus
stands for the journey (usually described as a sea-voyage – cf. *flodweg* 106)
which all Christians take through this life towards the Promised Land of
heaven. In *Rood* 88–9 the Cross reveals *lifes weg* to men; cf. John 14.6. For
the repetition of *lif-* in this line cf. *segn*(-) in 172.

105–6a] For the nautical imagery see note to 80b–84. As in 81 and 89

106 foron flodwege.   Folc wæs on salum,
    hlud herges cyrm.   Heofonbeacen astah   [p.148

107 hlud] lud *with space for large initial capital,* h *written in margin (probably
    by corrector) apparently as guide-letter;* herges] heriges *with* i *expuncted*

the sail is a metaphor for the cloud-pillar. Allegorically the sail is to be
equated with the Holy Spirit (note to 96) which in union with God had
control of the Israelite journey. Here for the first time in the poem the
Israelites are called 'sailors' (also at 133, 223, 331, 333, 479) and their
journey is described as a sea-voyage – that *flodweg* anticipates the crossing
of the Red Sea seems unlikely as the Israelites have not yet even reached its
shore.

107a] *hlud heriges cyrm*: so *Andreas* 1156a, where *cyrm* is associated with
evil-doers, a connotation which, according to B. F. Huppé, *Web of Words*
(New York, 1970) 181, is general in poetry except for *Ex* 107. For the
presumption that the MS large capital in *hlud* is misplaced see Intro. 9.

107b–11a] These lines, which have caused much difficulty, refer to the
fire-pillar. The difficulties are chiefly syntactical and semantic. Bright's im-
plied suggestion [*MLN* xvii (1902) 213] that *æfter* is a temporal conjunction
must be rejected because the word is not otherwise so used before the 14th
cent. (MED *after* conj. 1.(a)). C. Brady's assertion [*PMLA* lxvii (1952) 545]
'that *æfter sunnan setlrade* is a syntactic unit that will not bear tampering
with', though plausible [cf. *æfter sunnan setlgange* (*ASC* D 744)], deprives
beheold of its required object. Farrell's proposal [*NM* lxvii (1966) 369–72]
that lines 108b–9 be taken as a parenthesis, with *oðer wundor* denoting the
cloud-pillar, seems awkward. The precise reference of *oðer wundor* is am-
biguous: either it refers to the pillar appearing in a second form, or to the
pillar as a second marvel taking the place of the sun. Both references are
probably intended. The fire-pillar, here mentioned separately for the first
time, is *oðer wundor* after the cloud-pillar, but also after the sun. With this
second reference the pillar takes on its role of Cross (esp. the transverse bar)
which, as in *Christ* III 1101–2, is seen as supplanting the sun in men's view
(cf. note to 88–90 and Wisd. 18.3). This reading is supported by the use of
setlrad, a *hapax legomenon* which by association with *setlgang* suggests the setting
of the sun, for the course of the pillar and by the use of *heofoncandel* (115),
usually a word for the sun, for the fire-pillar itself. Thus *beheold* must be
taken in the sense 'kept to' as in *Menologium* 113 and cf. *Beowulf* 1498, *Elene*
1143, *Gen B* 366. Translate: 'Every evening a heavenly sign arose, the
flaming column, another wonderful marvel, to shine with fire over the
people, [and it] kept to a course in the manner of the sun'.

IRVING compares the passage with *Guthlac* 1282ff. in which a bright sign
appears in the night sky at Guthlac's death. The reason for the similarities
is that both poets evidently had in mind the Cross as the Sign of the Son of
Man in the Heavens (see note to 107b). Close verbal resemblances are indi-
cated in the appropriate notes below.

107b] *Heofonbeacen* refers to the fire-pillar. In view of the identification

æfena gehwam,   oðer wundor,
syllic æfter sunnan   setlrade beheold,
110 ofer leodwerum   lige scinan,
byrnende beam.   Blace stodon
ofer sceotendum   scire leoman,
scinon scyldhreoðan;   sceado swiðredon,
neowle nihtscuwan   neah ne mihton
115 heolstor ahydan.   Heofoncandel barn;

113 sceado *Thorpe*] sceaðo

---

of the pillar (whether of cloud or fire) and the Cross this term, found only
here, would almost certainly have suggested the *signum Filii hominis in caelo*
(Matt. 24.30) which was conventionally interpreted as the Cross (Reijners,
Holy Cross (1965) 122–3) See further Lucas in *FChristi* 199–200.

111] *byrnende beam* denotes the fire-pillar, but, like the phrase *beama
beorhtast* in *Guthlac* 1309, implicitly refers also to the Cross (see note to 94b).
However, yet another conception, confirmed by the term *heofoncandel* (115
and note), is envisaged here, the fusion of the fire-pillar and the Paschal
Candle familiar from the use of the word *columna* for both concepts in the
Exultet of the liturgy for Holy Saturday (*LM* 96ff.).

113a] *scinon scyldhreoðan*: cf. *blicon bordhreoðan* 159. Etymologically both
scyldhreoða and *bordhreoða* probably mean 'shield-cover'; the former occurs
also as a gloss for *testudo* 'phalanx' (WW i 532/8). As Gradon suggests (note
to *Elene* 122) the two words may have been interchangeable.

113b–15a] These verses were probably inspired by a statement from the
Exultet of the Paschal Vigil: 'Haec igitur nox est quae peccatorum tenebras
columnae ilumninatione purgauit' (*LM* 96) – 'This then is the night which
dissipated the darkness of sin by the light of the pillar'. As well as the fire-
pillar and the Paschal Candle the Cross too was considered by the Anglo-
Saxons as having the power to banish the dark shadows of evil by its bright-
ness (*Christ* III 1088ff.). All three, the fire-pillar, the Paschal Candle and
the Cross were symbols of Christ.

113b] *sceado swiðredon*: identical in wording with *Guthlac* 1288b. MS
sceaðo is possibly a scribal variant with *ð* for *d* (so BLACKBURN) but is more
probably an error, perhaps induced by the medial *ð* in the preceding and
following words. Two other instances of *ð* for *d* (*Gen* 2758, *Daniel* 615) by
the same scribe are cited by J. R. Hulbert, *JEGP* xxxvii (1938) 536.

115] *Heofoncandel*, usually a word for 'sun', here refers to the fire-pillar
and displays remarkable verbal economy. In the narrative sequence the
notion 'fire-pillar' is primary but through the use of a compound in -*candel*
the implicit reference to the Paschal Candle is given apparent priority. See
further Lucas in *FChristi* 203–4. In *Guthlac* 1290b *heofonlic condel* refers to
the sign of the Cross shining brightly in the night sky.

niwe nihtweard   nyde sceolde
wician ofer weredum,   þy læs him westengryre,
har hæðbroga,   holmegum wederum
on ferclamme   ferhð getwæfde.
120 Hæfde foregenga   fyrene loccas,
blace beamas,   belegsan hweop
in þam hereþreate,   hatan lige,
þæt he on westenne   werod forbærnde,

118 hæðbroga *Cosijn*] hæð
119 on ferclamme *Kluge*] ofer clamme ; getwæfde *Thorpe*] getwæf
121 belegsan *Blackburn*] bell/egsan *over line division*
122 hereþreate] *2nd* r *altered from* a

116] The *nihtweard* is *niwe* in the sense that the fire-pillar is the 'night'-time equivalent of the cloud-pillar (*dægsceld* 79); cf. *oðer wundor* 108.

118a] *hæðbroga*: although not recorded this compound is normal in formation and makes an excellent parallel in sense to *westengryre*. Cf. *herebroga*, *sperebroga*, *wæterbroga*.

118b] *holmegum wederum*: in this phrase the allegorical level of meaning is momentarily predominant since it must refer to the allegorical interpretation of the journey through life viewed as a sea-voyage; for the nautical imagery see notes to 80b–84 and 105–6a. The phrase may have been inspired by Isa. 4.6 which describes the cloud-pillar merged with the Tabernacle as a protection *a turbine et a pluvia*; see further Lucas in *FChristi* 205.

119] *on ferclamme*: possibly the mistake arose because a WS scribe failed to understand *fēr* as equivalent to regular WS *fǣr*.

120] *foregenga*: the fire-pillar. On the assumption that *fore-* relates to the pillar in its rôle as leader of the Israelite host, the fire-pillar has here been given one of the functions of the cloud-pillar, since it was the function of that pillar to lead (103b–6a); the function of the fire-pillar was to remain stationary, *wician ofer weredum* (117). Cf. note to 93–7.

121b–3] The notion of the fire-pillar as a means of coercing the Israelites into obedience, threatening to consume them in flames, is not in Ex., and BLACKBURN found 'such an addition . . . surprising'. IRVING attempted to explain it by reference to Num. 11.1–3 where *ignis Domini* is used to punish the Israelites for disobedience; as Irving notes Ps. 105 (106).18 alludes to the same idea. But the connection of the fire-pillar with nocturnal terror and the scorching of the unrighteous is clearer in the commentaries, e.g. Isidore *Quaestiones in Exodum* PL lxxxiii 296 cap. xviii.2 (cited by IRVING). There may also be an allusion to the pillar as Cross which, shining brightly in the sky, terrified sinners (*Christ* III 1103–6).

123] Grammatically *he* must refer back to *foregenga* but it is also possible that the reference is to God, represented through the physical phenomenon of the fire-pillar – cf. 88–92 and note to 489.

      nymðe hie modhwate   Moyses hyrde,
125 scean scirwerod –   scyldas lixton.
      Gesawon randwigan   rihte stræte,
      segn ofer sweoton,   oðþæt sæfæsten
      landes æt ende   leodmægne forstod,
      fus on forðweg.   Fyrdwic aras;
130 wyrpton hie werige,   wiste genægdon

---

128 leodmægne *Thorpe*] leo/mægne *over line division*

124] *hyrde*: on 'OE Plural Subjunctives in *-e*' for regular *-en* see L. Bloomfield, *JEGP* xxix (1930) 100–13.

125] *scean scirwerod*: 'it (the pillar) shone brightly clad'. The phrase is probably taken from Ps. 103 (104).2, *amictus lumine* 'cloaked in light', where it refers to the Lord. This allusion lends support to the suggestion that *he* (123) refers to God represented in the form of the pillar. Possibly *scan scirwered* was a formulaic phrase, as it occurs also in *Guthlac* 1288; cf. also *sweglwered* 'clothed in brightness' (*Beowulf* 606), and *scirmæled* 'brightly adorned' (*Judith* 230). The alternative reading (available here but not at *Guthlac* 1288) *scean scir werod* 'the bright troop shone' is unattractive: it seems unlikely (1) that *Ex* 125a and *Guthlac* 1288a are to be read differently, and (2) that *werod* (123) would be repeated in line 125 (but cf. 230/233).

126] *rihte stræte*: Helder [*AM* xvi (1975) 16] compares *via recta* in Ps. 106 (107). 7.

127] *segn*: the pillar (properly of cloud, but cf. note to 120) seen as a *labarum*, a battle-standard incorporating the Cross; see further Lucas in *FChristi* 199–200. *Sweoton* is dat. pl. for regular *sweotum*.

128] Emendation to *leodmægne* is preferable, though the MS reading *leomægne* has been defended by Robinson [*NM* lxvii (1966) 356–9]. He interprets *leomægen*, which would be a *hapax legomenon*, as 'lion host', and refers it to the Israelites, here said to take their name from the tribe of Judah, whose symbol was the Lion, and who led all the Israelites into the Red Sea (310ff.): just as later the Israelites follow the *segn* of the Lion of Judah (319–21) so they follow the same *segn* as a 'lion host' in 127–8. However *segn* (127) denotes the pillar of cloud and fire, seen as a battle-standard, which is raised when leading the host and made to descend when they rest (Ex. 40.34–5 (AV 36–7), Num. 9.17–23). Thus the Israelites only saw the *segn* and the *rihte stræte* until (*oðþæt*) they arrived at the sea where the pillar descended and the road ended.

129] *fus* qualifies *leodmægne*: as Campbell notes [*Eng. & Med. Stud.* (1962) 22] 'a parallel may be uninflected if the case is clearly indicated in the expressions which it parallels'.

130ff.] As Irving 218 notes these lines suggest a relaxed mood which is shattered by the *færspell* of 135.

modige meteþegnas, hyra mægen beton.
Bræddon æfter beorgum, siððan byme sang,
flotan feldhusum. Þa wæs feorðe wic,
randwigena ræst, be þan Readan Sæ.
[·XLIIII·] Ðær on fyrd hyra færspell becwom,
136 oht inlende. Egsan stodan,
wælgryre weroda. Wræcmon gebad
laðne lastweard, se ðe him lange ær

131] *bēton* is a possible 'Northumbrian' form: see Intro. 38. Mürkens (*BBA* ii (1899) 114], followed by SEDGEFIELD and IRVING, emended to *bētton*. Cf. *hab*(*b*)*að* 1, and *nið*(*ð*)*a* (*Daniel* 312).

133] *flotan feldhusum*. The juxtaposition of nautical imagery (the Israelites as sailors) and tents (repeated in 223) is reminiscent of 80b–85; see notes to 80b–84 and 85. Tents are appropriate for the Israelites on their travels.

133b–4] The fourth camp is that 'contra Phihahiroth' (Num. 33.7) in the region 'quae est inter Magdalum et mare, contra Beelsephon' (Ex. 14.2).

135–41] The section presumed to begin here apparently takes the Israelite fears arising from the Egyptian pursuit as a cue for explaining how the hostile relationship arose between the two peoples, but the lacuna after 141 (Intro. 15) leaves much only to be conjectured. It is generally agreed that the lost portion dealt with the relationship worked out between the Israelites and a former Pharaoh (*se yldra cyning* 141) by Joseph (inferred from *his* 146) and described in Gen. 47 (excluding 13–26 which applies to the Egyptians). The *wær* (140, 147) is presumably the undertaking by the Pharaoh of Joseph's time to allow the Israelites to settle the land of Goshen (Gen. 45.16–20, 47.5–6); this agreement was broken by the Pharaoh of the exodus who set officers over them 'ut affligerent eos oneribus' (Ex. 1.11), an action to which *onnied gescraf* (139) no doubt refers.

136] *inlende*: i.e. by the Egyptians, who are 'native to the land' by contrast with the homeless Israelites (see next note); for other compounds in *in-* see note to 142. The contrast implies that the Egyptians will never undertake the journey to the Promised Land and that allegorically they will never enter heaven but rather be confined in hell (cf. 49 and note). Through its second element the word is linked with another designation for the Egyptians, *landmenn* (179 and note). Robinson [*NM* lxix (1968) 166, n. 2] suggests that the phrase *oht inlende* reflects L *tribulatio coangustans* 'enclosing affliction', a name-etymology for *Aegyptus* given by Jerome.

137b–40a] Every Israelite (*wræcmon*) is an exile (*eðelleas*) until he reaches the Promised Land just as, at the allegorical level, every Christian (cf. *eðellease* 534) is an exile (cf. *wreccum* 533) until he reaches the heavenly home; for the motif of exile cf. 383b. Pharaoh (*lastweard*) is hateful to the Israelites; he oppressed them *lange ær*, i.e. from the time that he first ascended the throne (Ex. 1.8–14). Grammatically *wean*, qualified by *witum fæst*, is parallel with *onnied*.

eðelleasum   onnied gescraf,
140 wean witum fæst.   Wære ne gymdon,
ðeah þe se yldra cyning   ær gesealde ...

*   *   *

[·XLV·] Þa wearð yrfeweard   ingefolca   [p.149
manna æfter maðmum,   þæt he swa miceles geðah.
Ealles þæs forgeton,   siððan grame wurdon,

---

141 gesealde *Sedgefield*] ge
142 Þa] a *with space for large initial capital*

139] *onnied*: Kock (PPP 7) adduces the cognate ON word *ánauð* 'op-
pression'.

142-3] The subject of *wearð* is 'Pharaoh' (understood), i.e. the Pharaoh
of the exodus, who 'ignorabat Ioseph' (Ex. 1.8). Since line 142 begins a new
section there are no grounds for IRVING's remark that the lines are 'part of
an incomplete sentence'.

142] *ingefolca*: this word, together with *ingemen* (190) and *ingeðeode* (444),
has long caused difficulty, the most recent discussion being by J. L. Rosier
[*PMLA* lxxxi (1966) 342-6], who, however, omits reference to C. Ball
[*Anglia* lxxviii (1960) 403-10]. Rosier's view that the first element is *in-*
(prep.) and that *ge-* is a nominal prefix (BT records *ge-men* once and BTS
ge-þeod once) is probably correct as far as the words in *Ex* are concerned,
the element *in-* 'native' referring, like *land-* in *landmenn* (179), to the fact that
the Egyptians have no prospect of departure from their present condition
(see note to 136). Alternatively, as J. R. R. Tolkien suggested, *in-* could
mean 'belonging to the household of a lord'.

144-5] These lines are notoriously difficult. (1) As it stands in the manu-
script v.145b is metrically deficient and obscure in meaning. (2) If the
subject of *forgeton* is *cyn* the construction is abnormal in that where a collec-
tive noun is construed with more than one verb the first verb is usually sg.
to provide grammatical concord (Andrew, *Postscript* §65). (3) It is not clear
whether *ymb* should be construed with *grame* (so most previous editors) or
forgeton. With regard to (3) *forgietan ymb* is certainly closely paralleled by
the usages cited in BT *ymb* I 3.(c), but there is apparently no parallel to
gram ymb. On this basis a noun is required after *ymb* indicating what the
Egyptians forgot about. Difficulty (2) is thus disposed of since *siððan grame
wurdon* can now be taken as a complete clause. The subject of *forgeton* is
'they' (understood) and *Egypta cyn* is a variation of this subject. Difficulty
(1) has been met by assuming the manuscript point to be misplaced before
ða and by postulating a noun *antwigðu* 'hesitation' based on **ontweogan*: cf.
æbylgðu 'anger' formed on *abelgan*. The phrase *forgeton . . . ymb antwigða* (with
-a for regular *-e*) 'forgot about hesitation' may be taken as *litotes* for 'did not
delay'. So read, the passage is closely paralleled by *PPs* 118.38. Bammes-
berger [*Anglia* xciii (1975) 140-44] takes *ymb* (145b) with *grame* and reads

145 Egypta cyn,   ymb antwigða:
    heo his mægwinum   morðor fremedon,
    wroht berenedon,   wære fræton.
    Wæron heaðowylmas   heortan getenge,
    mihtmod wera;   manum treowum
150 woldon hie þæt feorhlean   facne gyldan,
    þætte hie þæt dægweorc   dreore gebohte,

145 antwigða] an twig . ða
146 heo] *written twice*
151 hie *Grein*] he

---

ymb andþingða 'concerning the Israelite prosperity at the expense of (*and-*) the Egyptians', but this explanation involves emendation and is semantically strained.

144] *Ealles þæs*: the agreement made by Joseph between the earlier Pharaoh and the Israelites (see note to 135–41). This Egyptian forgetfulness is probably taken over from Wisd. 19.4.

146a] *his*: Joseph's. Cf. 588 and note.

146b] *morðor*: the killing of the Israelite male children (Ex. 1.22).

147] *wære fræton*: a vivid metaphor – it is almost as if the Egyptians were beasts of prey; see Intro. 50. For the use of the mouth to perpetrate deceit cf. Ps. 49 (50).16. Cf. also 513 and note to *muðhæl* 553.

148ff.] Here, after the reference to past events, the focus is again on the Egyptian pursuit of the Israelites.

149] *manum treowum* is parallel with *facne* (150) and means in effect, as BLACKBURN notes, 'treacherously'. The emphasis is on the fact that the Egyptians are to be regarded as *wærlogan* 'treaty-breakers' (cf. 140b, 147b).

150] *feorhlean*: the recompense due to the Israelites for Joseph's saving of the Egyptians from the seven years of famine; BTS adduces Gen. 47.25 where the Egyptians say to Joseph 'Salus nostra in manu tua est'. With admirable concision the line both makes a statement about what the Egyptians intended to do and compares that action with what they ought to have done, give a proper reward. There is also a marked contrast between the Egyptians' perpetration of *morðor* (146) together with their intention to slaughter the Israelites (151–3 and note) and the Israelites' provision (through Joseph) of *feorh*.

151–3] These lines make it clear that the Egyptians intended to slaughter the Israelites *en masse*; cf. 197–9. What evidence there is in the Bible suggests that Pharaoh's purpose in pursuing the Israelites was to recapture them and restore them to hard labour (Ex. 14.5). But Ex. 14.12 is ambiguous: 'Multo enim melius erat servire eis, quam mori in solitudine' – it is not clear whether the Israelites expected to die because of 'the hardships they experienced in the desert' (Hyatt 152) or as a result of being overrun by the Egyptian chariots.

151] *dægweorc*: Joseph's action in saving the Egyptians from the seven

Moyses leode,   þær him mihtig God
on ðam spildsiðe   spede forgefe.
þa him eorla mod   ortrywe wearð,
155 siððan hie gesawon   of suðwegum
fyrd Faraonis   forð ongangan,
eoferholt wegan,   eored lixan –

157 eoferholt *Sedgefield*] ofer holt

---

years' famine.

Gebohte is p.t. pl. subj. for regular *gebohten*; see note to *hyrde* 124. Presumably *he* was substituted for *hie* in anticipation of what was erroneously taken to be a sg. verb.

153] The use of the term *spildsið*, which would more readily apply to the journey of the Passover Angel, to denote the Egyptians' intended genocide of the Israelites suggests that the one action is being described in terms of the other. This device serves to emphasize the feebleness of the Egyptians beside God.

154–6] Adapted from Ex. 14.10, 'levantes filii Israel oculos, viderunt Aegyptios post se et timuerunt valde'. The Egyptians approach *of suðwegum* because the Israelites had kept to a northerly route (68).

157] *Eoferholt* is closely paralleled by *eoferspreot* 'boar-spear' (*Beowulf* 1437), which is specifically stated to be barbed (*heorohocyhte*). To judge by the surviving examples [see M. J. Swanton, *The Spearheads of the AS Settlements* (London, 1973) 28–37] such a spear would not have been adequate for killing a boar; evidently a 'boar-spear', in poetry at least, was so called from its decoration rather than its function. The boar, sacred to (ON) Freyr, was associated with fertility and was thought to protect those who wore its image (cf. Tacitus, *Germania*, ch. 45). Figures of boars were either stamped or punched into the blade of the sword from the River Lark [H. R. E. Davidson, *The Sword in AS England* (Oxford, 1962) 49]. The animal was used to decorate helmets, such as that at Benty Grange, Derbyshire, and that from Sutton Hoo (eyebrow terminations), both illustrated in R. Bruce-Mitford, *Aspects of AS Archaeology* (London, 1974) plates 63–7 and 46–9 respectively. The association of the boar with the army of a non-Christian king (Pharaoh) is very appropriate. As R. J. Cramp points out [*MA* i (1957) 59–60, repr. in D. K. Fry, *The Beowulf Poet* 118], in *Elene* the *eoforcumbol* 'boar-banner' (76) seems to be associated with Constantine before he saw the image of Christ's cross, i.e. when still a pagan, and was worn conventionally by Constantine's soldiers (259); and W. A. Chaney, *The Cult of Kingship in AS England* (Manchester, 1970) 126, suggests that the boar was primarily associated with kings. On boar-symbolism in general see also H. Beck, *Das Ebersignum im Germanischen* (Berlin, 1965) esp. 51–2 on spears. Earlier editors' attempts to make sense of MS *oferholt* are unsatisfactory. Independently *holt* can mean a wooden shaft (*Riddle 56* 3) or handle (glossing

garas trymedon,   guð hwearfode,
blicon bordhreoðan,   byman sungon –
160 þufas þunian,   þeod mearc tredan.
Onhwæl þa on heofonum   hyrnednebba
(hreopon herefugolas   hilde grædige,

161-2] on hwæl . hwreopon . here fugolas . ;   þa on heofonum
hyrnednebba] *supplied;*   hreopon *Bouterwek*] hwreopon *with 2nd* o
above a *expuncted*

L *capulus*, WW i 375/16, 535/7) and it has this sense in the compound *garholt*
'spear' (*Beowulf* 1834). There is no support for the sense 'shield'. BLACK-
BURN's 'forest (of spears)' apparently derives the notion 'forest' from the
usual sense of *holt* but uses the word 'forest' to translate (rather loosely) the
first element *ofer-*. Usually *ofer-* means 'too much', sometimes 'upper',
'outer', but neither of these basic senses is appropriate here. The present
emendation is therefore necessary and assumes only a minor scribal error
(the omission of *e-*) – perhaps a scribe mistook the original to read *forð*
ongangan ofer holt.

158-9] GREIN and SEDGEFIELD placed these lines after 160 to avoid
taking them as a parenthesis.

158] *hwearfode*: lit. 'revolved'. The verb seems to imply that the Egyptian
army is a seething mass of active armed men who, as they draw nearer,
increasingly threaten to envelop and swamp the Israelites.

160a] *þufas*. A *þuf* was a kind of standard, a variant of the *vexillum* (see
note to *fana* 248), provided with foliage or possibly feathers. See further
M. Deanesly in *EHR* lviii (1943) 136-42 and R. Bruce-Mitford, *Aspects of
AS Archaeology* (1974) 15-16.

160b] *þeod* and *mearc* are acc. sg. for regular *þeode*, *mearce*, apparently
Anglian forms: see SB §252 Anm. 2.

161-9] This passage is an example of what have been called beast-of-
battle 'type-scenes', on which see F. P. Magoun in *NM* lvi (1955) 81-90,
also A. Bonjour in *PMLA* lxxii (1957) 563-73. As Bonjour points out (565-6)
such scenes conventionally anticipate battle, and accordingly *on wenan* (165)
and *beodan* (166) imply destruction that is only projected. In fact no battle
takes place because the two sides are cut off from each other (204-7) but
the doom-laden atmosphere indicates what might have happened to the
Israelites without God to direct events in their favour.

161] Evidently something is missing here. On the assumption (as the
pointing seems to suggest) that the original had two successive lines alliter-
ating on *h-*, the most probable explanation, the line has been completed
editorially. The MS reading *on hwæl* has been taken as the p.t. of *onhwelan*,
recorded with the sense 'resound' in a gloss (reboat *onhwileð*, WW i 528/39);
the simplex occurs with the sense 'roar' in poetry (*Andreas* 495, *Streamwelm
hwileð*) and the verbal noun in a gloss (in clangore *on hwelunge*, WW i 423/20).
Since *onhwæl* 'cried out (with pleasurable anticipation)' will make good

deawigfeðere)   ofer drihtneum,
wonn wælceasega.   Wulfas sungon   [p.151]
165 atol æfenleoð   ætes on wenan,
carleasan deor,   cwyldrof beodan
on laðra last   leodmægnes fyl.

167 fyl *Kluge*] ful

---

sense in the context it is in principle unacceptable to emend it to fit in with
whatever is supplied to reconstruct the rest of the line, and this principle
vitiates all previous attempts to make good the lacuna. The most recent
attempt, that by Robinson [*Anglia* lxxx (1962) 365–8], is also open to serious
metrical and syntactical objections.

162–3a] These verses have been taken as a parenthesis because *wonn
wælceasega* (sg.) cannot go with *hreopon* (pl.).

163] *ofer drihtneum* '[cried out (with pleasurable anticipation)] in regard
to dead troops'; for *ofer* in this sense see BT(S) *ofer* prep. I.(5) and OED
Over prep. I.4. Since no battle takes place the passage should not be in-
terpreted to imply the presence of corpses. The second element of *drihtneum*
is the same as in *orcneas* 'evil spirits of the dead' (*Beowulf* 112) and is related
to Gothic *naus* 'dead man'. Cf. also *nēfuglas* (*Gen* 2159), *nīobedd* (*Gen B* 343,
Phoenix 553) and *nēosīþ* (*Vainglory* 55).

164] *wælceasega* 'chooser of the slain'. This word probably implied asso-
ciations with Northern mythology in which the (ON) *valkyrjur* were god-
desses who hovered over battlefields with a view to conducting the slain to
Odin's hall, Valhalla; see H. R. E. Davidson, *Gods and Myths of Northern
Europe* (Harmondsworth, 1964) 61–6. OE *wælcyrge* was used to gloss such
classical personages as the Furies (WW 347/32, 417/12, 533/26), Bellona,
goddess of war (WW 360/3, 527/17), a Gorgon, and the Parcae or Fates
(assuming WW 189/11–12 to be interchanged and Napier 115/4449 to refer
to Venus Urania), but later the word was used by Wulfstan of witches
[*Sermo Lupi*, ed. D. Whitelock (1952 edn), note to 171].

165] *wenan* is dat. pl. for regular *wenum*.

166] *cwyldrof. Cwyld* either as a simplex or as the first element of a com-
pound does not otherwise occur in poetry. It is related to *cwellan* 'kill' and
always means 'death', 'destruction' except in the compounds *cwyldseten* 'first
hours of night' and *cwyldtid* 'evening'. No doubt with these exceptions in
mind J. R. R. Tolkien compared ON *kveld* 'evening' and translated *cwyldrof*
as 'bold at the dying of the light', a plausible alternative to the sense given
in the glossary.

Beodan shows back mutation and is for regular WS *bidon*: see Intro. 38.

167a] *laðra*: the Egyptians seen from the Israelite viewpoint.

167b] Two suggestions have been made which retain the MS reading,
but both are unsatisfactory. Farrell's reading *leodmægnes fūl* 'the foulness of
the people's army' [*NM* lxvii (1966) 372–3] involves the unlikely proposition
that *beodan* is an inf. (after *sungon*) meaning 'announce': I have been unable

Hreopon mearcweardas   middum nihtum,
fleah fæge gast,   folc wæs genæged.

170   Hwilum of þam werode   wlance þegnas
mæton milpaðas   meara bogum.
Him þær segncyning   wið þone segn foran,
manna þengel,   mearcþreate rad;
guðweard gumena   grimhelm gespeon,

168 middum] 2nd d *suprascript with caret to mark place of insertion*
169 genæged *Grein*] gehæged

---

to find any parallel example for the use with a dependent inf. either of
singan or any other verb with a similar meaning, and it seems preferable
to take *beodan* as p.t. pl. of *bīdan*, thus echoing the sense of *on wenan*. BTSA,
comparing 195b, suggests *leodmægnes ful* 'the whole of the people's army'
but there is no reason to suppose that part of the army has 'arrived' already
nor does this reading harmonize in sense with *ætes on wenan*. Consequently
the usual emendation to *fyl* has been adopted; on scribal confusion of *u* and
y see C. & K. Sisam, *The Salisbury Psalter*, EETS 242 (1959) 24 n.2.

168] *mearcweardas*: presumably the *wulfas* of 164.

169a] This verse relates to the Israelites' despair at the advance of the
Egyptians (cf. 154–6 and note) recorded in Ex. 14.10–12. Through ill-
founded and short-lived pessimism the Israelites are 'doomed' in their own
minds, though not in fact. Since, as D. M. E. Gillam shows [*SGG* iv (1962)
175], 'it is almost always the bad who are *fæge*' there is probably 'some
implication of condemnation at [the Israelites'] lack of faith in God'; cf.
Beowulf 2291–3a. Later (266ff) Moses tells the Israelites to shake off their
mood of despair and trust in God. Robinson's attempt [*Anglia* lxxx (1962)
365 n.2], followed by Irving, to interpret the verse as 'the accursed one (i.e.
Pharaoh) advanced rapidly' is not founded on what the OE words mean.

169b] If MS *gehæged* were retained, the metre (1A1b) would require it
to be read *gehǣged*, and in his glossary BLACKBURN posits a verb *gehǣgan*
'hedge in', comparing Ex. 14.3 in his note. However, a verb with this sense
would presumably be formed on *haga, hæg* 'enclosure', giving **hecgan*, pp.
*heged, which provides neither the required quality nor quantity of root
vowel. Emendation is therefore necessary and there is little to choose be-
tween *genǣged* and BOUTERWEK's *gehnǣged* 'brought low'. The former has
been preferred as palaeographically the more straightforward, since it as-
sumes merely the miscopying of *n* as *h* (cf. 280, 432); it also gives preferable
sense.

170–71] J. Grimm compared *Beowulf* 916–7 [*PQ* xliv (1965) 166]; cf.
also *Beowulf* 864–7a. The display of equestrian prowess was no doubt a
Germanic epic convention though IRVING thought the mention of horses
was probably inspired by Ex. 15.1, 'equum et ascensorem deiecit in mare'.

172] For the repetition of *segn*(-) in this line cf. *lif-* in 104.

175   cyning cinberge   (cumbol lixton)
      wiges on wenum,   wælhlencan sceoc,
      het his hereciste   healdan georne
      fæst fyrdgetrum.   Freond onsegon
      laðum eagan   landmanna cyme.
180   Ymb hine wægon   wigend unforhte,
      hare heorawulfas,   hilde gretton,
      þurstige þræcwiges,   þeodenholde.
      Hæfde him alesen   leoda dugeðe
      tireadigra   twa þusendo

176 wælhlencan *Bouterwek*] hwæl hlencan
178 fyrdgetrum *Wülker*] syrd getrum *;* onsegon *Dietrich*] onsigon

---

176] Emendation to *wælhlencan* restores sense and alliteration.

178a] MS *syrd getrum* was first read correctly by Sievers [*ZfdA* xv (1872) 459]; earlier editors misread *fyrd getrum*. WÜLKER was the first to print *fyrdgetrum* as a correction.

178b] *onsegon*: as Farrell notes [*NM* lxvii (1966) 374], the emendation is supported by Ex. 14.10, 'viderunt Aegyptios'.

178b–79] These verses constitute a brief shift of focus from the impressive display of martial vigour by the Egyptians to the awed hostility of the Israelites. Note the contrast between the Israelites' affection for each other (*Freond*) and hatred for the Egyptians (*laðum eagan*). The Egyptians are called *landmenn* by contrast with the Israelites, who are called 'sea-men' (105, 133, 223, 333, 479); see notes to 80b–84 and 105–6a. The contrast implies that the Egyptians will never embark on the voyage to the heavenly home but will be confined in hell; see note to 136.

179] *eagan* is dat. pl. for regular *eagum*.

180a] *hine*: Pharaoh. It seems best to retain the MS reading with *wægon*, though *wegan* is not recorded with an intransitive sense elsewhere. SEDGE-FIELD's proposal, *wæron* for *wægon*, 'enfeebles the line' (KRAPP). BTS suggested inserting *wæpen* before *wægon* to provide an object for the verb.

180b] This verse (also at 328b) scans as Type 1A*1a with *un-* unstressed; cf. *Beowulf* 1756a.

181] *heorawulfas*: lit. 'sword-wolves' – the first element is OE *heoru* with *-a* for regular *-u* in an unstressed syllable (Intro. 36). Cf. the description of the Vikings as *wælwulfas* in *Maldon* 96.

183a] KLUGE's proposed emendation to *alesene* on metrical grounds is unnecessary: the verse may be scanned as the comparatively rare Type e1 in which resolution is usual (Bliss §§67, 73); cf. 499a.

184] *twa þusendo* refers to the number of Egyptian unit-commanders, not the whole army. This number is not found in the Bible and its precise origin

185 (þæt wæron cyningas　　ond cneowmagas)
　　　on þæt ealde riht,　　æðelum deore:
　　　forðon anra gehwilc　　ut alædde
　　　wæpnedcynnes　　wigan æghwilcne
　　　þara þe he on ðam fyrste　　findan mihte.
190 Wæron ingemen　　ealle ætgædere,
　　　cyningas on corðre.　　Cuð oft gebead
　　　horn on heape　　to hwæs hægstealdmen,
　　　guðþreat gumena,　　gearwe bæron.
　　　Swa þær eorp werod,　　ecan læddon,
195 lað æfter laðum,　　leodmægnes worn

186 ealde *Kluge*] eade
191 gebead *Grein*] gebad

---

is obscure. Moore [*MP* ix (1911) 105–6] notes the occurrence of multiples of 2000 for the number of foot-soldiers in accounts by Josephus and Peter Comestor and in a Jewish legend, and conjectures that all four (including *Ex*) reflect a common source.

185] *þæt wæron*: *þæt* is dem. and the number of the verb is governed by the complement. For the construction, which is idiomatic, cf. *Gen* 389, *Christ & Satan* 357, *Vainglory* 25. The line is treated as a parenthesis in order to preserve the continuity of *alesen . . . on þæt ealde riht* (183–6). If *þæt* were a rel. pron. (so previous editors) the lack of numerical concord between *þæt* and *wæron* would be unusual [cf. B. Mitchell in *Anglia* lxxxi (1963) 313–4]; this problem could only be surmounted (other than by emendation) by expanding MS þ as *þe* or *þa* (cf. Klaeber, *Beowulf*, note to line 15, Andrew, *Postscript* §172) the propriety of which is dubious (cf. KRAPP, p. xxii). The *cyningas ond cneowmagas* are no doubt the *duces* and *electi principes* of Ex. 14.7 and 15.4.

186] *ealde*. Emendation is necessary as there is evidently no such adj. as *ead*; the only other possible instance is *Juliana* 352, where R. Woolf sensibly reads *eadmægden*.

190] *ingemen*: the 'land-bound' Egyptians (see note to 142). As Irving remarks J. C. Pope's suggested emendation *ingēmend* 'native rulers' 'lacks supporting evidence'.

191] *gebead*: BLACKBURN notes confusion of *bad*, *bead*, *bæd* as a scribal idiosyncrasy.

194] The subject of *læddon* is *ingemen*, *cyningas* understood from 190–91. Since the Egyptians are not called 'dark' in the Bible *eorp werod* probably subsumes an allusion to the explication, common in patristic name-etymology, of *Aegyptus* as *tenebrae* 'darkness'; see Robinson, *Anglia* lxxxvi (1968) 26–7.

195a] This verse cleverly uses repetition to combine the hostile attitude of both sides towards each other. Cf. *gelaðe* 206, and *Beowulf* 440.

þusendmælum;   þider wæron fuse.
Hæfdon hie gemynted   to þam mægenheapum [p.153
to þam ærdæge   Israhela cynn
billum abreotan   on hyra broðorgyld.
200   Forðon wæs in wicum   wop up ahafen,
atol æfenleoð,   egesan stodon,
weredon wælnet;   þa se woma cwom,
flugon frecne spel.   Feond wæs anmod,
werud wæs wigblac,   oðþæt wlance forsceaf

196b] A verb of motion must be understood: 'they were eager to go there'.

199] *on hyra broðorgyld* 'in revenge for their brothers', i.e. the first-born. There is a change here from the scriptural account. In Ex. 14.5 it is implied that Pharaoh's motive for pursuing the Israelites was to bring them back alive into servitude. Here he hopes to slaughter them and his motive is clearly that of Germanic vengeance. The addition of this motive is in harmony with the emphasis on kinship in the poem.

200a] *wicum*: in the Israelite camps.

200b] So *Beowulf* 128b.

201] *atol æfenleoð*. In 165a this phrase was used of the song of the wolves, eager for slaughter. Here, by contrast, it is used of the cries of the Israelites, afraid of slaughter.

202a] *wælnet* has been taken to mean 'net of death', giving some such translation as 'the nets of death held them back', i.e. they were trapped between the Egyptians and the sea, but this interpretation seems somewhat forced. With the sense 'coat of mail' for *wælnet* (cf. *wælhlencan* 176) the syntax is ambiguous: the verse could mean 'they [the Israelites] donned their corslets' (taking, *weredon* as p.t. of WEAR[1]) but is more likely to mean 'corslets hindered [the Israelites in their desire to run away]'. With this latter interpretation the verse complements what precedes and follows. Irving 219 and note 50, following Cosijn and Mürkens, recommends emendation to *weredum*, and *weredon* could be for *weredum*, but the interpretation of *wælnet* as 'death-trap(s)', parallel with *egesan*, seems awkward. Cf. Kock, JJJ 25–6.

203a] The primary meaning of this verse is probably 'bold speeches fled', i.e. the Israelites were so fearful that they forgot any vows they may have made to do great deeds – cf. 455a. There may be a contrast between the approach of the noise of battle and the departure of speeches of endeavour. Alternatively the verse could mean 'they fled the fearful tidings' (Johnson) or possibly 'The fatal tidings flew abroad' (Kennedy).

203b] If the first element of *anmod* were *ān* the verse would scan as 1A2a, a type found only in the *a*-verse. Cf. 334b.

204a] In the context *werud wæs wigblac* probably refers to the Egyptians, but it could apply to the Israelites if *wigblac* were taken to mean 'war-pale'.

204b–7] The reference here is to Ex. 14.19–20 (cf. also Josh. 24.7) where

205 mihtig engel,   se ða menigeo beheold,
    þæt þær gelaðe mid him   leng ne mihton
    geseon tosomne: sið wæs gedæled.
        Hæfde nydfara   nihtlange fyrst,   [p.154
    þeah ðe him on healfa gehwam   hettend seomedon,
210 mægen oððe merestream;   nahton maran hwyrft.
    Wæron orwenan   eðelrihtes,
    sæton æfter beorgum   in blacum reafum
    wean on wenum;   wæccende bad
    eall seo sibgedriht   somod ætgædere
215 maran mægenes,   oð Moyses bebead
    eorlas on uhttid   ærnum bemum
    folc somnigean,   frecan arisan,
    habban heora hlencan,   hycgan on ellen,

216 bemum *Thorpe*] benum

---

the angel of the Lord and the cloud-pillar move behind the Israelites and
in front of the Egyptians so that neither can see the other. Thus the momen-
tum of the Egyptian advance is broken. As Irving 219 notes, the verb *forsceaf*
emphasizes God's power effectively employed against the Egyptians. *Mid
him . . . geseon tosomne* is a circuitous way of saying 'see each other' perhaps
influenced by the L *ad se invicem . . . accedere* of Ex. 14.20.

205] *engel*: cf. *Daniel* 236–7 where the Holy Spirit is apparently described
as an angel.

207b] This striking phrase perhaps carries the implication that from now
on the Israelites and Egyptians will each go their separate ways: the time
for a moral distinction has come.

208] *nydfara*: every Israelite is a 'traveller by necessity' primarily in the
sense that he seeks a homeland; cf. 211.

209–10] The notion that the Israelites were caught between Pharaoh
and the Red Sea was probably not original with the poet. IRVING cites a
parallel from pseudo-Augustine and Irving compares a passage from Haymo
of Auxerre. Cf. also Mirsky, *ES* xlviii (1967) 396.

211] For God's covenant with the Israelites in which he promised them
the land of Canaan see Gen. 15.18.

212b] The Israelites' clothing symbolizes their mood. For purposes of
scansion *blacum* must show resolution and cannot therefore be from *blāc*
'shining'. Bright [*MLN* xxvii (1912) 16] compared *on blacum hrægle* (*Riddle 10*
7).

214] Cf. *Beowulf* 387, 729.

218] *heora hlencan*: almost certainly two words – cf. *habbað eowre linda*
(*Finnsburh* 11a). Sisam (*Studies* 38 n.1) suggests *heorahlencan* (i.e. *heoruhlencan*

       beran beorht searo,   beacnum cigean
220 sweot sande near.   Snelle gemundon
       weardas wigleoð   (werod wæs gefysed),
       brudon ofer burgum –   byman gehyrdon –
       flotan feldhusum: fyrd wæs on ofste.
       Siððan hie getealdon   wið þam teonhete
225 on þam forðherge   feðan twelfe
       mode rofra;   mægen wæs onhrered.
       Wæs on anra gehwam   æðelan cynnes
       alesen under lindum   leoda duguðe
       on folcgetæl   fiftig cista;

226 rofra *Bouterwek*] rofa

'sword-coat') but this reading produces a variety of verse in which the
second element of a compound alliterates in addition to the double alliter-
ation (Type 1D*2) that is already there. Such 'treble' alliteration would
be unique.

221] *wigleoð*, i.e. trumpet calls (*beacnum* 219). The contrast with *atol
æfenleoð* (201) is no doubt deliberate; the Israelites have changed their tune
overnight.

222] *burgum*: see note to *burhhleoðu* (70).

223a] See note to 133.

224] *teonhete*: note that the Egyptians are here viewed as an abstraction.
a hostile influence which the Israelites and Christians must overcome.

224–32] The Israelite army is said to comprise the 12 tribes descended
from the 12 sons of Jacob (listed 1 Chr. 2.1–2), each tribe having 50 com-
panies and each company 1,000 men, thus making a total of 600,000 men,
the number given in Ex. 12.37 and Num. 11.21. The internal organization
of this total number is not, however, given in the Bible. Reference to Num. 1
is unhelpful since the numbers given for each tribe vary considerably and
relate to a total of 603,550 – excluding Levites – arrived at by taking a
census in Sinai. As the origin of the division into thousands Moore [*MP* ix
(1911) 102] suggested Ex. 18.21 (AV 18.25) where the word *tribunos* was
evidently taken to mean 'rulers of thousands', e.g. in *The OE . . . Heptateuch*
(EETS 160) 258, which has *ðusendmen*; Irving compares Augustine, *Quaest.
in Hept.*, Num. I, CCSL xxxiii 234 (= PL xxxiv 717). Once it is known that
the total number of men is 600,000, that there are 12 of the largest units
and 1000 in each of the smallest units, the number of intermediate units (50)
is easily calculated.

227ff.] These lines are similar to 183ff. where the reference is to the
Egyptians. The likeness of the two sides in terms of the way men are selected
for military service helps to throw into relief the importance of God's power
in deciding the issue between them.

230 hæfde cista gehwilc   cuðes werodes
garberendra,   guðfremmendra,
tyn hund geteled,   tireadigra:
þæt wæs wiglic werod.   Wace ne gretton
in þæt rincgetæl   ræswan herges,
235 þa þe for geoguðe   gyt ne mihton
under bordhreoðan   breostnet wera
wið flane feond   folmum werigean,
ne him bealubenne   gebiden hæfdon
ofer linde lærig,   licwunde spor,
240 gylpplegan gares.   Gamele ne moston,

233 wace Grein] wac
239 spor Grein] swor

233] *wace* is evidently acc. pl. m. and emendation of MS *wac* is therefore
necessary to restore grammatical acceptability.

233–46] The basis for the notion of excluding those too young or too
old to fight, appropriate enough in a Germanic epic poem (cf. Tacitus
Germania ch. xv), is contained in the Bible, Num. 1.3, 45, and Ps. 104 (105).37
et non erat in tribibus eorum infirmus, expanded in *PPs* 104.32 to *næs þæra leoda
ða | ænig untrum yldra ne gingra*. Irving cites also Augustine, *Quaest. in Hept.*,
Ex. XLVII, CCSL xxxiii 88 (= PL xxxiv 610).

236a] So *Beowulf* 2203a, *Andreas* 128b. Cf. 320a.

239a] *lærig*, a word of uncertain origin, occurs only here and in *Maldon*
(*Bærst bordes lærig* 284 – see note to Gordon's edn). It is probably a borrowing
from L *lōrīca* 'shield' with subsequent shortening of *ō* and unrounding (cf.
Campbell §507). According to M. Förster [*Festgabe für Liebermann* (Halle,
1921) 171–2] the borrowing was probably made through OW, but the
phonology of *æ* in *lærig* is difficult in view of W *llurig*; possibly *lærig* could
be a WS 'back-spelling' (like *mæsse*) for Kt *lerig* from *lyrig*. The meaning
'rim' is based on a gloss containing a related verb, *syn emblærgide* 'provided
with a border (on a sleeve)' for *ambiuntur* (Napier 170/377), evidence which
seems to overrule Förster's view that *lærig* meant the metal-studded leather
covering of a (wooden) shield.

239b] Despite E. A. Kock [*Anglia* xliii (1919) 305] MS *swor*, a form not
found elsewhere, cannot be adequately defended and therefore requires
emendation. The choice is between *spor* and *swol* 'burning', the former being
palaeographically more plausible. In *Juliana* 623 (cf. *Andreas* 1180) *wæpnes
spor* means 'wound' and so probably does *licwunde spor*: the difference is
simply that between a phrase which indicates what gave the wound (a
weapon) and one which indicates what received the wound (the body).

240] *gylpplegan gares*: i.e. combat with spears in which there is an obli-
gation on the participants to live up to their vows. See also note to 455.

hare heaðorincas, hilde onþeon
gif him modheapum mægen swiðrade,
ac hie be wæstmum wigheap curon,
hu in leodscipe læstan wolde
245 mod mid aran, eac þan mægnes cræft
garbeames feng gretan mihte.
Þa wæs handrofra here ætgædere,
fus forðwegas. Fana up gerad,
beama beorhtost; bidon ealle þa gen
250 hwonne siðboda sæstreamum neah
leoht ofer lindum lyftedoras bræc.

---

243 wigheap *Blackburn*] wig
246 gretan mihte] *supplied by Kluge*
248 gerad *Sievers*] rad
249 bidon *Grein*] buton

242] *modheapum* 'among the bold troops'.

243b] As it stands in the MS this verse is evidently defective and requires to be completed both in metre and sense. For the sense what is needed is a word including *wig* which will denote those chosen (object of *curon*); *wigheap* supplies this need and restores metrical acceptability. Another possibility is *wigþreat* (BLACKBURN).

244] *hu* '(considering) how': the consideration is implicit in *curon*.

246] As the metre indicates a verse is missing from the MS and a verb phrase roughly parallel to *læstan wolde* (244) would complete the sense very satisfactorily. As the best available solution therefore *gretan mihte* has been supplied and it has been placed in the *b*-verse on the grounds that such a verb phrase is commoner in final than in medial position.

247] *wæs . . . ætgædere*: i.e. formed into a group.

248a] *forðwegas* is gen. sg. for regular *-weges*. KLUGE emended to *fus on forðwegas*; cf. *Gen* 2814.

248b] *fana*: the cloud-pillar seen as a battle-standard incorporating the Cross (*segn* 127 and note). Since the word occurs as a gloss for L *vexillum* (Napier 1/4804) and *labarum* (Napier 1/1762) it probably suggests the Cross itself as 'banner' or 'standard'. Such a standard could be military or ecclesiastical; see further Lucas *FChristi* 199–200. MS *rad* is emended to *gerad* to restore metrical acceptability.

249a] *beama beorhtost*: the cloud-pillar as Cross – the phrase is used of the Cross in *Rood* 6. See note to 94b.

249b–51] Translate 'they were all still waiting there when the guide of the journey, bright above the shields, broke the air-roofs near the sea'.

250] *siðboda*: the cloud-pillar, here made to seem animate by the use of a compound on *-boda* 'messenger' (cf. 475).

251b] *bræc* is the verb after *hwonne* (250), which can stand only if MS

·XLVI·   Ahleop þa for hæleðum   hildecalla,   [p.156
253 bald beodohata,   bord up ahof,

253 beodohata] beo/hata *over line division;* ahof] hof *over erasure, a supra-
script with caret to mark place of insertion — original point (after erased
letters) only partially erased*

---

buton is emended to *bidon*. Since *hwonne* 'always seems to take the subjunctive'
(cf. 472–5) the verse is 'suspect' [B. Mitchell, *Guide to OE* (1965) §174]. The
only exceptions to this general rule [as pointed out by Mitchell in *Neophil.*
xlix (1965) 160, n.5] seem to be *huoenne cymmeð* (LGosp. and sim. RGosp.)
glossing 'quando venit' (Luke 17.20) where the WS versions have the subj.
(Skeat 170–71). Emendation to the subj. *bræce* (so GREIN) is not acceptable
because it would produce an otherwise unknown metrical type, 3A, and
Cosijn thought *bræc* to be 'licentia poetica metri causa' [*PBB* xx (1895) 100].
However, as Bright argued [*MLN* xxvii (1912) 16–17], the Israelites were
not waiting *for* the pillar to move, but were still waiting *when* it moved, and
the indicative is appropriate, though *þa* would be more usual to convey this
sense. In general sense the verse resembles *on lyft lædan* (*Rood* 5) except that
here the description of the *sidboda* seems to imply some personification (cf.
mihtig engel, 205). For the sense of *lyftedoras* cf. *eoderas* in *Beowulf* 1037.

252] *hildecalla*: this herald is a separate person from Moses (*modiges* 255).
The second element has excited considerable comment because it is one of
the two instances of 'call'-words in OE, the other being *ceallian* in *Maldon* 91.
Some – rightly – think these words native, others consider them to be bor-
rowed from ON; the decision is important because if *-calla* were of Norse
origin the poem's date of composition would have to be after the Norse
settlements [so D. Hofmann, *Anglia* lxxv (1957) 31]. All the evidence, in-
cluding the distribution of *calle* in ME texts, is assembled by Stanley [*Med.
Lit.* (1969) 94–9], who concludes that the word is native.

253a] The various ingenious attempts to elucidate MS *beohata* have been
reviewed by Schabram [*Wortbildung* . . . (1968) 203–9]. The word is evi-
dently parallel to *hildecalla* of which it is almost certainly a variant. The
second element may be read either as *-hāta* 'promiser' or *-hata* 'hater';
Irving's observation that compounds in *-hāta* do not occur elsewhere in OE
poetry is hardly decisive. Some of the main possibilities for the whole com-
pound are: *bēohata* 'bee-hater, bear, warrior', described by Schabram as
'phantasievolle'; *behāta* 'promiser', but there is then no word to indicate
what is promised; *bēahhāta* 'ring-promiser', but this would be appropriate
only as a description for Moses; the same objection applies to *bodhāta*
'command-bringer' and *bēothāta* 'promiser of vows'. The present reading.
which provides 'a good parallel to *hildecalla*' (IRVING), is based on a sugges-
tion first made by G. Sarrazin [*ESt* xlii (1910) 19], and the *eo*-spelling is a
variant of *ea* such as is sometimes found in Mercian texts (Campbell §207).
Thus the MS form is explicable as simply due to scribal haplography. For
the word-formation cf. *winhāte* 'summons to wine' (*Judith* 8).

253b] Raising the shield conventionally indicated that a speech was

heht þa folctogan   fyrde gestillan
255 þenden modiges meðel   monige gehyrdon.
Wolde reordigean   rices hyrde
ofer hereciste   halgan stefne,
werodes wisa   wurðmyndum spræc:
'Ne beoð ge þy forhtran,   þeah þe Faraon brohte
260 sweordwigendra   side hergas,
eorla unrim.   Him eallum wile
mihtig Drihten   þurh mine hand
to dæge þissum   dædlean gyfan,
þæt hie lifigende   leng ne moton
265 ægnian mid yrmðum   Israhela cyn.
Ne willað eow andrædan   deade feðan,
fæge ferhðlocan,   fyrst is æt ende
lænes lifes.   Eow is lar Godes

about to be made. Cf. *Maldon* 42, 244, 309.

255] *monige*, i.e. the Israelite multitude; cf. 553b.

256] *rices hyrde*, a common expression for a ruler, is here applied rather loosely to Moses without regard to the fact that the Israelites are *eðellease* (139).

259–75] This speech by Moses corresponds to that in Ex. 14.13–14, from which it differs considerably. Irving compares Deut. 20.1–4.

261a] Cf. *Beowulf* 1238a.

262] *þurh mine hand*: so *Beowulf* 558b, *Judith* 198b. Cf. 486 and see note to 19.

265] *ægnian* is taken as a variant spelling for *ægnan* with scribal substitution of *-ian* for *-an*; this variation is paralleled by *neosan/neosian* in *Beowulf* (see Klaeber's edn, 277 §9). *Ægnan* may be assumed to derive from Pr.OE **aʒunjan-, aʒun-* being the stem of MnE *awn* (ODEE s.v.). This verb accords closely in form with, and is probably formed on the same stem as, the OE pl. n. *ægnan* 'chaff' found in the *Corpus Glossary* [ed. W. M. Lindsay (Cambridge, 1921) 133, 150] for *paleae* (P185) and *quisquiliae* (Q45), and the sense of the verb would thus be 'thresh'. Its semantic range may have been similar to L *flagello* 'whip', 'thresh'. The resulting expression is a metaphor not uncharacteristic of this poem. See further Lucas *NQ* ccxvi (1971) 283–4.

266a] *Ne willað* corresponds to L *Nolite (timere)* in Ex. 14.13. But the obvious Latinism and regular OE usage would be *Nellað*: cf. K. Suter, *Das Pronomen beim Imperativ im Alt- und Mittelenglischen* (Aarau, 1955) 32–3, §14, and C. M. Millward, *Imperative Constructions in Old English* (Janua Linguarum ser. pract. 124, 1971) 26–7, §2.2.3. *Ne willað* without contraction is apparently Anglian: see Intro. 38.

267b] Translate '(do not fear that) the time . . .'.

abroden of breostum.   Ic on beteran ræd,
270 þæt ge gewurðien   wuldres Aldor,
ond eow Liffrean   lissa bidde,
sigora gesynto,   þær ge siðien.
Þis is se ecea   Abrahames God,
frumsceafta Frea,   se ðas fyrd wereð,
275 modig ond mægenrof,   mid þære miclan hand.'
Hof ða for hergum   hlude stefne   [p.157
lifigendra þeoden,   þa he to leodum spræc:
'Hwæt ge nu eagum to   on lociað,

---

277 þeoden *Blackburn*] þeod

269b] The verb is *on* 'give' from *unnan*. Since this verb normally takes
the genitive Irving recommends acceptance of Cosijn's suggestion *Ic con*
[*PBB* xix (1894) 461] which is very plausible palaeographically. However,
as *geunnan* is certainly used with the acc. [BTS s.v. (3)], it is hard to rule
out the possibility that *on* is correct here.

271] *bidde*: on the pr. subj. pl. in *-e* see note to *hyrde* (124).

272] *gesynto*: for the levelling of the nom. sg. ending to other cases in
this noun-class see Campbell §589.6.

275] In *mid þære miclan hand* the word *hand* must be taken as dat. sg. for
regular *handa*, a variant permitted by SB §274 though no supporting evi-
dence is cited. The difficulty could be eliminated by omitting *þære* (J. R. R.
Tolkien's suggestion) on the assumption that it was added by a WS scribe,
in whose dialect *mid* took the dat. (in Anglian *mid* took the acc.); thus
hand could be taken as acc. However, it is impossible to be certain that the
text is incorrect as it stands. The image of God's mighty hand or arm (really
the divine power communicated through Moses's hand – see note to 19) is
frequent in the Psalms: see 76.16 (77.15), 88.11, 14 (89.10, 13), 97 (98).1,
135 (136).12.

277] *lifigendra þeoden*: Moses, but the term is equally applicable to God,
whose mouthpiece Moses is. *Þeoden* is by far the best emendation of MS *þeod*,
which will not make sense in the context; the emendation does not affect
the scansion (3E1) since the final *-en* is not to be counted as metrically
syllabic (Intro. 40). Of other proposals BOUTERWEK's *leod* results in having
both *leod* 'lord' and *leodum* in the one line and *l* for *þ* is not readily explicable
palaeographically. IRVING's reading (following Bright), *leoð* 'song', is even
less explicable palaeographically and involves him in taking *hlude stefne* as
dat. sg. f. even though the required form of the adj. would be *hludre*.

278–98] The division of the Red Sea is here described by Moses rather
than told in the third person as in Ex. 14.21–2. This device was presumably
employed to give the event greater immediacy, an impression reinforced by
the use of the *nu . . . nu* correlative construction (278/280). Cf. the remarks
by Shippey, *OE Verse* (1972) 138–40.

278] *to* is adverbial; cf. *Soul and Body II* 112. Bright [*MLN* xxvii (1912)

folca leofost,   færwundra sum
280   nu ic sylfa sloh   ond þeos swiðre hand
grene tacne   garsecges deop.
Yð up færeð,   ofstum wyrceð
wæter on wealfæsten.   Wegas syndon dryge,
haswe herestræta,   holm gerymed,

280 nu *Tolkien*] hu
283 on *Grein*] 7

17] advocated its omission, suggesting that the scribe was confused by the fact that *lōcian* could be construed with either *on* or *to* (cf. *Daniel* 418), but, as Dobbie [*JEGP* liii (1954) 231] pointed out, *to* is necessary 'to reinforce an expression of direction'.

279] *færwundra sum* 'a (particular) sudden awe-inspiring miracle'.

280a] Translate 'now I myself have stuck . . .'. MS *hu* gives a very awkward construction which does not make good sense.

280b] It is hard to distinguish the hand of Moses from that of God (275 and note); see also note to 19.

281] *grene tacne*: Moses's rod of living wood, a symbol of salvation (cf. Ex. 17.5–6, 9–13). Cf. note to 15b, where it is remarked that Moses's rod was conventionally interpreted as the Cross; the term *grene tacn* could also refer to the 'green' Cross, on which see H. R. Patch, *PMLA* xxxiv (1919) 247n. Emendation to *tane* 'rod' (BOUTERWEK) is unnecessary; so also Hermann, *ELN* xii (1975) 241–3.

283] In *wæter on wealfæsten, on* for MS 7 (abbreviation for *ond*) is extremely plausible palaeographically and produces excellent sense: 'the wave makes the water into a fortified wall'. Alternatively MS 7 may be omitted altogether and *wæter* taken as subject of *wyrceð*. For purposes of scansion the final *en* of *wealfæsten* must be taken as non-syllabic. Note that the sea, formerly seen as hostile (*hettend* 209), now provides protection for the Israelites.

283b–88] *Wegas, herestræta, staðolas* and *feldas* are all parallel. The sentence is an expansion of the biblical 'et vertit [mare] in siccum; divisaque est aqua' (Ex. 14.21). IRVING notes a similar expansion in *The OE . . . Heptateuch* (EETS 160) 250, where *7 læg an drige stræt ðurh ða sæ* is added, and compares 2 Sam. 22.16. BLACKBURN and Irving cite a passage from the *Joca Monachorum* which states that the path in the sea was exposed to the sun and wind only for 'una hora diei nec antea nec postea', and note that *antea* corresponds to 285b–6 and *postea* to 287b–8. Helder [*AM* xvi (1975) 17–19] suggests that the description in these lines evokes the original paradise.

284a] The precise sense of *haswe* offers difficulty and must be determined in relation to the terms *fage feldas* (287) and *grenne grund* (312) also used of the path through the sea. BT glosses *hasu* as 'grey' [see also M. Trautmann, *BBA* xix (1905) 216–8] and certainly the word comes midway on the AS light-dark axis [N. F. Barley, *ASE* iii (1974) 18] but 'silvery' or even 'glistening' would be a preferable rendering here; BTSA notes that the word is

285 ealde staðolas,   þa ic ær ne gefrægn
     ofer middangeard   men geferan,
     fage feldas,   þa forð heonon   [p.158
     in ece tid   yðe þeccað.
     Sælde sægrundas   suðwind fornam,
290 bæðweges blæst;   brim is areafod,

288 tid] *supplied by Holthausen;* þeccað] þeahton
290 brim *Thorpe*] bring

'used as a conventional epithet' in *Phoenix* 121, where it is paralleled by
beorht (cf. OHG *hasan* 'bright'). BTS suggests equivalency with L *glaucus*
'sea-green' but such a sense is not necessary to harmonize with *grenne grund*
since *hasu* and *grene* were roughly equivalent in brightness, a concept more
important than hue in AS colour classification.

284b] Understand *is*. Irving's suggested emendation to *holme* is un-
necessary.

287] The *fage feldas* are presumably the same as the *grenne grund* of 312;
see note to 284a. Normally *fah* means 'bright' or 'variegated' but neither is
particularly appropriate as a rendering here, though brightness and green-
ness are associated in *Phoenix* 78–80. Perhaps the best rendering would be
'mottled', indicating a variegation in brightness rather than hue.

287–8] If MS *þeahton* is allowed to stand the sequence of tenses becomes
confused: 'the open expanses of land which henceforth the waves have
covered'! Emendation to *þeccað* is therefore necessary and the gist of the
passage is that men have never before trodden the sea-bottom (285–6) and
that they will not do so again because the waves will cover it. In 288a the
addition of *tid* makes the verse metrically complete.

289a] *Sælde sægrundas*: the sea-depths are confined in the sense that they
are normally covered by the surface of the sea which is of a uniform level.
At the point of the crossing the wind cleared away all the water to make a
dry path flanked by the walls of water on either side.

289b] *suðwind* has received considerable attention because it indicates the
direction of the wind, a detail lacking in the corresponding statement in
the Vulgate, 'flante vento vehementi et urente' (Ex. 14.21); but cf. Ps. 77
(78).26. As noted by Cross and Tucker [*Neophil.* xliv (1960) 38–9] the OL
Bible, not yet reconstructed for this passage, probably had *auster*, as the
south wind appears in the Septuagint. Cross and Tucker also cite patristic
authorities, e.g. Ambrose, Cyprianus Gallus, from whom *suðwind* could have
derived. Their implied suggestion that the identification of *auster* with the
Holy Spirit in allegorical exegesis is subsumed in *suðwind* is not supported
by the text.

290] Although *blæst* elsewhere means 'flame', in this context the sense
must be one appropriate as a parallel for *suðwind*, and the same sense is
probably implicit in the compound *blæstbelg* 'bellows'.

sand sæcir spaw.   Ic wat soð gere
þæt eow mihtig God   miltse gecyðde,
eorlas ærglade.   Ofest is selost
þæt ge of feonda   fæðme weorðen
295 nu se Agend   up arærde
reade streamas   in randgebeorh.
Syndon þa foreweallas   fægre gestepte,
wrætlicu wægfaru,   oð wolcna hrof.'
Æfter þam wordum   werod eall aras,
300 modigra mægen;   mere stille bad.
Hofon herecyste   hwite linde,
segnas on sande.   Sæweall astah,
uplang gestod   wið Israhelum
andægne fyrst,   yðholmes hleo.

291 spaw *Krapp*] span
304 yðholmes hleo] *supplied*

291a] Emendation to *spaw* is necessary to give acceptable sense; cf. 450.
Translate 'the undertow (of the retreating waves) spewed out sand'. For
the expression cf. *Beowulf* 212–3.

293a] *eorlas ærglade* is vocative. The *eorlas* are 'happy as of old' because,
with the way of salvation open to them, they can escape *of feonda fæðme*. For
the sense of *ærglade* see W. F. Bryan in *MP* xxviii (1930–31) 159–60.

293b] So *Beowulf* 256b and cf. 3007.

295–6] These lines state explicitly that the Lord was responsible for the
division of the sea. The word *Agend* reminds us that the sea is not just a
natural phenomenon but a possession of God's, one which He uses as a
weapon against the Egyptians. By contrast the language of protective
armour is used to describe the sea in relation to the Israelites.

303–5] A verse is assumed to be lacking here probably because the orig-
inal had three consecutive lines with vocalic alliteration. Since all five half-
lines given in the MS have single vocalic alliteration, in theory each could
be either an *a*- or a *b*-verse. In practice the missing verse must be either
304b or 305b. If the latter alternative is followed the verse supplied must
include a subject for *heold*. Two previous proposals do just this, but both
Grein's *Hie ece Drihten* [*Germania* x (1865) 418] and IRVING's *Him se Alwalda*
are open to the objection that they are syntactically incomplete since the
usual constructions with *healdan wære* are *wið* + acc. or *mid* + acc./dat.;
moreover neither of these prepositions could be fitted in as either would have
to be postposited and therefore metrically stressed. In view of this difficulty
in taking the missing verse to be 305b it is preferable to assume the loss to
be at 304b. In the verse supplied here, which is modelled on 79b, the un-

305 Wæs seo eorla gedriht   anes modes,
    fæstum fæðmum   freoðowære heold:
    nalles hie gehyrdon   haliges lare
    siððan leofes leoþ   læste near
    sweg swiðrode   ond sances bland.
310 Þa þæt feorðe cyn   fyrmest eode,

307 hie *Thorpe*] hige

---

recorded compound *yðholm* is closely paralleled by *wægholm* (*Beowulf* 217),
sæholm (Andreas 529), and the second element is used as the first in *holmweall*
(468), a synonym for *sæweall*.

306] i.e. the Israelites clutched the covenant to their hearts, so firmly did
they adhere to it.

307] If MS *hige* is retained as a noun, 'in mind', as urged by Wrenn
[*RES* n.s. vi (1955) 186], the verse is metrically objectionable and idiomati-
cally suspect (*on hige* would be preferable). IRVING's assertion that '*hige* is a
form of *hīe*, *hī*' is arguable (cf. SB §24 Anm.) but unlikely; the misspelling
hige was probably induced by the initial *ge-* of the next word, *gehyrdon*. For
this form, from *gehyrwan*, see Campbell §753.5. Cosijn [*PBB* xx (1895) 101]
notes an expression similar to *gehyrdon haliges lare* in *Judgment Day I* 70.

308–9] Translate 'when the speech of the loved one (Moses), his voice,
and the variation of pitch dwindled away nearer to performance', i.e. as
the time approached to carry out Moses's injunctions in action. But the
passage may well be corrupt. J. R. R. Tolkien noted that *swiðrode* is perhaps
over-generously provided with a triple-headed subject in the form of *leofes
leoð*, *sweg* and *sances bland*; the latter would be more appropriate if it applied
to several persons rather than one, and there is no other instance of *læst*
meaning 'performance'.

309] The *c* in *sances* (instead of usual *sanges*) arises from sporadic un-
voicing of the final plosive consonant in *sang* being extended to an inflected
form (Campbell §450).

310–46] The entry of the Israelites into the Red Sea passage is described
in terms of an army going into battle, though the enemy are behind out of
fighting distance. In 326–30 there is apparently actual combat. As Cross &
Tucker point out [*Neophil.* xliv (1960) 122–7] citing Augustine and Gregory,
this mode of description is to be explained only by reference to the exegetical
tradition of interpreting the Crossing of the Red Sea as an allegory for
Baptism [Daniélou, *Bible & Liturgy* (1956) ch. 5]; cf. note to 519–48. The
Christian catechumen approaches Baptism as a soldier fighting off assailants
(sins). This fighting is described in relation to the tribe of Judah simply
because it goes first. The order of the tribes (Judah, Reuben, Simeon)
puzzled IRVING (also later Irving) but is simply the order of seniority except
for the precedence of Judah. This precedence stems from Gen. 49.8–12 and

wod on wægstream,   wigan on heape,
ofer grenne grund,   Iudisc feða,
on onette   uncuð gelad
for his mægwinum.   Swa him mihtig God
315 þæs dægweorces   deop lean forgeald,
siððan him gesælde   sigorworca hreð,
þæt he ealdordom   agan sceolde
ofer cynericu,   cneowmaga blæd.

313 on onette *Thorpe*] an on orette

---

was gained by Judah because his three elder brothers defaulted (Gen. 49.3–7); already in Gen. 43.3 Judah speaks for all the brothers.

311] The verb *wadan*, of which the basic sense is 'pass through', esp. water, is particularly appropriate here, but in OE poetry, as B. Weman has shown [*OE Semantic Analysis and Theory* (Lund, 1933) 118–23], it has the special sense 'advance with difficulty and with special effort'.

312a] The *grene grund* was perhaps suggested by the *campus germinans* of Wisd. 19.7 [Keenan, *NM* lxxiv (1973) 218]. KRAPP's remark that *grene* is 'not an appropriate adjective here' is true in the sense that it would hardly be 'realistic' for the sea to reveal a green grassy path (cf. note to 284a). The lack of 'realism' was probably a deliberate pointer to an allegorical interpretation whereby the path through the Red Sea is equated with the Green Street of Paradise: both are roads to salvation. Keenan [*NM* lxxi (1970) 456] points to the same motif in *Christ & Satan* 286–7 and *PPs* 141.4; it also occurs in *Gen* 1137 [cf. F. C. Robinson, *Archiv* cciv (1967) 267–8]. Cf. also A. N. Doane, *NM* lxxiv (1973) 456–65, and K. Sajavaara, *NM* lxxvi (1975) 34–8.

312b] *Iudisc*: see note to 330.

313] The present emended reading has been adopted because the MS reading and all other proposed readings are unacceptable on grounds of metre and/or sense. The reading *ān onōrette*, which could mean 'on its own won by effort' [cf. K. Malone (ed.) *Widsith*, Anglistica xiii (1962) note to line 41, and glossary s.v. *onōrettan*], will not scan, nor will *ān on onette* 'alone hastened on'. Readings with *onōrette*, which KRAPP takes to mean 'in battle', deprive the sentence of its verb. The word *on* is indispensable on grounds of sense because it links *onette* with *uncuð gelad* and is best retained at the beginning of the *a*-verse where it is stressed because in displaced position. 313b is identical with 58b.

314b–5] For the concept of reward for a day's work cf. 150–51. Here the divine reward relates to the fact that the tribe of Judah have been foremost in their adherence to the covenant with the Lord (306) because they enter the Red Sea first.

316] Translate 'when the glory of victorious deeds fell to Judah's lot (*him*)'.

317–8] An allusion to the fact that Judah later became the most powerful and prominent tribe.

·XLVII· Hæfdon him to segne,   þa hie on sund stigon, [p.160
320 ofer bordhreoðan   beacen aræred
    in þam garheape   gyldenne leon,
    drihtfolca mæst,   deora cenost.
    Be þam herewisan   hynðo ne woldon
    be him lifigendum   lange þolian,
325 þonne hie to guðe   garwudu rærdon,
    ðeoda ænigre.   Þraca wæs on ore,
    heard handplega,   hægsteald modige,

321 leon *Thorpe*] leor
327 handplega] hand *altered from* heard

319–22] The reference is to the Lion of Judah, introduced in the Bible in Gen. 49.9. The most famous reference, in Rev. 5.5 'ecce vicit leo de tribu Iuda', led to the interpretation of the Lion of Judah as a foreshadowing of Christ – Robinson [*NM* lxvii (1966) 357, n.4] cites Ambrose (PL xiv 679–80), Isidore (PL lxxxiii 106, 135), Bede (PL xciii 145) and others. This interpretation is encouraged in the present context by the use of *segn* and *beacen*, words already employed to refer to the pillar or the pillar as Cross: like the Lion of Judah the Cross was a symbol of Christ. See further Lucas, *FChristi* 200.

320a] Cf. 236a and note.

321] *leon*: Thorpe's emendation was privately anticipated by J. Grimm [*PQ* xliv (1965) 163].

322] *drihtfolca mæst*: parallel with the unexpressed subject of *Hæfdon* (319).

323–6] Translate 'They had no intention of enduring humiliation from any people for long ...'. *Be þam herewisan* and *be him lifigendum* are to be taken together as one absolute clause: 'while the leader (Moses) was alive'. Bright's observation that the action here is conceived 'in the spirit of the *comitatus*' [*MLN* xxvii (1912) 17] requires elaboration. Statements in OE poetry (which generally lacks suspense) such as *þa hwile þe hi wæpna wealdan moston* (*Maldon* 83, sim. 14, 235, 272) normally imply that the temporal condition will be fulfilled (as in *Maldon* 167–8), but in *Ex* Moses does not die, nor is there any threat of impending disaster should he do so. What is implied is that the people's leader will live for ever and will always protect them. This Moses can do only as a type or foreshadowing of Christ. The sudden shift of subject from Judah to Moses (and back again) reinforces this interpretation, for both were types of Christ.

326] *þraca* is nom. sg. for regular *þracu*.

327] *hægsteald modige*: on the usual assumption that *hægsteald* is a masc. noun, the phrase apparently consists of a sg. noun and pl. adj. On the analogy of 328 the phrase must presumably be pl., but emendation to

wæpna wælslihtes,   wigend unforhte,
bilswaðu blodige,   beadumægnes ræs,
330 grimhelma gegrind,   þær Iudas for.
     Æfter þære fyrde   flota modgade,
Rubenes sunu;   randas bæron
sæwicingas   ofer sealtne mersc,
manna menio,   micel angetrum
335 eode unforht.   He his ealdordom
synnum aswefede,   þæt he siðor for

---

334 manna *Sievers*] man

---

hægstealdas (m. pl.) produces unacceptable metre. It seems best to assume that *hægsteald* is in fact a pl. form, either because the word could be neut. (cf. *gesteald* 'dwelling', *hagosteald* 'celibacy') as well as masc. (but this means taking *modige* for regular *modigu*) or, as noted by B. Mitchell [*NM* lxx (1969) 73] following J. R. R. Tolkien, by analogy with *nd*-nouns (cf. *wigend* 328).

328] *wælslihtes* is probably nom. pl. for regular *-slihtas*, but if the possibility that it is gen. sg. is entertained it would have to be dependent on *modige* (SEDGEFIELD) or on *unforhte* [Bright, *MLN* xxvii (1912) 17].

328b] See note to 180b.

330] As in L, *Iudas* must have initial /j/, which alliterates with *g*-.

331–5] A recurrence of the nautical imagery whereby the Israelites are sailors: see notes to 80b–84 and 105–6a.

333a] *sæwicingas*: the second element is one of the earliest occurrences of *wīcing* in English. Evidently the word existed in English before the Norse invasions, and the influence of ON *víkingr* probably gave it its special signification: E. Björkman, *Scandinavian Loan-words in ME* (Halle, 1902) 258, also OED *Viking*.

333b] *ofer sealtne mersc*: note the use of an adj. appropriate to the sea to describe the path open across the seabed.

334a] Emendation is necessary to restore metre and sense.

334b] If the first element of *angetrum* were *ān* the verse would scan as 1D4, a type found only in the *a*-verse. Cf. 203b.

335–9] Reuben, Jacob's eldest son, forfeited his right to primacy by sleeping with his father's concubine (Gen. 35.22, 49.3–4, 1 Chr. 5.1; cf. also Deut. 27.20); this action may have implied an attempt to usurp his father's authority (cf. 2 Sam. 16.21–2). The careful elaboration of this point suggests concern with a moral ideal; cf. *Beowulf* 2435ff. where Hæðcyn still succeeds his father as king of the Geats even though he killed his elder brother Herebeald. By implication the seriousness with which the subject of *frumbearnes riht* is treated here emphasizes the severity of the slaughter of the first-born as a blow to the Egyptians.

on leofes last   (him on leodsceare
frumbearnes riht   freobroðor oðþah,
ead ond æðelo);   næs he earg swa þeah.
340   Þær æfter him foron   folca þryðum
sunu Simeones,   sweotum comon,
þridde þeodmægen   (þufas wundon
ofer garfare)   guðcyste onþrang,
deawig sceaftum.   Dægwoma becwom
345   ofer garsecge,   Godes beacna sum,
morgen meretorht.   Mægen forð gewat.
Þa þær folcmægen   for æfter oðrum
isernhergum   (an wisode

339 næs he earg *Irving*] he wæs gearu
340 foron] *supplied by Sedgefield*
345 garsecge *Graz*] gar secges; beacna] c *altered from minim (first stroke of* n)
346 meretorht *Kluge*] mære torht

337a] *on leofes last* 'behind the loved one' (Judah or Moses?).

337b–9a] Translate 'his own brother had taken from him the right of the first-born among the nation, his wealth and station'.

339] Since initial /j/ in *gearu* cannot alliterate with the initial vowels in *ead* and *æðelo* (cf. KRAPP's note to *Gen* 238) emendation is required to restore alliteration. Presumably a scribe substituted an equivalent positive statement for the negative one probably in the original. For the sense Irving compares *unforht* 335, and he notes similar verses in *Beowulf* 1929, 2967.

340a] It is necessary to supply an alliterating word. Only two suggestions have been made that are metrically acceptable, that by Holthausen in *Anglia Beiblatt* v (1895) 231, *þær æfter him fūse*, and that by SEDGEFIELD, which is adopted here because it gives more acceptable word-order. If *fuse* were supplied the only verb in the clause (*comon*) would come at the very end of it, and after *þær* this would imply a subordinate rather than a demonstrative clause.

340b] Translate 'with the might of the people'.

344a] J. R. R. Tolkien suggested reading *deawigsceaftum* as one word; cf. the adj. *deawigfeðera*.

344b] *Dægwoma*: see note to 100.

345a] The *-es* of MS *gar secges* is probably, as KRAPP suggests, a scribal anticipation of the ending of *Godes*, the next word.

345b] Cf. *Beowulf* 570a.

346] If accepted MS *mæretorht* 'splendidly bright' would be the only recorded compound in *mære-*. In view of *morgen meretorhtne* in *Meters of Boethius* 13, 61 emendation to *meretorht* seems preferable.

348b] Translate 'one person directed [them]'. Usually *an* is taken to refer to Moses, but God is also a possibility.

mægenþrymmum mæst,   þy he mære wearð)
350 on forðwegas,   folc æfter wolcne,   [p.161
cynn æfter cynne.   Cuðe æghwilc
mægburga riht,   swa him Moises bead
eorla æðelo.   Him wæs an fæder,
leof leodfruma,   landriht geþah,
355 frod on ferhðe,   freomagum leof.
Cende cneowsibbe   cenra manna
heahfædera sum,   halige þeode,
Israela cyn,   onriht Godes,
swa þæt orþancum   ealde reccað,
360 þa þe mægburge   mæst gefrunon,
frumcyn feora,   fæderæðelo gehwæs.
Niwe flodas   Noe oferlað,

350 wolcne] wolcnum

350b] *wolcne*: the cloud-pillar. The emendation is necessary on grounds of sense and is preferable stylistically since the construction in *folc æfter wolcne* is repeated precisely in *cynn æfter cynne*. No doubt the implied parallel between Christians following the divine guide and members of a family group following one another was deliberate; cf. note to 446.

351b] *æghwilc*: each tribe.

352] *mægburga riht*, i.e. the correct position for each tribe. The order of the tribes, as implied by *eorla æðelo* (353), was established by descent, and was according to seniority among the sons of Jacob, except for the primacy of Judah: see note to 310–46. For a different order cf. Num. 2.3–31, 10.14–28.

353b] The reference is to Abraham – 'Pater noster Abraham est' (John 8.39) – cf. note to 446. There is probably an allusion to Gen. 17.4–5 where we are told Abraham is to be 'pater multarum gentium'.

354] *landriht geþah* occurs also in *Deor* 40. The reference is to God's undertaking to provide the Promised Land, as recorded in Gen. 12.7, 13.15, 15.18, 17.8, Ps. 104 (105).9–11 etc.

358] *onriht Godes*: tr. L *rectus Domini*, a name-etymology for *Israel* given by Jerome, as pointed out by Robinson [*NM* lxix (1968) 166, n.2; *Anglia* lxxxvi (1968) 25–6].

359–61] Probably, as IRVING suggests, an allusion (in the AS manner) to the frequent genealogies in the Pentateuch (also Kgs., Chr.).

362–446] This passage was formerly thought to be an interpolation: see Intro. 30–31.

362–76] This passage concerning the story of Noah harmonizes with the nautical imagery used to describe the Israelite exodus from Egypt (notes to 80b–84, 105–6a). Both events, the escape from the Flood under Noah, and

þrymfæst þeoden,   mid his þrim sunum,
þone deopestan   drencefloda
365 þara ðe gewurde   on woruldrice.
Hæfde him on hreðre   halige treowa;
forþon he gelædde   ofer lagustreamas
maðmhorda mæst,   mine gefræge.
On feorhgebeorh   foldan hæfde
370 eallum eorðcynne   ece lafe,

364 drencefloda *Cosijn*] dren floda
368 gefræge *Thorpe*] fr fræge

the escape from Egypt under Moses, demonstrate how God provides salvation for the Israelites, and both the Deluge and the Crossing of the Red Sea were interpreted allegorically by the Church Fathers as standing for Baptism.

362a] As J. R. Hall notes [*NQ* ccxx (1975) 243–4] the masses of flowing water (*flodas*) are *niwe* not in the sense of being unprecedented (the world was similarly inundated at the time of the Creation, Gen. 1.1–10) but in the sense of being a change from what immediately preceded and a renewal of what had gone before that. Hall sees the implication of 'new beginning' in *niwe* as alluding to Baptism.

362b] BLACKBURN – followed by IRVING, who ignored Bright [*MLN* xxvii (1912) 18] – thought it necessary to read *ofer lað* for metrical reasons, remarking that *ofer* is postposited and therefore takes stress. If so the verse would scan as Type 2A2, a type found only in the *a*-verse with double alliteration. Thus metrical criteria in fact establish that the correct reading is *oferlað*, and the verse scans as Type 2E1b.

364] *drencefloda*: Cosijn [*PBB* xx (1895) 103] cites *drenceflod* (*Gen* 1398).

365] *gewurde* is subj. in a restrictive relative clause after a superlative antecedent [for which see B. Mitchell in *Anglia* lxxxi (1963) 321–2 and *Guide to OE* (1965) §165.4]. Its number, however, is unclear since it could be sg. in concord with *þone deopestan* or (with *-e* for regular *-en*, on which see note to *hyrde* 124) pl. in concord with *þara* (see Mitchell, *Anglia* lxxxi 314).

366] *treowa* is acc. sg. for regular *treowe*. The reference is to Gen. 6.18, 9.9–17.

368] *maðmhorda mæst*: Noah's Ark with its contents.

369–74] Translate 'In the saving of lives of all the race of earth the wise seafarer had counted in number the everlasting survivors, the first generation of each, father and mother of those that produce descendants, more diverse than men know.'

370] Calder [*NM* lxxiv (1973) 87] sees here 'the identification of Noah as *ece lafe*', connecting this with the usual patristic name-etymology of Noah, *requies* 'remnant', but since Noah (*snottor sæleoda*) is already the subject of the sentence he cannot be the object as well.

frumcneow gehwæs,   fæder ond moder
tuddorteondra,   geteled rime,
missenlicra   þonne men cunnon,
snottor sæleoda.   Eac þon sæda gehwilc
375 on bearm scipes   beornas feredon
þara þe under heofonum   hæleð bryttigað.
Swa þæt wise men   wordum secgað
þæt from Noe   nigoða wære
fæder Abrahames   on folctale.
380 Þæt is se Abraham   se him engla God

371 gehwæs *Junius*] gehæs
373 missenlicra *Bosworth-Toller*] mis micelra

373] MS *mis micelra* is obscure; *micel* can hardly be accepted since the context requires a comparative and the comparative of *micel* is *māra*. The emendation adopted here was first suggested by BT *mis-micel*. In *Studies for E. Haugen* (The Hague, 1972) 328 W. P. Lehmann defends the MS reading on the grounds that a positive adj. followed by *þonne* can be comparative in sense but this is not idiomatic OE and, despite Lehmann, does not occur at *Beowulf* 69–70 (MS *þone*) nor *Elene* 646–7 (see note in Gradon's edn).

377–9] Abraham's father, Terah, was the ninth in line from Noah. The order was (in the spellings of the New English Bible) Noah, Shem (1), Arphaxad (2), Shelah (3), Eber (4), Peleg (5), Reu (6), Serug (7), Nahor (8), Terah (9): Gen. 11.10–26, 1 Chr. 1.24–6.

380–446] This passage concerning the story of Abraham and Isaac (Gen. 22.1–19) emphasizes the renewal of the covenant between God and the Israelites. In return for obedience God provides deliverance in need. The passage may be compared with the treatment of the same episode in *Gen* 2846–2936; cf. R. P. Creed in *OE Poetry: Fifteen Essays* (Providence, 1967) 69–92. In *Ex* the treatment is more selective (e.g., Abraham's servants do not appear, God's speeches before the offering are omitted, there is no mention of the wood which Isaac carried for the fire nor the ram which was substituted for Isaac in the actual sacrifice) and more allusive (e.g. in identifying the place of offering with the site of Solomon's Temple). But the interpretation is not primarily typological; the offering is not seen primarily as a prefiguration of the Crucifixion. On the treatment of the episode in early texts (and monuments) see Daniélou, *Shadows to Reality* (1960) 115–30, and van Woerden, *Vigiliae Christianae* xv (1961) 214–55.

380] *se him* is an unusual form of the relative [cf. B. Mitchell, *Guide to OE* (1965) §162]. In view of the parallels in (Exeter) *Maxims I* 37, 38 indicated by Mitchell in *RES* n.s. xv (1964) 134 BLACKBURN's suggestion that *se* be emended to the more usual *þe* can hardly be accepted.

naman niwan asceop;   eac þon neah ond feor
halige heapas   in gehyld bebead,
werþeoda geweald.   He on wræce lifde.
Siððan he gelædde   leofost feora
385 Haliges hæsum;   heahlond stigon
sibgemagas,   on Seone beorh.   [p.162
Wære hie þær fundon –   wuldor gesawon –
halige heahtreowe,   swa hæleð gefrunon.
Þær eft se snottra   sunu Dauides,

---

381 feor] e *suprascript with caret to mark place of insertion*
384 gelædde] gelifde *with* æ *altered from* if *and descender of* f *imperfectly
erased, 2nd* d *suprascript*

381] *naman niwan*: Abraham rather than Abram (Gen. 17.5).

382] *heapas*: the nations descended from Abraham (Gen. 17.6).

383] *He on wræce lifde.* In Gen. 12.1 Abraham is summoned to make a
complete break with his past and set out on a nomadic life of wanderings in
search of the Promised Land. Abraham is *on wræce* in the sense that he never
reached the new homeland (cf. Heb. 11.13). Here the word *wræce* carries
no overtones of 'punishment'. For the motif of exile cf. 137b–40a and note.

384–6] Irving points out that the OE seems to be modelled on the OL
text of Gen. 22.2, 'accipe filium tuum amantissimum, quem diligis, Isaac,
et vade in terram excelsam'. (The Vulgate has 'filium tuum unigenitum,
quem diligis' and 'terram visionis'.) Cf. *Gen* 2855 *hean landes*, and 2878 *hea
dune*.

386] Mt Zion, a hill in Jerusalem, was where the Tabernacle was erected
by David to house the Ark of the Covenant. Strictly speaking the Offering
of Isaac took place on an adjacent hill, Mt Moriah, and this was the site of
Solomon's Temple. But the two hills, linked by a wide bridge, became as
one, for which the name Zion, so familiar from its incorporation in the
devotional literature, esp. three of the 'Hymns of Zion', Pss. 47 (48), 75 (76),
86 (87), was commonly used. For other occurrences of the name in OE and
its declension see P. Gradon, *SN* xx (1947–48) 199–202.

389–96] The identification of the place of offering with the site of the
Temple (usually arrived at by collating Gen. 22.2 and 2 Chr. 3.1) is not in
the Vulgate (Gen. 22.2 has 'unum montium quem monstravero tibi'), nor
the OL Bible, but is explicit in the commentaries. Moore [*MP* ix (1911) 101]
cites Jerome, *Quaest. in Gen.* CCSL lxxii (1959) 26/13 (= PL xxiii 969 [2nd
edn 1019]) and Irving adds Bede *De Templo* i 472ff., CCSL cxix/A (1969)
159 (= PL xci 747). The allusion to the Temple no doubt takes up the earlier
reference to the Tabernacle (85 and note), its portable antecedent; allegori-
cally both stood for the Church. Hall [*Neophil.* lix (1975) 616–21] thinks
the exceptional 'piling up' of superlative epithets in 394–5 points to the
identification of the Temple and the Church. As in the Tabernacle (86–7)

390 wuldorfæst cyning,   witgan larum
      getimbrede   tempel Gode,
      alh haligne,   eorðcyninga
      se wisesta   on woruldrice,
      heahst ond haligost,   hæleðum gefrægost,
395 mæst ond mærost   þara þe manna bearn
      fira æfter foldan   folmum geworhte.
      To þam meðelstede   magan gelædde
      Abraham Isaac,   adfyr onbran
      (fyrst ferhðbana   no þy fægra wæs),

---

392 alh *Bouterwek*] alhn
399 fægra] fæg ra *with point imperfectly erased after* fæg, *clear under ultra-violet light*

---

the Lord dwelt in the Temple with the Israelites, a notion probably alluded to in the word *meðelstede* 397 (cf. 543); cf. Hall 617.

390] In his glossary Irving takes *witgan* as gen. sg. of *wit(e)ga* WITIE 'prophet', but it is David who exhorts Solomon to build the Temple (1 Chr. 28.10).

391] *tempel Gode*: for other examples of this type of verse see H. Schabram in *Britannica* [H. M. Flasdieck *Festschrift* (Heidelberg, 1960)] 233–7.

393] *se wisesta* is parallel with *sunu* (389). Solomon was specially endowed with wisdom by God: 1 Kgs. 3.5–15, 1 Chr. 1.7–12. For some account of the medieval legend of Solomon see R. J. Menner, *The Poetical Dialogues of Solomon and Saturn*, MLA Monographs xiii (New York, 1941) 21ff.

396] *geworhte* is p.t. pl. subj. for regular *geworhten* on which see note to *hyrde* 124. For the use of the subj. see note to *gewurde* 365.

399] A difficult line. The main problem is the identification of *ferhðbana*. Abraham is perhaps the most obvious candidate, but is open to the objection that he is only a potential, not an actual, slayer; also emendation of *fægra* to *fægenra* 'more joyful' would be necessary. Irving (following Cosijn) favours the devil, emending *fyrst* to *fyrn* 'ancient', but this reading produces an abrupt and arbitrary interruption of the narrative sequence. Hill [*NQ* ccix (1974) 204–5], citing Gregory on Gen. 3.3 and Bede on Gen. 2.17, argues plausibly for Adam (*in Adam omnes moriuntur*, 1 Cor. 15.21) who was the first soul-slayer in the sense that his own soul died in sin when he ate the forbidden fruit. As a consequence of this act all human beings share like spiritual death as well as the physical death of the body. Adam was not more doomed (to death by burning) than that (than Isaac was) because God provided Christ to save him and the rest of mankind just as He provided a ram in place of Isaac. Krapp's doubts about *fyrst* as an adj. in OE seem unnecessary in view of the evidence cited in BTS (despite its support for Abraham).

400 wolde þone lastweard   lige gesyllan,
     in bælblyse   beorna selost,
     his swæsne sunu   to sigetibre,
     angan ofer eorðan   yrfelafe,
     feores frofre,   ða he swa forð gebad,
405 leodum to lafe,   langsumne hiht.
     He þæt gecyðde,   þa he þone cniht genam
     fæste mid folmum,   folccuð geteag
     ealde lafe   (ecg grymetode),
     þæt he him lifdagas   leofran ne wisse
410 þonne he hyrde   Heofoncyninge.

401] *beorna selost*: Isaac, presumably as an adult. According to one tra-
dition Isaac was of mature age at the Offering: see M. E. Wells, 'The Age
of Isaac at the Time of the Sacrifice', *MLN* liv (1939) 579–82. Consequently
BLACKBURN's suggestion that *beorna* may be a variant of *bearna* 'of sons' is
probably ruled out.

402] *to sigetibre*: cf. *to tibre* (*Gen* 2853). The intended sacrifice is perhaps
victorious in the sense that it has a meritorious power which ensures the sal-
vation of the Israelites. But the most obvious sense in which the intended
sacrifice could be thought of as a victory is the typological: as a foreshadow-
ing of the Crucifixion. In *Juliana* 255 the use of *sigortifre* seems to be ironic.

403–5] Translate 'his sole heir on earth, the comfort of his life, which he
had awaited so long, his long-enduring hope, as a bequest to men.' The
pathos of Abraham's situation is emphasized by referring to Isaac as *frofre*
and *hiht*. Abraham's 'bequest' is one of example to others to show similar
faith and obedience; Abraham is held up as such an example in Heb. 11.8–
12.

406] *þæt* is proleptic and is taken up by the *þæt*-clause of 409.

407] *folccuð*: Abraham.

408a] There is probably a play on the word *lafe* 405/408. The inheritor-
to-be is to be killed by the inherited.

408b] The verb *grymetian* is normally used of animals. Here the blade
'roared' as if it were animate, perhaps, as BLACKBURN suggested, an allusion
to 'the ringing of the blade when drawn from the sheath', but the phrase
may simply be a vivid metaphor to convey menace.

409–10] Translate '. . . that he did not consider his (Isaac's) life dearer
than that he should obey the King of Heaven'. This statement is the climax
to the stress on kinship throughout the treatment of the Abraham and Isaac
episode (*sibgemagas* 386, *magan* 397, *sunu* 402): Abraham's loyalty to God is
stronger even than the closest bond of kinship.

    Abraham æðeling   up aræmde,
    wolde se eorl slean   eaferan sinne,
    unweaxenne,   ecgum reodan,
    magan mid mece,   gif hine Metod lete;
415 ne wolde him beorht fæder   bearn ætniman
    halig tiber,   ac mid handa befeng.

411 Abraham æðeling] *supplied*
412 wolde se eorl] se eorl wolde
413 ecgum *Thorpe*] eagum
414 Metod *Grein*] god

411–2] According to A. J. Bliss these lines display 'deep-seated corruption' [*NQ* ccxvi (1971) 447]. The following difficulties occur: (1) there are evidently three lines in succession with vocalic alliteration from which a verse is missing (cf. 303–5); (2) verse 412a, as the MS has it, breaks Kuhn's Law (Bliss §20) whereby it is not permissible to have both a particle (*wolde*) before the second stress and a proclitic (*se*) before the first stress; (3) the syntax of 411 is unparalleled in that there is no other instance in OE poetry of *up* + finite verb at the beginning of a sentence. In the present text difficulties (1) and (3) are overcome by supplying the missing verse before *up aræmde*. It is assumed that the omission of *Abraham æðeling* occurred because the copyist's eye strayed forward from *cyninge* to *æðeling* the two words being mistakenly identified because of their similar endings. Difficulty (2) has been overcome by transposing the word-order to accord with the idiomatic construction described by Andrew, *Postscript* §60(i), whereby a co-ordinate clause begun by a verb can be subordinate in sense to the preceding clause. Possibly a scribe transposed *wolde se eorl* to *se eorl wolde* because he failed to realize that *slean* can be metrically disyllabic; if *slean* were monosyllabic *wolde se eorl slean* would be unacceptable, but *se eorl wolde slean* would be satisfactory – apart from the breach of Kuhn's Law. For a parallel to the infinitive standing at the end of the first half-line of the verse-clause see 256a. Translate 'The noble man Abraham rose up, for that warrior intended to kill his son . . .'.

413] *ecgum reodan* (i.e. with bloody blade) is parallel with *mid mece*; *reodan* has *eo* for *ea*. It is hardly likely that *reodan* is a verb 'to stain red', 'kill?'. If preserved the MS reading *eagum reodan* might mean 'with red (i.e. weeping) eyes' but this would probably not be appropriate to Abraham's obedient act of faith.

414] *Metod* has been substituted for MS *god* to restore alliteration. Cf. 467a.

415] The *beorht fæder* is Abraham. Though reluctant to kill his son he is poised to strike when the voice from heaven interrupts him. See also note to 446.

Þa him styran cwom   stefn of heofonum,
wuldres hleoðor,   word æfter spræc:
'Ne sleh þu, Abraham,   þin agen bearn,   [p.163
420 sunu mid sweorde.   Soð is gecyðed,
nu þin cunnode   Cyning alwihta,
þæt þu wið Waldend   wære heolde,
fæste treowe,   seo þe freode sceal
in lifdagum   lengest weorðan
425 awa to aldre   unswiciendo.
Hu þearf mannes sunu   maran treowe?
Ne behwylfan mæg   heofon ond eorðe
His wuldres word,   widdra ond siddra
þonne befæðman mæge   foldan sceattas,
430 eorðan ymbhwyrft   ond uprodor,

423 freode *Graz*] freoðo
428 widdra] id *over erasure, 2nd erased letter still legible as* r

---

417–8] According to Gen. 22.11 the voice from heaven was that of the *angelus Domini* and this must be so here since God is referred to in the third person in 432.

419–46] This divine speech combines and expands the two speeches made by the angel of the Lord in Gen. 22.11–12, 16–18.

423b] Translate 'which will turn into goodwill for you . . .'. Although sense can be made of it the verse will not scan as it stands in the MS since *freoðo* 'protection' has a short stem-vowel. Emendation is therefore necessary and that adopted here is palaeographically very plausible. IRVING's *to freode* may make 'the sentence . . . clearer' but there is no authority for *to* in the MS.

426] Translate 'In what way does the son of man need a stronger pledge?'

427–31] Bright [*MLN* xxvii (1912) 18] suggested several biblical passages which may have acted as a stimulus for this sentence. Of these the closest are Mark 13.31 and Luke 21.33.

427] Since, according to Andrew, *Syntax* §72, *ne* 'not' 'was always prefixed to [the finite verb]' the MS word order could be made consistent with this observation by reading *Ne mæg behwylfan*; cf. 488a. The subject of the sg. verb *mæg* is *heofon ond eorðe*, presumably understood as a sg. entity, 'the universe'; for other instances of a dual subject with a sg. verb see Ælfric, *Cath. Hom.* ed. B. Thorpe (London, 1844–6) i 364/22, ii 60/28, 192/2. The general sense is that the efficacy of God's word is so great that *heuene my3te nou3te holden it* (Langland, *Piers Plowman* i 151, of love).

428] *widdra* and *siddra* are acc. pl. n. in concord with *word* but are uninflected in predicative use: see note to 129.

garsecges gin   ond þeos geomre lyft.
He þe að swereð,   engla Þeoden,
wyrda Waldend   ond wereda God,
soðfæst sigora,   þurh His sylfes lif,
435 þæt þines cynnes   ond cneowmaga,
randwiggendra,   rim ne cunnon
yldo ofer eorðan   ealle cræfte
to gesecgenne   soðum wordum,
nymðe hwylc þæs snottor   in sefan weorðe

432 He þe *Thorpe/Kock*] ne

431] *þeos geomre lyft*: there seems to be no particular reason why the air should be described as sad, unless it is an allusion to the motif of this life as transitory, a journey of exile before reaching the heavenly home.

432–46] Irving compares *Azarias* 32–41, to which corresponds *Daniel* 315–24. Verses 432a and 434b correspond to 'Per memetipsum iuravi' of Gen. 22.16.

432a] Most editors emend MS *ne* to read *He*, which is palaeographically very plausible (cf. 280), but better sense is given by Kock's proposal of *þe* (JJJ 27). On the analogy of *Beowulf* 472 *he me aðas swor*, adduced by Kock, both *he* and *þe* have been included here. It is assumed that the scribe misread *he* as *ne* and then overlooked *þe*, the second of two consecutive two-letter words ending in *-e*. Bright's suggestion of *nu* [*MLN* xxvii (1912) 18] does not give good sense since it implies that God's undertaking is new rather than confirmatory.

433] *wyrda Waldend*. The semantic range and development of the word *wyrd* has been well studied by B. J. Timmer, 'Wyrd in AS Prose and Poetry', *Neophil.* xxvi (1941) 24–33, 213–28, repr. in J. B. Bessinger & S. J. Kahrl (eds), *Essential Articles for . . . OE Poetry* (1968) 124–58; see also G. W. Weber, *Wyrd*, Frankfurter Beiträge zur Germanistik 8 (1969), K. Otten, *König Alfreds Boethius* (Tübingen, 1964) 60–70 and 123, and E. G. Stanley, *The Search for AS Paganism* (1975) 92–4. Etymologically *wyrd* is related to the stem of *weorðan* 'become' and its basic sense is 'what happens'. Its meaning in Christian contexts emerges particularly clearly from the Alfredian translation of the *De Consolatione Philosophiae* by Boethius (d.*c*.524), esp. Bk IV, Prose 6; see W. J. Sedgefield, *King Alfred's . . . Boethius . . .* (Oxford, 1899) esp. 128. Divine providence (*Godes foreþonc*) is what is in God's mind; when it comes to pass (*siððan hit fullfremed bið*) it is called *wyrd*; *þæt þæt we wyrd hata*ð, *þæt bið Godes weorc* which *færð æfter his forþonce*. *Wyrd* is the course of events for which God is responsible (458); before it has occurred it is *witod wyrd* (472). Thus God controls what happens: He is *wyrda Waldend*.

437] *yldo* is nom. pl. for regular *ylde*. See note to 28.

439–42] These lines are an expansion of Gen. 22.17 under the influence of 13.16; cf. also Heb. 11.12. Irving points out that the text of Gen. 13.16

440 þæt he ana mæge   ealle geriman
     stanas on eorðan,   steorran on heofonum,
     sæbeorga sand,   sealte yða;
     ac hie gesittað   be sæm tweonum
     oð Egipte   ingeðeode
445 land Cananea,   leode þine,
     freobearn fæder,   folca selost.'

                 *   *   *

442 sand *Thorpe*] sund
444 ingeðeode *Grein*] incaðeode

---

in the OL Bible, 'si potest quis enumerare *harenam maris*' [Vulgate *pulverem*],
is more likely to have stimulated the phrase *sæbeorga sand*.

443] *be sæm tweonum* occurs also at 563 and is a stock phrase (cf. *Beowulf*
858 etc.) perhaps meaning 'in entirety'. Possibly the phrase originated in
the peninsular continental home of the Anglo-Saxons between the North
Sea and the Baltic. Trahern [*AS Poetry* (1975) 295–7] notes that its use here
may be based on the phrase *a mari usque ad mare* in Ecclus. 44.23 [also
Ps. 71 (72).8, Zech. 9.10]. Mürkens [*BBA* ii (1899) 76–7] attempted to link
the instance at 563 with Ex. 23.31 'a mari Rubro usque ad mare Palaestin-
orum' (i.e. between the Red Sea and the Mediterranean), but reference to
Num. 34.6–12 (between the Mediterranean and the line of the Jordan
taking in the Sea of Kinnereth (Galilee) and the Dead Sea) would be just as
appropriate here.

444] *ingeðeode*: the 'land-bound' Egyptians (see note to 142). Attempts to
make sense of the MS reading *incaðeode* by taking the first element *inca*
'quarrel' to mean 'hostile' are philologically forced and semantically un-
satisfactory. Rosier [*PMLA* lxxxi (1966) 345] cites *PPs* 112.4 where *ofer ealle
ingeþeode* renders L 'super omnes gentes'.

446] *fæder* is ambiguous and could refer either to Abraham or God; cf.
353ff. and 415ff. where the momentary ambiguity is eliminated in both
instances by the next clause having Abraham as subject. The Lord con-
sidered the nation of Israel as his first-born son (Ex. 4.22).

446–7] Line 446 ends Section XLVII and line 447 begins Section
XLVIIII. There is thus a lacuna between these lines which comprised
Section XLVIII; see Intro. 15. The subject-matter of the lost portion, cor-
responding to Ex. 14.23–6, presumably dealt with the completion of the
crossing, the pursuit into the path through the sea by the Egyptians, and
Moses's action to bring about the return of the waters over the path through
the sea. Vickrey [*Traditio* xxviii (1972) 124–5] offers a different view of the
lost portion in order to accommodate his theory that there is a battle in
the sea between the Israelites and the Egyptians face to face.

·XLVIIII· Folc wæs afæred; flodegsa becwom   [p.166]
          gastas geomre, geofon deaðe hweop.
          Wæron beorhhliðu blode bestemed,
   450   holm heolfre spaw, hream wæs on yðum,
          wæter wæpna ful, wælmist astah.
          Wæron Egypte eft oncyrde,
          flugon forhtigende, fær ongeton,
          woldon herebleaðe hamas findan –
   455   gylp wearð gnornra. Him ongen genap
          atol yða gewealc, ne ðær ænig becwom
          herges to hame, ac behindan beleac
          wyrd mid wæge. Þær ær wegas lagon

447–515] The text resumes with the Egyptians (*Folc*) in the path through the Red Sea and the waters about to engulf them. The passage, which corresponds to a mere two verses in the Bible (Ex. 14.27–8), is a *tour de force* of dramatic description; cf. Intro. 42–3, 44–5. As Trask has argued, though not always convincingly [*Neophil.* lvii (1973) 295–7], the terms used to describe the drowning of the Egyptians are strongly suggestive of the Day of Judgment; these allusions are indicated below as and when appropriate.

447a] Fear on the part of people on earth was a sign of the Day of Judgment (Luke 21.25–6); sim. 490a and 491b.

449–50a] The sea turning to blood was a sign of the Day of Judgment (Rev. 8.8 and 16.3, after Ex. 7.17ff., the first plague of the Egyptians whereby the Nile was turned to blood). There is probably also a punning allusion to the Red Sea as having bloody water; so also 463b, 478.

449a] *beorhhliðu*: i.e. the walls of water on either side of the path through the sea. Gordon translates 'The mountainous waters'.

450b] *hream* could refer to the waters or to the Egyptians trapped in the sea.

451] *wælmist*: presumably a reference to spray caused by the churning of the water, but the main function of the word is to evoke a deathly atmosphere.

453a] The metre (Type 1D*1) requires that the *-ig-* of *forhtigende* is non-syllabic and the original probably had *forhtende*, an Anglian form (Campbell §757).

453b] Sudden disaster is a sign of the Day of Judgment (1 Thess. 5.3).

454–5a] Acts of cowardice, even in the face of certain defeat, were considered ignominious in Germanic heroic society. On the semantic range of *gylp* see *Wanderer*, ed. Bliss & Dunning (1969) 54–8.

456a] Cf. *atol yða geswing* (*Beowulf* 848a).

456b–7a] Cf. 508–12 and note, also *Beowulf* 2365b–6.

458a] On *wyrd* see note to 433.

458b–60a] *mere modgode* involves a 'pathetic fallacy' since *modgian* is nor-

mere modgode   (mægen wæs adrenced),
460 streamas stodon.   Storm up gewat
heah to heofonum,   herewopa mæst;
laðe cyrmdon   (lyft up geswearc)
fægum stæfnum.   Flod blod gewod:
randbyrig wæron rofene,   rodor swipode
465 meredeaða mæst.   Modige swulton,
cyningas on corðre.   Cyrm swiðrode

466 Cyrm *Cosijn*] cyre

---

mally used with a personal subject (as at 331). The implication is that the
sea was regarded as animate; see further notes to 469, 480 and 489, and
Intro. 48. The sea raging was a sign of the Day of Judgment (Luke 21.25,
Jude 13); sim. 490b.

460b–63] Since *cyrman* is intransitive *herewopa mæst* must be taken as
parallel with *storm*, which is to be understood figuratively; cf. *Andreas* 1236ff.
Darkness and lamentation were signs of the Day of Judgment (Amos 5.18,
Matt. 22.13); cf. *Judith* 269b–72a and the discussion by B. F. Huppé, *Web
of Words* (New York, 1970) 180–81. For a defence of the reading *lyft up
geswearc fægum stæfnum* (i.e. no parenthesis for 462b) as an 'unusually bold . . .
use of synaesthetic imagery' see F. C. Robinson in *Philological Essays* (H. D.
Meritt *Festschrift*), ed. J. L. Rosier (The Hague, 1970) 106; IRVING con-
sidered the reading 'extraordinary'.

463b] See note to 449–50a. The verse is an outstanding example of in-
ternal rhyme; see Intro. 43.

464a] It is perhaps relevant that the destruction of walls was a sign of
the Day of Judgment (Isa. 25.12). Cf. 484a, 485a.

465b–66a] *modige* used of the Egyptians perhaps connotes 'proud'. This
impression is reinforced by the ironic repetition of *cyningas on corðre* from 191
where it was used in a passage describing the martial splendour of the
Egyptians.

466b] *Cyrm swiðrode*: i.e. the Egyptians, shouting before (462), now be-
came silent as they drowned. The Egyptian *cyrm* is in contrast with that of
the joyful Israelites (107) and the phrase varies the usual associations of the
word. Generally *cyrm* occurs in collocations which stress its relative loudness
(in contrast with previous quietness), e.g. 107 and *cyrm up astah* (*Andreas*
1125). As it stands the MS reading *cyre swiðrode* might mean 'the choice
diminished', i.e. the Egyptians had no means of escape, but *cyre* seems to
be a prose word – it does not occur elsewhere in OE poetry either on its
own or in compounds [cf. K. R. Brooks, *Andreas* (1961) note to line 171] –
and the phrase seems unidiomatic (cf. BT *sweðrian*). An alternative emen-
dation would give *cyrr swiðrode* 'the retreat disappeared' but *cyrr* is not re-
corded elsewhere in OE with this sense; cf. *sæcir* 291, *oncyrde* 452. Cosijn
[*PBB* xx (1895) 104] took the verse as a parenthesis.

wæges æt ende;   wigbord scinon.
Heah ofer hæleðum   holmweall astah,
merestream modig.   Mægen wæs on cwealme
470 fæste gefeterod,   forðganges nep,
searwum asæled.   Sand basnodon
witodre wyrde,   hwonne waðema stream,

467 wæges *Grein*] sæs
471 asæled *Junius*] æsæled; basnodon *Dietrich*] barenodon
472 wyrde *Dietrich*] fyrde

467a] *wæges* has been substituted for MS *sæs* to restore alliteration. Cf. 414b.

469a] *modig* is here applied to the sea as if it were animate (cf. 459). The adj. has previously been used of God (275). See further notes to 480 and 489.

469b–70a] Probably an allusion to the binding of the devil (Rev. 20.2); cf. notes to 14b–15, 49.

470b] *forðganges nep*: a notorious crux. As first suggested by OED *Neap* adj. the word *nep* is probably the same as the first element of *nepflod* 'neap tide' found in OE glosses but then not recorded until the 15th cent. A neap tide is that having the smallest range between high and low water in a cycle. However, the etymology of OE *nep(-)* is obscure. The basic sense of the word is probably 'lacking power', 'enfeebled', and the general sense of the verse is thus that the Egyptians were unable to move in any direction. Emendation is therefore unnecessary. Bright's suggested reading *forðganges weg* [*MLN* xxvii (1912) 18], followed by KRAPP, is awkward in that it involves taking *weg* as the subject of *(wæs) asæled*. Mürkens [*BBA* ii (1899) 76] suggested *forðgange neh* but it is semantically disharmonious to have the Egyptians simultaneously 'close to death' and *on cwealme* 'in death'. Both emendations involve substantial alteration of the MS reading.

471a] The Egyptians caught in their own armour perhaps suggests the evil bound by their own sins (Prov. 5.22), a sign of the Day of Judgment.

471b–76] Translate 'The sands waited for the ordained course of events, until the time when the perpetually cold sea, the surge of the waves, accustomed to deviations of course, the naked messenger of hardship, the hostile warlike spirit, which crushed enemies, came seeking out the eternal foundations with salt waves'.

471b–2a] These verses will not make sense without emendation, and an appropriate verb is provided by reading *basnodon* in 471b. Irving revives the older view that MS *witodre fyrde* may mean 'doomed army' but the only use of the adj. to describe a person or group of persons recorded by BT (which Irving cites) has the sense 'certain'. Emendation of *fyrde* to *wyrde* is therefore preferable. On *wyrd* see note to 433. Irving's suggested reading, following BOUTERWEK, for 472a, *on witodre fyrde*, will not scan unless anacrusis is allowed, hardly satisfactory in a reconstructed verse having the caesura in position (i) – cf. Intro. 40–41.

sincalda sæ,   sealtum yðum,
æflastum gewuna,   ece staðulas,
475 nacud nydboda,   neosan come,
fah feðegast,   se ðe feondum gehneop.
Wæs seo hæwene lyft   heolfre geblanden.
Brim berstende   blodegesan hweop
sæmanna sið,   oðþæt soð Metod

---

476 gehneop *Dietrich*] geneop

473a] Extreme cold is a familiar hellish torment, usually alternated with
extreme heat; cf. *Gen B* 316.

474a] This phrase presumably refers to the contrary tidal movements of
the sea.

475] A compound in -*boda* implies a person (cf. 250) and thus the adj.
nacud appears appropriate, yet in fact *nydboda* denotes an inanimate object
(the sea) which can only be *nacud* either in the sense of an unsheathed sword
(BT I.(c); cf. 495) or in the sense of an unadorned message (BTS IIc); the
implication is probably that the hardship was so severe that no protection
could be found from it. Cf. *nacod nydgenga* (*Daniel* 632). Arguing that com-
pounds in *nyd*- always imply compulsion or necessity affecting the subject
rather than the object (as in *nydfara* 208), and comparing *nacud niðdraca*
(*Beowulf* 2273), J. R. R. Tolkien suggested reading *niðboda* 'bringer of
enmity'.

476a] The precise meaning of *feðegast* depends on whether the second
element is interpreted as (1) GHOST or (2) GUEST. If (1) is preferred, as here,
the sense must be something like 'warlike spirit', which goes well with the
relative clause in 476b. The sea is described in terms of an animate force.
If (2) is preferred the sense would be 'visitor', 'enemy' (but cf. *Beowulf* 1976,
Elene 845) and would go well with 475, but the form -*gast* would have to
be explained analogically (cf. Campbell §204.5) and does not occur in any
compound of which WS *giest* is the second element.

476b] MS *geneop* is usually taken as the p.t. of some otherwise unrecorded
verb of unknown etymology but it seems preferable to emend to *gehneop* (for
scribal confusion of *h* and *n* cf. 169, 280) and assume formation on the same
verb as *āhnēop* 'plucked' (*Guthlac* 847). OE **hnēopan* (related to Gothic
(*dis*)*hniupan* 'tear to pieces') presumably meant 'pull', 'push down'. Both
p.t. forms apparently have North. *ēo* for *ēa* (Campbell §278; cf. *heald* 61).
So emended the verb can be both etymologically and semantically explained
rather than having its meaning merely deduced from the context.

477] Cf. Rev. 8.7.

478-9a] See note to 449-50a. Cf. 121, where the Israelites are threatened
with terror of fire. In 479a there is a recurrence of the nautical imagery
whereby the Israelites are sailors: see notes to 80b-84 and 105-6a. Vickrey
[*Traditio* xxviii (1972) 127-8], noting that elsewhere (*Gen* 2637, *Guthlac* 190)

480 þurh Moyses hand　　mod gerymde,　　　　　　[p.167
　　　wide wæðde,　　wælfæðmum sweop,
　　　flod famgode　　(fæge crungon),
　　　lagu land gefeol –　lyft wæs onhrered.
　　　Wicon weallfæsten,　wægas burston,
485 multon meretorras,　þa se Mihtiga sloh
　　　mid halige hand,　heofonrices Weard,

hwopan takes the dat. of the person threatened (but cf. 448b), suggests that *sið* is nom. and would translate 479a as 'the journey of the seamen (into baptism)', a reading which harmonizes with his view that there is a battle between the Israelites and the Egyptians face to face in the Red Sea.

480a] *þurh Moyses hand*: cf. 486 and see note to 19.

480b] *mod gerymde* means 'manifested His will'. GREIN, followed by all subsequent editors except BLACKBURN, preferred to alter the MS word-division to *modge rymde* 'swept away the valorous', but this reading obscures an important feature of the passage: that, although the subject of *sweop* is *Metod*, the action of the verb is one very appropriate for *flod*, and thus the *Metod* and the *flod*, the agent of the destruction He wills, become difficult to distinguish. See further note to 489 and Lucas, *NQ* ccxiv (1969) 206–7. Cf. 459, 465.

482–3] In these lines, in addition to each verse being syntactically independent, the *a*- and *b*-verses have the same number of syllables, possibly a deliberate rhetorical device: cf. J. J. Campbell, *MP* lxiii (1965–6) 197.

483a] The ocean flooding dry land was one of the signs of the Day of Judgment (Matt. 24.39, an allusion to the story of Noah's Flood).

484a/485a] See note to 464a.

485b–7] These lines have caused considerable difficulty. The main problems are: (1) the syntactical place of *wlance ðeode* – whether it is the object of *sloh* (485) or the subject of *mihton* (488); (2) the metrical incompleteness of MS *wer beamas* in 487a; (3) the meaning of *werbeamas*, a hapax legomenon. (1) *wlance ðeode* must be the object of *sloh*. If it were taken as subject of *mihton*, then by Kuhn's Law of Sentence Particles (see note to 19–20) *mihton* would have to be stressed, and, if stressed, it would have to alliterate – which it does not. (2) The MS pointing indicates that *heofonrices Weard* forms one unit and *werbeamas* another, and the former is such a common formula that it would be undesirable to alter it. *Waldend* has therefore been supplied to complete v.487a. A close metrical parallel is provided by *wigend weorðfullost* (*Beowulf* 3099). (3) The best explanation of *werbeamas* is that it is gen. sg. (cf. *forðwegas* 248) of *wǣr-bēam* 'covenant-pillar', with *ē* for WS *ǣ*[1] in the first element; *bēam* is used elsewhere in the poem of the pillar of cloud and fire, the provision and guidance of which is one of the ways in which God keeps his *wǣr* with the Israelites. Another possible explanation is that the compound is *wǣrbēam* 'sea-bond', but *bēam* is not attested in the sense

Waldend werbeamas,   wlance ðeode.
Ne mihton forhabban   helpendra pað
merestreames mod,   ac He manegum gesceod
490 gyllende gryre;   garsecg wedde,

487 Waldend] *supplied*

'fetter'. For the expression *sloh . . . wlance ðeode* Irving compares Ps. 134 (135).9–10; cf. also 1 Cor. 15.25.

488] *helpendra pað* 'the course of the helpers', i.e. the waters which assisted the Israelites by destroying the Egyptians; *pað* (for more usual *pæð*) is by analogy with pl. forms whose inflections contained a back vowel (Campbell §160(1)). The word *pað* is to some extent prosaic, occurring only here in verse, though compounds with *pæð* as second element are common in verse [see E. G. Stanley, *NM* lxxii (1971) 411–2]. Though the sense 'course' is unusual the word probably had a semantic range similar to that of L *trames* 'path', 'course'. Irving's suggestion of reading *wað* 'wandering' (cf. *wæðde* 481) is unhappy because the acc. of *wað* f. *ō*-stem would be *wāðe*. Vickrey [*Traditio* xxviii (1972) 128–9] thinks the 'helpers' are the angels who assist at baptism.

489] *merestreames mod* means God's will manifested in the rejoining of the sea-waters – cf. 459, 469, 480, and see Intro. 48. This meaning becomes explicit through the use of *He*, which, though it could just conceivably refer to *pað* m. (*mod* is n.), almost certainly refers to God. The syntactical running together of God and the sea occurs in Ex. 14.27, where *Dominus* comes to be represented in terms of *aquae* (cf. also Ex. 9.23). Similarly God, 'in person' so to speak (91), directed the Israelites by means of the physical phenomenon of the cloud-cover – cf. note to 123.

490a] *gyllende gryre*: Kennedy translates 'in shrieking terror'. See note to 447a.

490b] *garsecg*: a notoriously difficult word to explain. R. L. M. Derolez [*MLQ* vii (1946) 445–52] summarizes the evidence and reviews earlier proposals. The usual interpretation is 'spear-warrior', which for F. Candelaria [*ELN* i (1964) 243–4] is a kind of dolphin whose description became a designation for the sea. F. G. Cassidy [*Names* xx (1972) 95–100] suggests that *garsecg* was a name for Woden through whom it became associated with the sea; he finds *Ex* 488–95 particularly Wodenesque. L. G. Heller [*Names* xxi (1973) 75–7] links the AS 'spear-warrior' with Greek Triton. Others take the second element to mean 'sea'. Thus C. Brady [*Studies in Honor of A. M. Sturtevant* (Lawrence, Kansas, 1952) 41–2] suggests the meaning 'stormy ocean', and T. Gardner [*Archiv* ccii (1966) 431–6] interprets *garsecg* as 'ocean of the primeval wind'. Most of these suggestions are, in Heller's words, 'highly speculative'. For the sea raging as a sign of the Day of Judgment see note to 458b–60a.

491   up teah, on sleap   (egesan stodon,
        weollon wælbenna),   witrod gefeol
        heah of heofonum   handweorc Godes,

491 teah *Sedgefield*] ateah

491a] Since this verse will not scan as it stands in the MS, metrical acceptability has been restored by emending *ateah* to *teah*, allowing scansion as Type 2A4. Although there are only five examples in *Beowulf*, all are *a*-verses with double alliteration (330, 193, 485, 1719, 1881), as here. However this instance is unusual in having four separate words; of the instances in *Beowulf* all have two words except 330 which has three. The expression *up teah* '[the sea] reared up', i.e. drew itself up, is also unusual but unexceptional.

491b] See note to 447a.

492a] Several interpretations are possible for *weollon wælbenna*. In *wælbenna* the first element may be *wæl* 'slaughter' or *wǣl* WEEL[1] 'sea', and the second element *benn* (f. *jō*-stem) 'wound' or *bend* 'bond'. (As Sisam suggested [*MLN* xxxii (1917) 48] *-benna* may be the pl. of *bend* with assimilation of *d* to *n* (Campbell §484) as in *benne* nom. pl. *Daniel* 434, *bennum* dat. pl. *Andreas* 962 (see Brooks's note), 1038, *Juliana* 519.) For *weollon* either '[wounds] flowed (with blood)' or '[the sea] raged' is permissible. Three possibilities merit consideration: (1) with *wælbenna* 'the deadly wounds gushed'; (2) with *wælbenna* (= *-benda*) 'the deadly bonds (of the sea) seethed'; (3) with *wǣlbenna* (= *-benda*) 'the bonds of the sea seethed'. On balance it seems more likely that the fearfulness of the Egyptians (491b) and the ferociousness of the sea (492a) are being contrasted than that a progression from fear (491b) to destruction (492a) is being indicated; on this basis (1) can be eliminated. Of the other two possibilities (2) seems the more poetic and has the advantage of using a compound also found in *Beowulf* 1936. For the sea as a binding agent cf. *wælfæðmum* 481, *fæste befarene* 498, *heorufæðmum* 505.

492b] The interpretation of MS *wit rod* and the decision as to whether it is subject or object of *gefeol* have caused difficulty. Here *witrod*, *wī(g)* 'war' + *trod* 'path' with vocalization of *-g* in the first element (Campbell §267), is taken as object; for the construction cf. 483a. All other proposed solutions involve emendation: BOUTERWEK's *wīterōd* obstructs scansion; SEDGEFIELD's *wīgrōd* 'war-pole', supposedly connected with *seglrōd* (83), is scarcely credible; Sisam's *wiþertrod* [*MLN* xxxii (1917) 48], which means 'path back, retreat, return' (*Gen* 2084, *Judith* 313), forces the sense of the word to 'returning waters'.

493] *handweorc Godes*: the sea. The overwhelming force of the surging waters has already been associated with the power of God's hand at 486; cf. also note to 19.

famigbosma;   Flodweard gesloh
495   unhleowan wæg   alde mece,
þæt ðy deaðdrepe   drihte swæfon,
synfullra sweot.   Sawlum lunnon
fæste befarene,   flodblac here,
siððan hie onbugon   brimyppinge,

494 Flodweard gesloh *Cosijn*] flod wearde sloh
496 deaðdrepe] r *altered from* a
499 onbugon *Grein*] on bogum; brimyppinge *Bright*] brun yppinge

494a] *famigbosma* applies to the sea, *handweorc Godes*. However, if *famig-bosma* nom. sg. m. is not for *famigbosme*, the use of the masc. form of the adj. with a neut. noun is a further indication of the tendency towards identifying God with the sea, the agent of destruction with the means of it. Cf. note to 480b.

494b] Without the emendation there is no one to wield the sword in line 495.

495a] *wæg* is ambiguous: (1) it can mean 'wave', the water which surges back to cover the passage made for the Israelites, or (2) it can be a form of *wāg* WOUGH[1] 'wall' (i.e. of water; cf. *wealfæsten* 283, *randgebeorh* 296, *foreweallas* 297, *sæweall* 302, *randbyrig* 464, *holmweall* 468, *weallfæsten* 484, *meretorras* 485, *weallas* 572). In either sense *wæg* may be *unhleowan* 'unprotective': if (1) then there is *litotes*, for the wave is in fact destructive; if (2) then the wall is *unhleowan* towards the Egyptians in contrast to its protectiveness towards the Israelites. The former seems marginally preferable (cf. 280–1 [Moses] *sloh . . . garsecges deop*): in that case the *wæg* which, through God's provision, is unprotective of the Egyptians contrasts with the *dægsceldes hleo* (79) which God provides for the protection of the Israelites. Irving suggests that *wæg* is a form of *weg* (Anglian? – cf. Campbell §328) but, if it were, the adj. *unhleowan* would hardly be appropriate.

495b] What BLACKBURN called the 'bold figure' of the sword was probably suggested by Wisd. 18.16; cf. also 1 Chr. 21.16 and Rev. 19.11–15, 21. Irving 206 adduces Ps. 7.13 (12).

497a] In allegorical exegesis the Egyptians sometimes represented men's sins: Daniélou, *Bible & Liturgy* (1956) 86–98.

497b] i.e. they died.

498] *flodblac* may mean 'pale as the flood' or 'pale through fear of the flood'; thus it suggests both an affinity with the water and potential subjugation by it. The uncertainty of the precise semantic relationship between the first and second elements makes the impact of the adj. particularly intense. Cf. *flodgræg*, *Maxims II* 31. For a different interpretation, FLOOD + BLACK, see Robinson, *Anglia* lxxxvi (1968) 27.

499–500a] Translate '. . . when they (the Egyptians) bowed down to the manifestation of God's will, the greatest of sea-waves'. As they stand in the MS these verses lack a verb and verses 499a and 500a are metrically un-

500 modwæga mæst.   Mægen eall gedreas,
ða þe gedrecte,   dugoð Egypta,
Faraon mid his folcum.   He onfond hraðe,
siððan grund gestah,   Godes andsaca,
þæt wæs mihtigra   mereflodes Weard –

500 modwæga *Grein*] mode wæga
502 onfond *Thorpe*] on feond
503 grund] *supplied by Grein*

satisfactory. Emendation of *on bogum* to *onbugon* 'bowed down (to)' provides
a verb, and verse 499a will now scan as Type e1d with the characteristic
resolution of the last two syllables (Bliss §§67, 73); cf. 183a. (The alternative
reading *on bugon* 'broke over' will not scan.) BT and BTS *on-bugan* III record
the verb as being used elsewhere of persons submitting to a superior, es-
pecially the Lord, and it would seem appropriate that the Egyptians should
bow down in submission under the waters which sweep 'super currus et
equites eorum' (Ex. 14.26). In 499b *-yppinge* is taken as dative, after *onbugon*,
of the vbl. n. (from *yppan* 'manifest') recorded by BT *ypping* only once else-
where (Durham *Ritual*) where it glosses L *manifestatio*, and *brun* (of which
the dative would be *brunre*) has been emended to *brim* and taken as the
first element of a compound. In 500a emendation to *modwæga mæst* renders
the verse metrically acceptable, and this phrase is in apposition with
brimyppinge, though *mæst* is not dative to agree with it (and could not be so
emended without violating the metre) because 'a parallel may be un-
inflected if the case is clearly indicated in the expressions which it parallels'
[Campbell, in *Eng. & Med. Studs* (1962) 22]. As regards sense, 499b and
500a must be taken together as an example of hendiadys (cf. Campbell,
ibid. 19): *brim-/-wæga* are the sea-waves which are the manifestation
(*-yppinge*) of God's will (*mod-*). On *mod* in the sense of God's will expressed
through the *flod* see notes to 480, 489. BT and BTS *yppan* II record the verb
as being used of God manifesting a characteristic in, e.g., *PPs* 71.7.

501] *ða þe gedrecte* 'those who afflicted', an onomastic allusion (cf. 37),
as Robinson points out [*Anglia* lxxxvi (1968) 28; *NM* lxix (1968) 167]. The
'standard meaning [in name-etymology] of *Ægyptus* ... was [*persequens*],
affligens, tribulans [Robinson cites Jerome, Ambrose and Augustine], or, as
Rabanus phrases it, "affligentes, eo quod afflixerunt Dei populum" [*De
Universo*, PL cxi 439]'. The pl. subject *ða* is construed with the verb *gedrecte*,
which, because it must be indic., is taken as p.t. pl. for regular *gedrecton* [cf.
Farrell's note to *Daniel* 77 (2nd)]; Robinson's attempt (*Anglia* lxxxvi 28
n.41) to take *ða* as fem. sg. agreeing with *dugoð* is unacceptable because *ða*
must be nominative and can therefore only be pl. In the light of this expla-
nation previous attempts to alter the MS reading to, e.g., *ða he gedre(n)cte*
or *deaþe* ..., are unnecessary.

503a] Grammar, sense and metre are restored by supplying *grund*.
503b] See note to 14b–15.

505 wolde heorufæðmum   hilde gesceadan,
     yrre ond egesfull.   Egyptum wearð
     þæs dægweorces   deop lean gesceod,
     forðam þæs heriges   ham eft ne com
     ealles ungrundes   ænig to lafe,
510 þætte sið heora   secgan moste,
     bodigean æfter burgum   bealospella mæst,   [p.169
     hordwearda hryre,   hæleða cwenum,
     ac þa mægenþreatas   meredeað geswealh,
     eac þon spelbodan.   Se ðe sped ahte
515 ageat gylp wera.   Hie wið God wunnon.
        Þanon Israhelum   ece rædas
     on merehwearfe   Moyses sægde,
     heahþungen wer,   halige spræce,

505 heorufæðmum *Kluge*] huru fæðmum
510 heora *Thorpe*] heoro
514 eac þon] *supplied*
517 Moyses *Thorpe*] moyse

506a] So *Christ* III 1528.
506b–7] Cf. 314b–5. Here the adj. *deop* is used with wry double meaning.
508–12] An elaboration of 456b–7a. No doubt both passages are based on Ex. 14.28 'nec unus quidem superfuit ex eis'.
509] *ealles ungrundes* qualifies *heriges* (508).
512a] Identical with 35a, where the reference was to the first-born.
513] Another metaphor from the language of feeding; cf. *wære fræton* (147). If the two metaphors are considered together we have here a case of the eater eaten.
514a] For the completion of this verse with *eac þon* cf. 546b.
514b] *Se*: God.
515a] The verb *ageotan* is recorded only once elsewhere in the sense 'destroy' (Wulfstan; BTS s.v. III) and may well retain here much of its basic sense 'pour out'. Thus men's vows are poured out of the wounded and dying like drops of blood, a forceful image achieved by using a verb with concrete sense to convey an abstract notion.
515b] Cf. the description of the damned *þa ær wiþ Gode wunnon* in *Christ* III (The Last Judgment) 1526; also *Beowulf* 113, *Gen B* 303.
516] *ece rædas* probably refers to the content of the following reported speech (see next note), though Earl [*NM* lxxi (1970) 548–50] tries to link the phrase with Deut. The same phrase occurs in *Beowulf* 1760 (cf. 1201 and Wrenn's note) where it refers to what Beowulf is advised (by Hroðgar) to choose for himself in life.

deop ærende.   Dægweorc ne mað,
520   swa gyt werðeode   on gewritum findað
doma gehwilcne,   þara ðe him Drihten bebead
on þam siðfate   soðum wordum.
Gif onlucan wile   lifes wealhstod,

519 ne mað *Tolkien*] nemnað

519–48] Although a case could be made for taking this didactic passage
as an actual speech (if so, the verbs *healdeð* (535) *murnað* (536), *witon* (536)
would have to be taken as 2 pl.), it seems more likely that the speech is
being reported in the third person; KRAPP notes the 'informality' of *Moyses
sægde* (517) as pointing to this conclusion. Ostensibly the reported speech
was made by Moses *on merehwearfe*, but the viewpoint is more Pauline than
Mosaic (cf. 2 Cor. 3.6). Moreover, the content of the speech is so inappro-
priate to the *narrative* context that Moses must be considered here as a type
of Christ ['Moyses typum Christi gestavit', wrote Isidore, PL lxxxiii 109,
and see Daniélou, *Shadows to Reality* (1960) 159–60]; cf. note to 310–46.
(Considerations of aesthetic tact no doubt led to the speech being reported
rather than uttered.) The passage is, however, very appropriate notionally,
for it serves as a guide to interpretation: it is an exhortation to all men to
understand human activity in general (and the Israelite exodus in particu-
lar) as a foreshadowing of better things to come and to conduct their lives
so as to ensure a favourable assessment at the Last Judgment.

519] *Dægweorc ne mað*: i.e. the significance of the exodus events has be-
come known. The reading adopted here is to be found in BTSA *dægweorc*
but the interpretation of it there is different.

520–22] Cosijn [*PBB* xx (1895) 105] astutely compared 521 with Deut.
6.1 and the reference is no doubt to the Ten Commandments. The *swa*-
clause indicates a comparison: the significance of the exodus has been no
more hidden than the Decalogue. This accords with patristic interpretation
of the Bible: according to Augustine (*De Trinitate* xv ix 15, PL xlii 1069)
the foreshadowing of NT events in the OT was a historical fact, 'non in
verbis . . . sed in facto'.

523–6] These lines clearly refer to the Pauline distinction between the
Letter and the Spirit (2 Cor. 3.6), a distinction which became a patristic
and medieval commonplace. Any informed Christian will interpret the
scriptures not only for their literal meaning but also for their spiritual
meaning, to be perceived by means of typological and allegorical exegesis
(cf. Gal. 4.24, 'These things contain an allegory'). As Origen put it, 'Blessed
are the eyes which see divine spirit through the letter's veil' [quoted by
B. Smalley, *Study of the Bible* (1952) 1].

523] *lifes wealhstod*: the intellect. *Wealhstod* usually means 'translator' or
'mediator' and the word clearly implies elucidation of the correspondence
between two sets of information, in this context the correspondence between
literal and allegorical and the typological connection between historically

beorht in breostum,   banhuses weard,
525 ginfæsten god   Gastes cægon,
run bið gerecenod,   ræd forð gæð;
hafað wislicu   word on fæðme,
wile meagollice   modum tæcan,
þæt we gesne ne syn   Godes þeodscipes,
530 Metodes miltsa.   He us ma onlyhð,
nu us boceras   beteran secgað,
lengran lyftwynna.   Þis is læne dream
wommum awyrged,   wreccum alyfed,
earmra anbid.   Eðellease

separate events or personages. The perception of those correspondences is
a source of life (cf. 2 Cor. 3.6).

525a] *ginfæsten* is acc. pl. n. wk. for regular *ginfæstan*.

525b] *cægon* is dat. pl. for regular *cægum*. For the image of the key (specifi-
cally the 'key of David') in biblical exegesis see R. B. Burlin, *The OE Advent*
(New Haven, 1968) 75; one of the standard interpretations was as the 'key
of the scriptures', i.e. typology itself.

527] The subject of *hafað* is *lifes wealhstod* (523).

531] By *boceras* is probably meant principally the Church Fathers (rather
than just the evangelists) who, after Christ has ensured the salvation of
mankind (*nu*), can teach the rewards of heaven (*beteran*) through the in-
terpretation of the scriptures.

532] Most editors emend *lyftwynna* to *lifwynna* 'life-joys', but, as Robinson
points out in his defence of the MS reading [*Anglia* lxxx (1962) 370–72],
'*lifwynn* always refers specifically to the joys of life *on earth*' whereas here the
lyftwynna are contrasted with the *læne dream* of this life. *Lyftwynn* is a com-
pound of the *heofondream* type and the interpretation of the first element as
meaning 'heaven' is supported by the Ælfrician phrase for God, *lyftes Weard*,
presumably modelled on the common formulae *swegles Weard*, *rodora Weard*
etc. Possibly, as suggested by Trahern [*AS Poetry* (1975) 297–8], the colloca-
tion *beteran . . . lengran lyftwynna* echoes the *meliorem . . . id est caelestem* [*terram*]
of Heb. 11.16.

532b] The motif of the transitoriness of life is commonplace in OE
poetry: cf. *Rood* 109, 138, *Seafarer* 65–6, etc.

533a] So also *Christ* III 1561.

533b/534b–5] For the motif of life as a state of exile from the heavenly
home cf. 137b–40a (and note) and 383. The word *gystsele* perhaps suggests
the 'tabernacle' (2 Cor. 5.4) used for the abode of the Christian soul on its
journey through this life; so A. S. Cook, *The Christ of Cynewulf* (Boston, 1909
edn repr. 1964) note to line 820. Just as the Israelites dwell in tents (133,
223), so Christians dwell in the Church (85) and the soul dwells in the bodily
'tabernacle'.

535 þysne gystsele   gihðum healdeð,
    murnað on mode,   manhus witon
    fæst under foldan,   þær bið fyr ond wyrm,
    open ece scræf   yfela gehwylces,
    swa nu regnþeofas   rice dælað,
540 yldo oððe ærdeað.   Eftwyrd cymeð,
    mægenþrymma mæst,   ofer middangeard,
    dæg dædum fah.   Drihten sylfa
    on þam meðelstede   manegum demeð,
    þonne He soðfæstra   sawla lædeð,   [p.170
545 eadige gastas,   on uprodor,
    þær bið leoht ond lif,   eac þon lissa blæd.
    Dugoð on dreame   Drihten herigað,
    weroda Wuldorcyning,   to widan feore.
    Swa reordode   ræda gemyndig

538 gehwylces *Junius*] gehylces
540 cymeð *Thorpe*] cymð
546 þær bið leoht] þær / leoht *over line division*, bið *supplied by Irving*

535] *healdeð* is pr. 3 pl. for regular *healdað*.

539–40a] The first element in *regnþeofas* 'arch-thieves' is etymologically related to ON *regin* 'gods' and originally probably denoted something like 'supernatural power'; cf. *regnheard* in *Beowulf* 326. In *Resignation* 15 *regnþeof* refers to the devil. Here *yldo* and *ærdeað* are *regnþeofas* in the sense that they rob men of life; Irving notes a similar personification of abstractions in *Solomon & Saturn* 348–9a. For the interpretation of *rice dælað* as 'share dominion' see Klaeber, *Archiv* cxiii (1904) 147.

540b] *Eftwyrd*: strictly 'what happens afterwards' – see note to 433. The Last Judgment for sinners corresponds to the drowning in the Red Sea for the Egyptians: see note to 447–515. The metre requires the uncontracted form *cymeð*.

542a] Kennedy translates 'a day of wrath upon the [evil] deeds of men'.

542b–3] On the treatment of God giving judgment, usually from his throne, in OE literature see J. F. Vickrey, *Speculum* xliv (1969) 88.

544–6] The Last Judgment for the faithful corresponds to the deliverance of the Israelites through the Red Sea. Note that the Lord Himself will *lead* the way to heaven just as through the cloud-pillar He led the Israelites on the way to the Promised Land.

546a] For the completion of this verse with *bið* cf. 537b.

547] *Dugoð* (coll. sg.) is construed with *herigað* (pl.). *Dream* in heaven perhaps contrasts with *dream* on earth (532); cf. *Seafarer* 80/86.

549] *Swa reordode* probably refers forward to Moses's speech (554–64)

550 manna mildost,   mihtum swiðed,
     hludan stefne –   here stille bad
     witodes willan   (wundor ongeton),
     modiges muðhæl –   he to mænegum spræc:
     'Micel is þeos menigeo,   mægenwisa trum,
555 fullesta mæst,   se ðas fare lædeð.
     Hafað us on Cananea   cyn gelyfed,
     burh ond beagas,   brade rice;
     wile nu gelæstan   þæt He lange gehet
     mid aðsware,   engla Drihten,
560 in fyrndagum   fæderyncynne,
     gif ge gehealdað   halige lare,
     þæt ge feonda gehwone   forð ofergangað,
     gesittað sigerice   be sæm tweonum,
     beorselas beorna: bið eower blæd micel.'
565   Æfter þam wordum   werod wæs on salum,
     sungon sigebyman   (segnas stodon)

556 us on *Bouterwek*] ufon

---

rather than backwards to the reported speech by Moses as a type of Christ. Cf. Bliss & Dunning, *Wanderer* (1969) 30–36.

553] *muðhæl*: for the endingless form of this fem. noun (historically from the *īn*-declension) extended beyond the nom. sg. see Campbell §589.7. The second element occurs independently in *Beowulf* 653, though in his glossary, s.v. *hǣl*, Klaeber confuses it with *hǣl* (n. *i*-stem) 'omen' both of which (after SB §288 Anm.) are wrongly ascribed to the noun-class of the related word *hǣlor* (n. *os/es*-stem) 'salvation'. With the notion of the Israelites receiving salvation from the mouth (of Moses, as God's 'mouthpiece'), probably derived, as Irving suggests, from Deut. 32.1, contrast the use of an eating metaphor, *wǣre frǣton* (147), to describe the action of the Egyptians in going back on their word.

552] *witodes*: Moses, the appointed leader.

554–64] This speech bears some resemblances to the Song of Moses (Ex. 15.1–19). Earl [*NM* lxxi (1970) 556] adduces Deut. 6.17–19.

555a] Irving compares this phrase with the *adiutor et protector* of Ex. 15.2 (OL version).

556] Cf. Ex. 15.15, 'obriguerunt omnes habitatores Chanaan'. The preposition *on* is in postponed position and governs *us*: 'into our hands'. BLACKBURN retained MS *ufon* translating 'from above' but this leaves unclear to whom the tribes of Canaan were *gelyfed*.

562] Cf. Deut. 6.19, also Ex. 23.31.

563] *be sæm tweonum*: see note to 443.

on fægerne sweg. Folc wæs on lande;
hæfde wuldres beam   werud gelæded,
halige heapas,   on hild Godes.
570 Lindwigan life gefegon   þa hie oðlæded hæfdon
feorh of feonda dome,   þeah ðe hie hit frecne
                                    geneðdon,
weras under wætera hrofas. Gesawon hie þær
                                    weallas standan,
ealle him brimu blodige þuhton,   þurh þa heora
                                    beadosearo wægon.
Hreðdon hildespelle,   siððan hie þam herge wiðforon;

570 Lindwigan] *supplied;* gefegon *Dietrich*] gefeon
574 herge] *supplied by Grein*

567b] Presumably an allusion to the nautical imagery (notes to 80b–84, 105–6a) whereby the Israelites were described as sailors. Now they have crossed the Red Sea they have arrived at their terrestrial destination and are sailors no longer.

568] *wuldres beam*: the cloud-pillar described metaphorically as the Cross – see note to 94b.

570–74] These five lines, all probably hypermetric originally, are the only hypermetric lines in the poem. For their scansion see Bliss 167.

570a] The MS reading *life gefeon* cannot be accepted as it stands: in the context *gefeon* inf. will not make sense, and, since loss of intervocalic *g* is not a known OE sound-change (Campbell §467), the form cannot be interpreted as p.t. pl. Emendation to *gefegon* produces good sense but suspicious metre, for, as Pope implies (*Rhythm of Beowulf* 103), the combination of normal verse plus hypermetric verse, while possible, seems extremely unlikely as the first of five otherwise entirely hypermetric lines. A word or words may therefore be assumed to be missing, probably at the beginning of the verse. If IRVING's suggestion is followed the verse might begin *Ongunnon þa . . .*, but, although it would facilitate the retention of *gefeon* inf., this reading would be unsatisfactory in a reconstruction because a hypermetric first half-line usually begins with a stress. The present reading is unexceptionable in terms of sense, syntax and metre and the omission could be explained as scribal haplography.

570b–71] Lit. 'when they had brought away life from . . .', i.e. when they had escaped alive from. . . . Cf. *Beowulf* 2141a.

572] *wætera hrofas*: the waters of the Red Sea, towering over the Israelites, were both a protective covering (cf. 295ff.) and an awesome threat.

574–7] These lines refer to the Song of Moses (Ex. 15.1–19).

574b] *herge* is necessary both to complete the sense and provide alliteration; translate 'when they had escaped from the (Egyptian) army'. Vickrey [*Traditio* xxviii (1972) 126] translates *wiðforon* as 'had gone against' a reading which harmonizes with his view that there is a battle between the Israelites

575 hofon hereþreatas   hlude stefne –
    for þam dædweorce   Drihten heredon –
    weras wuldres sang.   Wif on oðrum,   [p.171
    folcsweota mæst,   fyrdleoð golan
    aclum stefnum,   eallwundra fela.
580 Þa wæs eðfynde   Afrisc meowle
    on geofones staðe   golde geweorðod.
    Handa hofon   halswurðunge,

578 golan *Wülker*] galan
582 Handa hofon *Thorpe*] hand ahofon

and the Egyptians face to face in the Red Sea.

576a] *dædweorce*: perhaps *dægweorce* might be preferable.

576b] Cf. 547 and Ex. 15.1 'Cantemus Domino'.

577b] The reference to women derives from Ex. 15.20.

578] *golan* is p.t. pl. for regular *golon*. MS *galan* 'is plainly an error' (BLACKBURN). Cf. MS *faran* for *foran* (*Daniel* 53).

579a] The voices are excited by fear of God; BLACKBURN compares Ex. 14.31, 'timuitque populus Dominum'.

580] Translate 'Then the Ethiopian woman was easy to find', i.e. was conspicuous. As pointed out by Robinson [*Anglia* lxxx (1962) 373–8] the *Afrisc meowle* is Moses's Ethiopian wife, 'uxor aethiopissa' (Num. 12.1). This is presumably Zipporah (Ex. 2.21); for the identification of 'Ethiopian' and 'Midianite' see Hab. 3.7, and Robinson adduces patristic authority for the same identification. In allegorical exegesis Moses's Ethiopian wife was more important than the passing references in Ex. 2.21–2, 4.18–26, 18.1–6 might indicate; for, as Isidore put it, 'Uxor Moysi Aethiopissa figuravit Ecclesiam ex gentibus Christo conjunctam' (*Alleg. Script. Sac.* 61, PL lxxxiii 109). There is, however, no evidence that the poem was intended to suggest this allegorical equation here. Irving's objection that *wæs eðfynde* should introduce a pl. (cf. *Beowulf* 138, *Gen* 1993, *Andreas* 1547) seems pedantic. Moses's wife is as conspicuous at these celebrations as was Wealhþeow at the celebrations in the Danish court after Beowulf's victory over Grendel, and she is conspicuous not only because she was the leader's wife but also because, as the poem tells us, she was *golde geweorðod*. The adj. *Afrisc* is presumably formed on the root of the pl. n. *Africe* 'Africans' (see BT *Affric*) with almost inevitable assimilation and contraction of *-icisc* to *-isc*, though BTSA records an uncontracted variant *Africisc*. The attempts by previous editors to emend *Afrisc* to *Ebrisc* 'Hebrew' or *meowle* to *neowle* 'prostrate' are unnecessary.

582–9a] For the notion that the Israelites acquired the treasure which belonged to the Egyptians drowned in the Red Sea see Wisd. 10.19.

582] *Handa hofon*: this alteration of the MS word-division is necessary on grounds of sense.

blíðe wæron,   bote gesawon,
heddon herereafes –   hæft wæs onsæled.
585 Ongunnon sælafe   segnum dælan
on yðlafe   ealde madmas,
reaf ond randas;   heo on riht sceodon
gold ond godweb,   Iosepes gestreon,
wera wuldorgesteald.   Werigend lagon
590 on deaðstede,   drihtfolca mæst.

587 sceodon *Thorpe*] sceo
590 mæst *Junius*] mæ *followed by erasure; original reading irrecoverable under ultra-violet light*

583] Through the word *bote* there is probably a reference to the beginning of the poem where men are said to have been told about *bote lifes* (5). This reminiscence reinforces the allegorical interpretation of the exodus as man's journey through life.

584b] The placing of this verse here links the destruction of the Egyptians with the liberation of the Israelites. This juxtaposition of ideas (repeated in 589) suggests the interpretation of the Crossing of the Red Sea as prefiguring eschatological death and resurrection. For an even more remarkable instance of repeated antithesis (buttressed by alliteration and rhyme) to juxtapose ideas similar to those here see *Christ* II 591–5.

585] *sælafe*: the Israelites, those who have survived the sea-crossing (the term would be equally appropriate for those on Noah's Ark); cf. 567b and note. For a similar compound cf. *wealafe* 'survivors of a misfortune' (*Beowulf* 1084, 1098). Alternatively *sælafe* is acc. pl. meaning 'spoils of the sea' and is to be taken as parallel to *ealde madmas*.

586] *mádmas*: for the lOE change of *ð* to *d* before a nasal see Campbell §424.

587] MS *sceo* is evidently defective; *scēodon* is from *sceádan*, though the usual p.t. is *sceád, scēd*. Cf. *togiscēode* (RGosp.) and *swēop* from *swápan*.

588] As in L, *Iosepes* must have initial /j/, which alliterates with *g*-. For an account of how Joseph accumulated wealth for the Egyptians see Gen. 47.13–26. Cf. note to 135–41.

589b–90] Irving compares the Judgment Day scene in Rev. 20.13, 'Et dedit mare mortuos'.

589b] *Werigend*, i.e. the Egyptians, whose responsibility it was to guard the treasure in their keeping. Since the 'protection' afforded to the treasure was in fact impotent the use of this term serves to emphasize the ignominy of the Egyptians' defeat and to point up the irony of *drihtfolca mæst* (590).

Select Bibliography

1 BIBLIOGRAPHICAL LISTS

The most comprehensive bibliographical list is that contained in IRVING pp.36–41 and 130–4. The present bibliography includes the more important works and those not included in IRVING.

2 FACSIMILE

1927   I. Gollancz, *The Cædmon Manuscript of Anglo-Saxon Biblical Poetry*. [GOLLANCZ]

3 MANUSCRIPT

(See also 4 EDITIONS)

1888   F. H. Stoddard, 'The Cædmon Poems in MS. Junius XI', *Anglia* x, 157–67.

1893   J. Lawrence, 'The Metrical Pointing in Codex Junius XI', in *Chapters on Alliterative Verse*, 1–37.

1925   M. D. Clubb, *Christ and Satan*, Yale Studies in English lxx, pp. ix–xvii.

1932   G. P. Krapp, *The Vercelli Book*, ASPR II, pp. liii–lxxx (list of accents).

1948   B. J. Timmer, *The Later Genesis*, 1954 edn, 1–18.

1952   B. J. Timmer, 'The History of a Manuscript', *The Book Collector* i, 6–13.

1954   G. C. Thornley, 'The Accents and Points of MS. Junius 11', *TPS*, 178–205.

1957   N. R. Ker, *Catalogue of Manuscripts containing Anglo-Saxon*, no. 334, pp.406–8.

1959   J. I. Young, 'Two Notes on the *Later Genesis*', in *The Anglo-Saxons* (B. Dickins *Festschrift*), ed. P. Clemoes, 204–11.

1964 M.-M. Larès, 'Échos d'un rite hiérosolymitain dans un manuscrit du haut Moyen Age anglais', *Revue de l'Histoire des Religions* clxv, 13–47.

1972 T. H. Ohlgren, 'Five New Drawings in the *MS Junius 11*: their Iconography and Thematic Significance', *Speculum* xlvii, 227–33.

1972 T. H. Ohlgren, 'The Illustrations of the *Cædmonian Genesis*', *Medievalia et Humanistica* iii, 199–212.

1972 T. H. Ohlgren, 'Visual Language in the Old English *Cædmonian Genesis*', *Visible Language* vi, 253–76.

1973 O. Pächt & J. J. G. Alexander, *Illuminated Manuscripts in the Bodleian Library Oxford* III (British, Irish and Icelandic Schools) no. 34, p. 5.

1974 R. T. Farrell, *Daniel and Azarias*, pp. 1–10.

1975 G. Henderson, 'The Programme of Illustrations in Bodleian MS Junius XI', in *Studies in Memory of David Talbot Rice*, ed. G. Robertson & G. Henderson, 113–45.

1976 E. Temple, *Anglo-Saxon Manuscripts 900–1066*, no. 58, pp.76–8.

4 EDITIONS

1655 F. Junius, *Cædmonis Monachi Paraphrasis Poetica Genesios ac praecipuarum Sacrae paginae Historiarum...* (Amsterdam). [JUNIUS]

1832 B. Thorpe, *Cædmon's Metrical Paraphrase of Parts of the Holy Scriptures.* [THORPE]

1849–54 K. W. Bouterwek, *Cædmon's des Angelsachsen biblische Dichtungen* (Gütersloh and Elberfeld). [BOUTERWEK]

1857 C. W. M. Grein, *Bibliothek der angelsächsischen Poesie* (Göttingen) Bd 1. [GREIN]

1888 F. Kluge, *Angelsächsisches Lesebuch* (Halle). (Lines 1–361, 447–590) [KLUGE]

1894 R. P. Wülker, *Bibliothek der angelsächsischen Poesie* (Leipzig) Bd 2. [WÜLKER]

1907 F. A. Blackburn, *Exodus and Daniel* (Boston). [BLACKBURN]

1922 W. J. Sedgefield, *An Anglo-Saxon Verse Book*. (Lines 1–361, 447–590) [SEDGEFIELD]

1931 G. P. Krapp, *The Junius Manuscript*, ASPR I. [KRAPP]

1953 E. B. Irving, *The Old English Exodus* (Yale Studies in English cxxii, repr. with supplementary bibliography 1970). [IRVING]
Supplemented by two articles, (1) '*Exodus* retraced' (= Introduction) in *Old English Studies in Honour of John C. Pope* ed. R. B. Burlin & E. B. Irving (Toronto, 1974) 203–23 [Irving (always qualified by page number)], and (2) 'New Notes on the Old English *Exodus*' (= Notes) in *Anglia* xc (1972) 289–324 [Irving (never qualified by page number because reference is to the relevant note)].

1958 R. Kaiser, *Medieval English* (Berlin). (Lines 1–20, 154–304a, 447–515).

5 TRANSLATIONS

1903 W. S. Johnson, 'Translation of the Old English *Exodus*', *JEGP* v, 44–57.

1916 C. W. Kennedy, *The Cædmon Poems*, repr. 1965.

1926 R. K. Gordon, *Anglo-Saxon Poetry*, rev. ed. 1954. (Lines 1–306, 447–590).

6 TECHNICAL STUDIES

1882 H. Balg, *Der Dichter Cædmon und seine Werke* (Bonn).

1883 E. J. Groth, *Composition und Alter der altenglischen (angelsächsischen) Exodus* (Göttingen).

1883 H. Ziegler, *Der poetische Sprachgebrauch in den sogen. Cædmonschen Dichtungen* (Münster).

1894 F. Graz, *Die Metrik der sog. Cædmonschen Dichtungen mit Berücksichtigung der Verfasserfrage* (Weimar) 1–40, 109.

1913 R. Wieners, *Zur Metrik des Codex Junius XI* (Cologne).

1915 L. L. Schücking, *Untersuchungen zur Bedeutungslehre der angelsächsische Dichtersprache* (Heidelberg).

1918 F. Klaeber, 'Concerning the Relation between *Exodus* and *Beowulf*', *MLN* xxxiii, 218–24, supplemented in *Anglia* l (1926) 202–3.

1933 H. Kuhn, 'Wortstellung und -betonung im Altgermanischen', *PBB* lvii, 1–109. [Kuhn]

1939 C. T. Carr, *Nominal Compounds in Germanic* (St Andrews Univ. Publ. xli) 412–6.

1940 S. O. Andrew, *Syntax and Style in Old English*, repr. 1966. [Andrew, *Syntax*]

1940 H. Marquardt, 'Zur Entstehung des *Beowulf*', *Anglia* lxiv, 152–8.

1942 J. C. Pope, *The Rhythm of Beowulf*, 1966 edn.

1948 S. O. Andrew, *Postscript on Beowulf*, repr. 1969. [Andrew, *Postscript*]

1958 A. J. Bliss, *The Metre of Beowulf*, 1967 edn. [Bliss]

1959 E. B. Irving, 'On the Dating of the Old English Poems *Genesis* and *Exodus*', *Anglia* lxxvii, 1–11.

1961 E. D. Clemons, *A Metrical Analysis of the Old English Poem Exodus* (Unpubl. Dissertation, Texas).

1962 A. Campbell, 'The Old English Epic Style', in *English and Medieval Studies* (J. R. R. Tolkien *Festschrift*) ed. N. Davis & C. L. Wrenn, 13–26.

1968 A. G. Brodeur, 'A Study of Diction and Style in Three Anglo-Saxon Narrative Poems', in *Nordica et Anglica* (S. Einarsson *Festschrift*), ed. A. H. Orrick, 97–114, esp. 109–13.

1968 Sr. C. Wall, 'Stylistic Variation in the Old English *Exodus*', *ELN* vi, 79–84.

1969 R. Frank, *Wordplay in Old English Poetry* (Unpubl. Dissertation, Harvard) 56–79.

7 TEXTUAL STUDIES

1856 F. Dietrich, 'Zu Cädmon', *ZfdA* x, 310–67, esp. 339–55.

1872 E. Sievers, 'Collationen Angelsächsischer Gedichte', *ZfdA* xv, 456–67, esp. 459.

1885 E. Sievers, 'Zur Rhythmik des germanischen Alliterationsverses. II', *PBB* x, 451–545, esp. 513–4.

1894 P. J. Cosijn, 'Anglosaxonica', *PBB* xix, 441–61, esp. 457–61.

1895 P. J. Cosijn, 'Anglosaxonica II', *PBB* xx, 98–116, esp. 98–106.

1895 F. Graz, 'Beiträge zur Textkritik der sogenannten Cædmon'schen Dichtungen', *ESt* xxi, 1–27, esp. 2–7.

1895 F. Holthausen, untitled review of Wülker, *Anglia Beiblatt* v, 231.

1899 G. Mürkens, 'Untersuchungen über das altenglische Exoduslied', *BBA* ii, 62–117, esp. 113–7.

1902 J. W. Bright, 'Notes on the Cædmonian *Exodus*', *MLN* xvii, 212–3.

1904 F. Klaeber, 'Zu altenglischen Dichtungen', *Archiv* cxiii, 146–9, esp. 146–7.

1911 A. S. Napier, 'The Old English "Exodus", ll. 63–134', *MLR* vi, 165–8.

1912 J. W. Bright, 'On the Anglo-Saxon Poem *Exodus*', *MLN* xxvii, 13–19.

1917 K. Sisam, 'The Cædmonian *Exodus* 492', *MLN* xxxii, 48.

1918 E. A. Kock, 'Jubilee Jaunts and Jottings', *Lunds Universitets Årsskrift*, N. F., Avd 1, Bd 14, Nr 26. [Kock JJJ]

1920 R. Imelmann, *Forschungen zur altenglischen Poesie* (Berlin), 382–420.

1922 E. A. Kock, 'Plain Points and Puzzles', *Lunds Universitets Årsskrift*, N.F., Avd 1, Bd 17, Nr 7. [Kock PPP]

1929 L. L. Schücking, 'Noch einmal: "enge ānpaðas, uncūð gelād" ', in *Studies in English Philology* (F. Klaeber *Festschrift*) ed. K. Malone & M. B. Ruud (Minneapolis), 213–6.

1938 J. R. Hulbert, 'On the Text of the Junius Manuscript', *JEGP* xxxvii, 533–6.

1955 C. L. Wrenn, untitled review of IRVING, *RES* n.s. vi, 184–9.

1960 J. E. Cross and S. I. Tucker, 'Appendix on *Exodus* 11. 289–90', *Neophil.* xliv, 38–9.

1962 F. C. Robinson, 'Notes on the Old English *Exodus*', *Anglia* lxxx, 363–78.

1966 R. T. Farrell, 'Eight Notes on Old English *Exodus*', *NM* lxvii, 364–75.

1966 F. C. Robinson, 'Notes and Emendations to Old English Poetic Texts', *NM* lxvii, 356–64, esp. 356–9.

1968 F. C. Robinson, 'The Significance of Names in Old English Literature', *Anglia* lxxxvi, 14–58, esp. 25–9.

1968 F. C. Robinson, 'Some Uses of Name-Meanings in Old English Poetry', *NM* lxix, 161–71, esp. 166–7.

1968 H. Schabram, 'AE. *Beohata, Exodus* 253', in *Wortbildung Syntax und Morphologie* (H. Marchand *Festschrift*), ed. H. E. Brekle & L. Lipka, 203–9.

1969 P. J. Lucas, ' "Exodus" 480: "mod gerymde" ', *NQ* cciv, 206–7.

1969 P. J. Lucas, 'An Interpretation of "Exodus" 46–53', *NQ* cciv, 364–6.

1969 E. G. Stanley, 'Old English "-calla", "ceallian" ', in *Medieval Literature and Civilization* (G. N. Garmonsway memorial studies), ed. D. A. Pearsall & R. A. Waldron, 94–9.

1970 H. T. Keenan, '*Exodus* 312', *NM* lxxi, 455–60.

1971 P. J. Lucas, ' "Exodus" 265: ægnian', *NQ* ccvi, 283–4.

1973 D. G. Calder, 'Two Notes on the Typology of the OE *Exodus*', *NM* lxxiv, 85–9.

1973 H. T. Keenan, '*Exodus* 312a', *NM* lxxiv, 217–9.

1973 J. Vickrey, ' "Exodus" and the Tenth Plague', *Archiv* ccx, 41–52.

1974 T. D. Hill, 'The "Fyrst Ferhðbana": Old English "Exodus", 399', *NQ* ccix, 204–5.

1975 A. Bammesberger, 'Zu *Exodus* 145b', *Anglia* xciii, 140–44.

1975 J. R. Hall, ' "Niwe flodas": Old English "Exodus" 362', *NQ* ccxx, 243–4.

1975 J. R. Hall, 'The Building of the Temple in *Exodus*: Design for Typology', *Neophil.* lix, 616–21.

1975 J. P. Hermann, 'The Green Rod of Moses in the Old English *Exodus*', *ELN* xii, 241–3.

8 SOURCES AND COMPARATIVE MATERIAL

(i) *The Bible*

1751 P. Sabatier, *Bibliorum sacrorum Latinae versiones antiquae* (Paris). [OL Bible]

1874 F. P. Dutripon, *Bibliorum Sacrorum Concordantiae.*

1926– Biblia Sacra iuxta Latinam Vulgatam Versionem ad codicum fidem iussu Pii PP.XI (Rome). [Benedictine Vulgate]

1949– B. Fischer o.s.b. et al., *Vetus Latina, Die Reste der altlateinischen Bibel* (Freiburg). [OL Bible]

1965 *Biblia Sacra Vulgatae Editionis Sixti V Pont. Max. iussu recognita et Clementis VIII auctoritatae edita* (Rome).[Clementina Vulgate]

(ii) *Modern biblical commentary on Exodus*

1962 M. Noth, *Exodus A Commentary,* tr. J. S. Bowden (Old Testament Library). [Noth]

1971 J. P. Hyatt, *Commentary on Exodus* (New Century Bible). [Hyatt]

1974 B. S. Childs, *Exodus A Commentary* (Old Testament Library) [Childs]

(iii) *Bibliographical guides to patristic authorities*

1946 C. P. Farrar and A. P. Evans, *Bibliography of English Translations from Medieval Sources* (New York).

1950–55 F. Stegmüller, *Repertorium Biblicum Medii Aevi* (Madrid).

1961 E. Dekkers o.s.b., *Clavis Patrvm Latinorvm* (*Sacris Erudiri* iii).

1967 J. D. A. Ogilvy, *Books Known to the English, 597–1066* (Cambridge, Mass.).

1974– M. Geerard, *Clavis Patrvm Graecorvm* (Turnhout).

(iv) *Patristic commentaries on Exodus*

(The dates in the left-hand column are those of the author's death.)

d.*c.*254 Origen, *In Exodum Homiliae,* PG xii 297–396, GCS xxix (1920) 145–279: as *Homélies sur l'Exode,* SC xvi (1947).

d.430 Augustine, *Quaestiones in Heptateuchum,* lib ii (Quaest. Exodi), CCSL xxxiii (1958) 70–174, PL xxxiv 597–674.

d.636 Isidore of Seville, *Quaestiones in Exodum*, PL lxxxiii 287–322.

?c.800 Pseudo-Bede, *In Pentateuchum Commentarii* (lib. ii, Exodus), PL xci 285–332.

d.856 Rabanus Maurus, *Commentaria in Exodum*, PL cviii 9–246.

(v) *Modern studies based on the Church Fathers*

1956 J. Daniélou s.j., *The Bible and the Liturgy* (Notre Dame Liturgical Studies iii) esp. ch. v.

1960 J. Daniélou s.j., *From Shadows to Reality*, tr. W. Hibberd o.s.b.

1961 I. S. van Woerden, 'The Iconography of the Sacrifice of Abraham', *Vigiliae Christianae* xv, 214–55.

1963 H. Rahner s.j., 'Odysseus at the Mast', in *Greek Myths and Christian Mystery*, tr. B. Battershaw, ch. vii.

1964 J. Daniélou s.j., 'The Ship of the Church', in *Primitive Christian Symbols*, tr. D. Attwater, ch. 4.

1965 G. Q. Reijners o.s.c., *The Terminology of the Holy Cross in Early Christian Literature* (Graecitas Christianorum Primaeva ii, Nijmegen).

(vi) *The Liturgy*

1883 F. E. Warren (ed.), *The Leofric Missal*. [*LM*] (On the date and provenance of this missal see D. H. Turner (ed.), *The Missal of the New Minster, Winchester*, HBS xciii (1960) p. vi.)

1932 B. Capelle, 'La Procession du Lumen Christi au Samedi-Saint', *Revue Bénédictine* xliv, 105–19.

1932 J. W. Tyrer, *Historical Survey of Holy Week* (Alcuin Club Collections xxix).

1942 P. Lundberg, *La Typologie Baptismale dans l'Ancienne Église* (Acta Seminarii Neotestamentici Upsaliensis 10).

1958 A. Baumstark, *Comparative Liturgy*, rev. B. Botte o.s.b., tr. F. L. Cross.

1969 T. Klauser, *A Short History of the Western Liturgy*, tr. J. Halliburton.

(vii) *Studies relating to the OE poem Exodus*

1905 F. Holthausen, 'Zur Quellenkunde ... der altengl. Exodus', *Archiv* cxv, 162–3.

1911   S. Moore, 'On the Sources of the Old English *Exodus*', *MP* ix, 83–108.

1912   J. W. Bright, 'The Relation of the Cædmonian *Exodus* to the Liturgy', *MLN* xxvii, 97–103.

1967   A. Mirsky, 'On the Sources of the Anglo-Saxon *Genesis* and *Exodus*, *ES* xlviii, 385–97.

1969   E. McLoughlin, 'OE *Exodus* and the *Antiphonary of Bangor*', *NM* lxx, 658–67.

1975   J. B. Trahern, 'More Scriptural Echoes in the Old English *Exodus*', in *Anglo-Saxon Poetry: Essays in Appreciation* (J. C. McGalliard *Festschrift*), ed. L. E. Nicholson & D. W. Frese, 291–8.

1976   M. J. B. Allen & D. G. Calder, *Sources and Analogues of Old English Poetry*, 219–20.

9   LITERARY STUDIES

1943   C. W. Kennedy, *The Earliest English Poetry*, 175–83.

1959   B. F. Huppé, *Doctrine and Poetry* (New York), 217–23.

1960   J. E. Cross and S. I. Tucker, 'Allegorical Tradition and the Old English *Exodus*', *Neophil.* xliv, 122–7.

1966   S. B. Greenfield, *A Critical History of Old English Literature*, 154–9.

1966   G. Shepherd, 'Scriptural Poetry', in *Continuations and Beginnings*, ed. E. G. Stanley, 1–36, esp. 30–31.

1968   N. D. Isaacs, '*Exodus* and the Essential Digression', in *Structural Principles in Old English Poetry* (Knoxville, Tennessee), 151–9.

1969   R. T. Farrell, 'A Reading of OE. *Exodus*', *RES* n.s. xx, 401–17.

1970   J. E. Cross, 'The Old English Period', in *The Middle Ages*, ed. W. F. Bolton (Sphere History of Literature in the English Language 1), 12–65, esp. 28–30.

1970   J. W. Earl, 'Christian Tradition in the Old English *Exodus*', *NM* lxxi, 541–70.

1970   P. J. Lucas, 'The Cloud in the Interpretation of the Old English *Exodus*', *ES* li, 297–311.

1970   P. Rollinson, 'Some Kinds of Meaning in Old English Poetry', *AM* xi, 5–21, esp. 16–18.

1972   A. A. Lee, *The Guest-hall of Eden*, 41–8.

1972   T. A. Shippey, *Old English Verse*, ch. 6.

1972   J. F. Vickrey, ' "Exodus" and the Battle in the Sea', *Traditio* xxviii, 119–40.

1972   J. F. Vickrey, '*Exodus* and the treasure of Pharaoh', *ASE* i, 159–65.

1973   R. M. Trask, 'Doomsday Imagery in the Old English *Exodus*', *Neophil.* lvii, 295–7.

1974   T. Rendall, 'Bondage and Freeing from Bondage in Old English Religious Poetry', *JEGP* lxxiii, 497–512, esp. 505–9.

1974   J. H. Wilson, *Christian Theology and Old English Poetry* (The Hague), ch. v.

1975   W. Helder, 'Etham and the Ethiopians in the Old English *Exodus*', *AM* xvi, 5–23.

1975   J. F. Vickrey, ' "Exodus" and the "Herba Humilis" ,' *Traditio* xxxi, 25–54.

1976   P. J. Lucas, 'Old English Christian Poetry: the Cross in *Exodus*', in *Famulus Christi: Essays in Commemoration of the Thirteenth Centenary of the Birth of the Venerable Bede*, ed. G. Bonner, 193–209.

10   CULTURAL BACKGROUND

1904   W. O. Stevens, *The Cross in the Life and Literature of the Anglo-Saxons* (Yale Studies in English xxiii).

1940   D. Knowles o.s.b., *The Monastic Order in England*, 1963 edn.

1952   B. Smalley, *The Study of The Bible in The Middle Ages*, 2nd edn.

1953   K. Sisam, *Studies in the History of Old English Literature*.

1957   M. L. W. Laistner, *Thought and Letters in Western Europe: A.D. 500 to 900*.

1959   E. Auerbach, ' "Figura" ', tr. R. Manheim, in *Scenes from the Drama of European Literature*, 11–76.

1959   R. P. C. Hanson, *Allegory and Event.*

1959–64 H. de Lubac s.j., *Exégèse Médiévale* (Paris).

1962   C. J. Godfrey, *The Church in Anglo-Saxon England.*

1962   J. Leclercq o.s.b., *The Love of Learning and the Desire for God*, tr. C. Misrahi.

1962   P. Riché, *Éducation et Culture dans l'Occident Barbare* (Patristica Sorbonensia 4, Paris).

1963   B. Fischer o.s.b., 'Bibelausgaben des frühen Mittelalters', *Settimane di Studio del centro Italiano sull'alto Medioevo* x, 519–600.

1966   A. C. Charity, *Events and their Afterlife.*

1969   G. W. H. Lampe (ed.), *The Cambridge History of the Bible, Volume 2, The West from the Fathers to the Reformation.* [*CHB*]

1970   P. H. Blair, *The World of Bede.*

1971   P. Gradon, *Form and Style in Early English Literature.*

1972   H. Mayr-Harting, *The Coming of Christianity to Anglo-Saxon England.*

1973   G. Bonner, 'Bede and medieval civilization', *ASE* ii, 71–90.

Glossary

In the glossary all words used in the text are recorded and are to be found under the forms in which they occur, except that nouns and adjectives (excluding irregular comparatives, etc.) are entered under the nom. sg. (m.) or nom. pl., and verbs under the infinitive; pronouns are to be found under the nom. sg. m., except that in regard to the personal pronouns those of the 1st and 2nd persons are entered under the nom. sg. and nom. pl. Irregular grammatical or phonological forms liable to cause difficulty are noticed in their proper places with cross-references to the words under which they are dealt with.

Line-references are exhaustive unless followed by 'etc.'. References to words supplied by the editor and to forms that have been emended are printed in italics. When a reference is followed by 'n.' the relevant note in the Commentary should also be consulted. An asterisk before a headword indicates that it is a *hapax legomenon* and is recorded only in the instance cited from this text. Cross-references to compound nouns and adjectives are given under the second element as simplex.

In the alphabetical arrangement æ is treated as a separate letter after *a*; þ/ð are placed after *t*, and their use is normalized, so that þ is printed at the beginning of a word or element of a compound, but ð in other positions. The prefix *ge-* is always ignored in the arrangement of the glossary.

Reference is made to *OED* by printing the *OED* word (under which the Old English word is found) as the first meaning in small capitals; if the word is not the true phonological descendant of the OE form in the glossary it is in italic capitals. If it is radically different in meaning or if it is obsolete it is enclosed in square brackets. Unless the *OED* word provides the sense required by the context, it is followed by a semicolon and the sense required printed in ordinary lower-case type.

The abbreviations employed are in common use.

A

ābrecan, *v.* (*5*), [ABREAK]; destroy. *pp. acc. pl.* **abrocene** 39n.

ābregdan, *v.* (*3*), [ABRAID]; remove. *pp.* **ābrōden** 269

ābrēotan, *v.* (*2*), [A- +]; destroy 199

ac, *conj.*, [AC]; but 443, but on the contrary 243, 457, 489, 513, but nevertheless 416

ācol, *adj.*, excited by fear. *dat. pl.* **āclum** 579

*ādfȳr, *n. a-stem*, [AD + FIRE]; fire of the funeral pyre; *acc. sg.* 398

ādrencan, *w.v.* (*1b*), [ADRENCH]; drown. *pp.* **ādrenced** 459

ādrincan, *v.* (*3*), [ADRINK]; be quenched. *p.t. sg.* **ādranc** 77

āfǣran, *w.v.* (*1b*) [AFEAR]; terrify. *pp.* **āfǣred** 447

āfæstnian, *w.v.* (*2*), [A- + FASTEN]; fasten. *pp.* **āfæstnod** 85

*Afrisc, *adj.*, African, Ethiopian 580

āgan, *pret. pr.*, [OWE]; have, possess 317. *p.t. sg.* **āhte** 514; *pl. neg.* **nāhton** 210

āgen, *adj.*, OWN; *acc. sg. n.* 419.

Āgend, *m. nd-stem*, owner, Lord 295

āgēotan, *v.* (*2*), [AGETE(N)]; pour forth, destroy. *p.t. sg.* **āgēat** 515

āhebban, *v.* (*6*), [*AHEAVE*] ; lift, raise up. *p.t. sg.* **āhof** 253. *pp.* **āhafen** 200

āhlēapan, *v.* (*7*), [A- + LEAP]; leap forward. *p.t. sg.* **āhlēop** 252

āhte, see **āgan**

āhȳdan, *w.v.* (*1b*), [A- + HIDE[1]]; conceal 115

ālǣdan, *w.v.* (*1b*), [A- + LEAD[1]]; lead forth. *p.t. sg.* **ālǣdde** 187

ald, see **eald**

aldor, *m. a-stem*, [ALDER[2]]; commander 12, *acc. sg.* 31, Lord 270. Cf. **ealdordōm**

aldor, *n. a-stem*, life; *dat. sg.* **aldre** in *awa to aldre* for ever and ever 425

ālesan, *v.* (*5*), [A- + LEASE[1]]; select. *pp.* **ālesen** 183, 228

alh, *m. a-stem*, temple; *acc. sg. 392*

Alwalda, *m. n-stem*, [ALL +]; omnipotent ruler, Lord 11

alwihte, *f. pl. i-stem*, [ALL + WIGHT]; all creatures; *gen. pl.* **alwihta** 421

ālȳfan, *w.v.* (*1b*), [A- + LEVE[1]]; allow, grant. *pp.* **ālȳfed** 44, 533

ān, *adj.*, ONE 353; *gen. sg. n.* **ānes** 305. *nom. sg. m. wk.* **āna** alone 440. *pron.* one man 348; *gen. pl.* **ānra** of them 187, 227. [See M. Rissanen, *Uses of One in Old & e.ME* (Helsinki, 1967)]

anbid, *n. a-stem*, [ON-[1] + BIDE]; expectation 534

āndæge, *adj.*, [ONE + DAY]; lasting one day; *acc. sg. m.* **āndægne** 304

andrǣdan, *v.* (*7*), [ON-[1] + DREAD]; fear (*w. refl. dat.*) 266

andsaca, *m. n-stem*, [AND- +]; adversary 503; (prob.) *acc. sg.* **andsacan** *15*

ānga, *adj.*, only; *acc. sg. f.* **āngan** 403

anmōd, *adj.*, [ON-[1] + MOOD[1]]; resolute 203

ānpæð, *m. a-stem*, [ONE + PATH]; lonely track. *acc. pl.* **ānpaðas** 58

*angetrum, *n. a-stem*, [ON-[1] +]; host 334

*antwigðu, *f. ō-stem*, [ON-[1] +]; hesitation; *acc. sg.* **antwigða** 145

ārǣman, *w.v.* (*1b*), [A- +]; arise. *p.t. sg.* **ārǣmde** 411

ārǣran, *w.v.* (*1b*), [AREAR]; raise (up). *p.t. sg.* **ārǣrde** 295. *pp.* **ārǣred** 320

āre, *f. n-stem*, [ARE[1]]; honour; *dat. sg.* **āran** 245

*ārēafian, *w.v.* (*2*), [A- + REAVE[1]]; remove, draw back. *pp.* **ārēafod** 290

ārisan, *v.* (*1*), ARISE 217. *p.t. sg.* **ārās** 100, 299, was established 129

āsǣlan, *w.v.* (*1b*), [A- + SEAL[2]]; bind, hold down. *pp.* **āsǣled** *471*

āscieppan, *v.* (*6*), [A- + SHAPE]; create. *p.t. sg.* **āscēop** 381

āstīgan, *v.* (*1*), [ASTY(E)]; rise, mount up, arise. *p.t. sg.* **āstāh** 107, 302, 451, 468

āswebban, *w.v.* (*1a*), [ASWEVE]; destroy. *p.t. sg.* **āswefede** 336

atol, *adj.*, [ATEL]; terrible 201, 456; *acc. sg. n.* 165

āð, *m. a-stem*, OATH; *acc. sg.* 432

āðswaru, *f. ō-stem*, [OATH + SWARE]; swearing of oaths; *dat. sg* **āðsware** 559

āwa, *adv.*, always 425

āwyrgan, *w.v.* (*1b*), [*AWORRY*]; suffocate, corrupt. *pp.* **āwyrged** 533

Æ

æfen, *n. ja-stem,* EVEN; evening. *gen. pl.* **æfena** in *æfena gehwam* every evening 108

æfenlēoð, *n. a-stem,* [EVEN +]; evening song 201; *acc. sg.* 165

****æflāst,** *m. a-stem,* [OF-[1] + LAST[1]]; deviation of course. *dat. pl.* **æflāstum** 474

æfter, *adv.,* AFTER; behind 105; then 418. *prep. w. dat.* (of place) following 331, 340, 347, etc.; (spreading) over 132, 212, throughout 396, among 511; in pursuit of 195; (of time) after 5, 299, 565; (of manner) in the manner of 109; in consequence of (obtaining), by means of 143

æghwæðer, *pron.,* EITHER; each (of two) 95

æghwilc, *adj.,* EACH; every; *acc. sg. m.* **æghwilcne** 188. as *pron.* each one 351

****ægnian,** *w.v.* (*1b*), thrash 265n.

æht, *f. i-stem,* [AUGHT[1]]; possession, power; *acc. sg.* 11

ælfer, *n. a-stem,* [ALL + FARE[1]]; whole host; *dat. sg.* **ælfere** 66. Cf. **eall-**

ænig, *pron.,* ANY 456, 509; *dat. sg. f.* **ænigre** 326

ær, *adv.,* ERE; before, previously 28, 138, 141 etc.

ærdæg, *m. a-stem,* [ERE + DAY]; dawn; *dat. sg.* **ærdæge** 198

****ærdēað,** *m. a-stem,* [ERE + DEATH]; premature death 540

æren, *adj.,* brass. *dat. pl.* **ærnum** 216

ærende, *n. ja-stem,* [ERRAND]; message; *acc. sg.* 519

****ærglæd,** *adj.,* [ERE + GLAD]; happy as of old. *nom. pl. m.* **ærglade** 293

æt, *prep. w. dat.,* (of time) AT 267, in 37; (of place) AT 128, 467

æt, *m. a-stem,* [EAT]; food; *gen. sg.* **ætes** 165

ætgædere, *adv.,* together 190, 247n.; *somod ætgædere* together 214

****ætniman,** *v.* (*4*), [AT-[2] + NIM]; take away, kill 415

æðele, *adj.,* [ATHEL]; noble; *gen. sg. n. wk.* **æðelan** 227

æðeling, *m. a-stem,* [ATHELING]; noble man *411*

æðelo, *n. pl. ja-stem,* [ATHEL[1]]; station determined by descent; *acc.* 339, 353; *dat.* **æðelum** lineage 186. See also **fæderæðelo**

B

(ge)bād, see **(ge)bīdan**

bald, *adj.,* BOLD 253

bana, *m. n-stem,* [BANE[1]]; slayer 39. See also **ferhðbana**

band, see **bindan**

bānhūs, *n. a-stem,* [BONE + HOUSE[1]]; body; *gen. sg.* **bānhūses** 524

barn, see **byrnan**

bāsnian, *w.v.* (*2*) *w. dat.,* await. *p.t. pl.* **bāsnodon** *471*

bælblyse, ?*m. i-stem,* [BALE[2] +]; blazing (funeral) fire; *acc. sg.* 401

****bælc,** *m. a-stem,* [BALK]; central beam in roof, ceiling (of Tabernacle); *dat. sg.* **bælce** 73n.

bæron, see **beran**

bæðweg, *m. a-stem,* [BATH[1] + WAY[1]]; sea; *gen. sg.* **bæðweges** 290

be, *prep. w. dat.,* (of place) BY 134, to 69, in *be . . . tweonum* between 443, 563; (of time) while 323–4n.; (of manner) according to 243

bēacen, *n. a-stem,* [BEACON]; standard, sign; *acc. sg.* 320. *gen. pl.* **bēacna** signs 345; *dat. pl.* **bēacnum** (prob.) audible signals 219. [See *NQ* ccxxi (1976) 200-07]. See also **heofonbēacen**

(ge)bēad, see **(ge)bēodan**

*beadosearo, n. wa-stem, war-gear; acc. sg. 573

*beadumægen, n. a-stem, [+ MAIN¹]; army; gen. sg. beadumægnes 329

bēah, m. a-stem, [BEE²]; treasure. acc. pl. bēagas 557

*bealospell, n. a-stem, [BALE¹ + SPELL¹]; bad news. gen. pl. bealospella 511

*bealubenn, f. jō-stem, [BALE¹ +]; serious wound; acc. sg. bealubenne 238

bealusīð, m. a-stem, [BALE¹ + SITHE¹]; terrible journey; dat. sg. bealusīðe 5n.

bēam, m. a-stem, BEAM¹, pillar, Cross 111n., 568. nom. pl. bēamas 94n.; acc. pl. rays of light 121; gen. pl. bēama 249. See also gārbēam, wērbēam

bearhtm, m. a-stem, noise, clamour; dat. sg. bearhtme 65

bearm, m. a-stem, [BARM¹]; bosom; acc. sg. 375

bearn, n. a-stem, [BAIRN]; child, son; acc. sg. 415, 419. nom. pl. 28, 395. See also frēobearn, frumbearn

bebēodan, v. (2), [BIBEDE]; order. p.t. sg. bebēad 101, 215, 382, commended 521

becuman, v. (4), [BECOME]; come. p.t. sg. bec(w)ōm 46, 135, 344, 456, (trans.) came over 447

befaran, v. (6), [BE- + FARE¹]; surround. pp. nom. pl. m. befarene 498

befæðman, w.v. (1b), [BE- + FATHOM]; enclose 429

befōn, v. (7), [BEFONG]; seize. p.t. sg. befēng 416

beforan, prep. w. dat., BEFORE 93

behealdan, v. (7), [BEHOLD]; guard. p.t. sg. behēold 205, kept to 109n.

behindan, adv., BEHIND 457

behwylfan, w.v. (1b), [BE- +]; cover over, confine 427

*bēlegsa, m. n-stem, [BALE² +]; terror of fire; dat. sg. bēlegsan 121. Cf. bǣl-

belūcan, v. (2), (BELOUKE]; shut in. p.t. sg. belēac 457. pp. nom. pl. m. belocene clasped shut 43

bēmum, see byme

-bend, see wælbend

-benn, see bealubenn

bēodan, v. (2), [BID]; announce. p.t. sg. bēad 352

gebēodan, v. (2), [I-¹ + BID]; proclaim. p.t. sg. gebēad 191

beodan p.t., see bidan

*beodohāta, m. n-stem, announcer of battle 253. Cf. beado-

bēon, anom. v., BE. pr. 3 sg. is 267, 273, 293 etc., (w. pp.) 268, 290, 420; bið freq. 537, 546, fut. 526, 564; 3 pl. syndon 283, 297; 1 pl. subj. sȳn 529. imper. 2 pl. bēoð 259. p.t. sg. wæs 12, 19, 22 etc.; neg. næs 339; pl. wǣron 43, 60, 148 etc.; sg. subj. wǣre 378

beorh, m. a-stem, [BARROW¹]; hill, mountain; acc. sg. 386. dat. pl. beorgum 132, 212, burgum 222. See also sǣbeorh

-gebeorh n., see feorhgebeorh, randgebeorh

beorhhlið, n. a-stem, [BARROW¹ + LITH²]; hillside, steep slope. nom. pl. beorhhliðu 449; acc. pl. burhhleoðu 70n.

beorht, adj., BRIGHT, pure 524, noble 415; acc. sg. n. gleaming 219. superl. beorhtost 249

*beorhtrodor, m. a-stem, BRIGHT sky; acc. sg. 94

beorn, m. a-stem, [BERNE]; warrior, man. nom. pl. beornas 375; gen. pl. beorna 401, 564

bēorsele, m. i-stem, BEER¹-hall. acc. pl. bēorselas 564

bēoð, see bēon

beran, *v.* (*4*), BEAR[1], carry, wear 219. *p.t. pl.* **bǣron** 59, 193, 332

berēafian, *w.v.* (*2*), [BEREAVE]; rob. *pp.* **berēafod** 45

berēnian, *w.v.* (*2*), [BE- +]; arrange, bring about. *p.t. pl.* **berēnedon** 147

berēofan, *v.* (*2*) *w. dat.*, [BE- +]; deprive (of). *pp. nom. pl. m.* **berofene** 36

berstan, *v.* (*3*), BURST, crash. *pr.p.* **berstende** 478. *p.t. pl.* **burston** 484

bestēman, *w.v.* (*1b*), [BE- + STEAM]; make wet, spatter. *pp.* **bestēmed** 449

bētan, *w.v.* (*1b*), [BEET]; restore. *p.t. pl.* **bēton** 131

betera, *compar. adj.,* BETTER; *acc. sg. m.* **beteran** 269. *acc. pl.* as *sb.* **beteran** better things 531

beþeccan, *w.v.* (*1c*), [BE- + THATCH]; cover. *pp.* **beþeaht** 60

-bid, *see* **anbid**

bīdan, *v.* (*1*), [BIDE]; remain, wait (for). *p.t. sg.* **bād** 300, (*w. gen.*) 213, 551; *pl.* **bidon** *249,* **beodan** 166

gebīdan, *v.* (*1*), (I-[1] + BIDE]; wait for, experience. *p.t. sg.* **gebād** 137, 404. *pp.* **gebiden** 238

biddan, *v.* (*5*) *w. acc. of person of whom, refl. dat. of person for whom, and gen. of thing requested,* [BID]; ask. *pr. 2 pl. subj.* **bidde** 271n.

bill, *n. ja-stem,* [BILL[1]]; sword. *dat. pl.* **billum** 199

***bilswæð,** *n. a-stem,* [BILL[1] + SWATH[1]]; wound. *nom. pl.* **bilswaðu** 329

bindan, *v.* (*3*), BIND. *p.t. sg.* **band** 15

bið, *see* **bēon**

blāc, *adj.,* [BLOK(E); bright. *nom. pl. m.* **blāce** 111; *acc. pl. m.* 121. See

also **wigblāc.** Cf. **flōdblāc**

***bland,** *n. a-stem,* mixture, harmonization 309

geblandan, *v.* (*7*), [I-[1] + BLAND[1]]; mingle. *pp.* **geblanden** 477

blæc, *adj.,* BLACK. *dat. pl.* **blacum** 212

blǣd, *m. a-stem,* [BLEAD]; abundance 546, glory 564; *acc. sg.* 318

blǣst, *m. a-stem,* [BLAST]; strong gust of wind 290n.

-blēað, *see* **hereblēað**

blīcan, *v.* (*1*), [BLIK]; shine. *p.t. pl.* **blicon** 159

blīðe, *adj.,* BLITHE, joyful. *nom. pl. m.* 583

blōd, *n. a-stem,* BLOOD 463; *dat. sg.* **blōde** 449

***blōdegesa,** *m. n-stem,* [BLOOD +]; terror of blood; *dat. sg.* **blōdegesan** 478n.

blōdig, *adj.,* BLOODY. *nom. pl. n.* **blōdige** 329, 573

-blyse, *see* **bǣlblyse**

bōcere, *m. ja-stem,* writer. *nom. pl.* **bōceras** 531n.

-boda, *see* **nȳdboda, siðboda, spelboda**

bodigean, *w.v.* (*2*), [BODE[1]]; announce 511

bōh, *m. a-stem,* [BOUGH]; shoulder. *dat. pl.* **bōgum** back (of horse) 171

gebohte, *see* **gebycgan**

bord, *n. a-stem,* [BOARD]; shield; *acc. sg.* 253. See also **wigbord**

bordhrēoða, *m. n-stem,* [BOARD +]; shield; *dat. sg.* **bordhrēoðan** 236. *nom. pl.* 159; *dat. pl.* 320

-bōsma, *see* **fāmigbōsma.**

bōt, *f. ō-stem,* [BOOT[1]]; reward; *acc. sg.* **bōte** 5, 583

brād, *adj.,* BROAD; *acc. sg. n. wk.* **brāde** 557

brǣdan, *w.v.* (*1b*), [BREDE[2]]; spread out. *p.t. pl.* **brǣddon** 132

brecan, *v.* (*5*), BREAK (through).
p.t. sg. **bræc** 251

bregdan, *v.* (*3*), [BRAID[1]]; move.
p.t. pl. **brūdon** 222

brengan, *w.v.* (*1c*), BRING.
p.t. sg. **brōhte** 259

brēost, *n.* *a-stem*, BREAST. *dat. pl.*
brēostum heart 269, 524

brēostnet, *n.* *ja-stem*, [BREAST +
NET[1]]; coat of mail; *acc. sg.* 236

brim, *n.* *a-stem*, [BRIM[1]]; sea *290*,
478. *nom. pl.*

brimypping, f. *ō-stem*, [BRIM[1] +];
sea-manifestation; *dat. sg.* **brim-
yppinge** *499*n.

-brōga, see **hǣðbrōga**

brōhte, see **brengan**

-brōðor, see **frēobrōðor**

brōðorgyld, n. a-stem, [BROTHER +
YIELD]; retribution for brothers;
acc. sg. 199

brūdon, see **bregdan**

brūn, *adj.*, BROWN. *acc. pl. m.* **brūne**
70

-bryne, see **fǣrbryne**

bryttian, *w.v.* (*2*), enjoy the use of.
pr. 3 pl. **bryttigað** 376

-būend, see **eorðbūend**

burgum (= **beorgum**), see **beorh**

burh, *f.* *monos. stem*, [BOROUGH];
city; *acc. sg.* 557; *dat. sg.* **byrig** 66.
dat. pl. **burgum** 511. See also
randburh

burhhleoðu, see **beorhhlið**

burhweard, *m. a-stem*, [BOROUGH +
WARD[1]]; guardian of the city.
acc. pl. **burhweardas** 39n.

burston, see **berstan**

gebycgan, *w.v.* (*1c*), [I-BYE]; pay
for. *p.t. pl. subj.* **gebohte** 151n.

bȳme, *f.* *n-stem*, [BEME]; trumpet
132. *nom. pl.* **bȳman** 159; *acc. pl.*
222; *dat. pl.* **bēmum** *216*. See
also **herebȳme, sigebȳme**

byrnan, *v.* (*3*), BURN[1], scorch. *pr.p.*
byrnende 111, *acc. sg. m.* **byr-
nendne** 73. *p.t. sg.* **barn** 115

C

-cald, see **sincald**

-calla, see **hildecalla**

camp, *m.* *a-stem*, [CAMP[1]]; battle;
inst. sg. **campe** 21

-candel, see **heofoncandel**

carlēas, *adj.*, CARELESS; reckless.
nom. pl. n. wk. **carlēasan** 166

cǣg, *f.* *jō-stem*, KEY[1]. *dat. pl.* **cǣgon**
525

-cēasega, see **wælcēasega**

cēne, *adj.*, KEEN; bold. *gen. pl.* **cēnra**
356. *superl. acc. sg. n.* **cēnost** 322

cennan, *w.v.* (*1a*), [KEN[2]]; beget,
bring forth. *p.t. sg.* **cende** 356

cēosan, *v.* (*2*), CHOOSE. *p.t. pl.* **curon**
243

cigean, *w.v.* (*1b*), summon 219

cinberg, f. *ō-stem*, [CHIN +
BERGH]; chin-guard (on helmet);
acc. sg. **cinberge** 175

-cir, see **sǣcir**

cist, *f.* *i-stem*, (picked) company.
gen. pl. **cista** 229, 230. See also
gūðcyst, herecist

-clamm, see **fērclamm**

cnēoriss, *f.* *jō-stem*, generation.
dat. pl. **cnēorissum** 3

-cnēow, see **frumcnēow**

cnēowmǣg, *m.* *a-stem*, [+ MAY[2]];
kinsman. *nom. pl.* **cnēowmāgas**
185; *gen. pl.* **cnēo(w)māga** 21,
318, 435

cnēowsibb, f. *jō-stem*, [+ SIB[2]];
nation; *acc. sg.* **cnēowsibbe** 356

cniht, *m.* *a-stem*, [KNIGHT]; boy;
acc. sg. 406

-colu, see **heofoncolu**

cōm(-), see **cuman**

corðor, *n.* *a-stem*, troop; *dat. sg.*
corðre 191, 466

cræft, *m.* *a-stem*, [CRAFT]; power;
acc. sg. 245; *inst. sg.* **cræfte** in *ealle
cræfte* by any skill 84, 437. *dat. pl.*
cræftum 30

cringan, *v.* (*3*), [CRINGE]; fall
dead. *p.t. pl.* **crungon** 482

cuman, *v.* (*4*), COME. *pr. 3 sg.* (*fut.*)
cymeð *540. p.t. sg.* **c(w)ōm** 91,
202, 417, 508, *pl.* **cōmon** 341;
sg. subj. **cōme** 475

cumbol, *n. a-stem,* standard. *nom. pl.*
175

cunnan, *pret. pr.* (*3*), *CAN*[1]; know.
pr. 3 pl. **cunnon** 373, (*fut.*) be
able (to) 436. *p.t. sg.* **cūðe** 351,
pl. **cūðon** 28, 82

cunnian, *w.v.* (*2*) *w. gen.,* [CUN];
make trial of. *p.t. sg.* **cunnode**
421

curon, see **cēosan**

cūð, *adj.,* [COUTH]; familiar 191;
gen. sg. n. **cūðes** famous 230. See
also **folccūð, uncūð**

cwealm, *mn. a-stem,* [QUALM[1]];
death; *dat. sg.* **cwealme** 469

cwēn, *f. i-stem,* QUEEN, wife. *dat. pl.*
cwēnum 512

cwōm, see **cuman**

*****cwyldrōf,** *adj.,* brave in scaveng-
ing. *nom. pl. n.* 166n.

cyme, *m. i-stem,* [*COME*[1]]; ap-
proach; *acc. sg.* 179

cymeð, see **cuman**

cynerice, *n. ja-stem,* [KINRICK];
kingdom. *acc. pl.* **cynericu** 318

cyning, *m. a-stem,* KING 141, 175,
390, (of God) 9, 421. *nom. pl.*
cyningas 185, 191, 466. See also
**eorðcyning,   Heofoncyning,
segncyning, Wuldorcyning**

cyn(n), *n. ja-stem,* KIN[1]; race 29, 145,
tribe 310, 351; *acc. sg.* 14, 198,
265 etc.; *gen. sg.* **cynnes** 435,
family 227; *dat. sg.* **cynne** tribe
351.   See   also   **eorðcynn,
fæderyncynn,   frumcyn,
wǣpnedcynn**

cyrm, *m. i-stem,* [CHIRM]; clamour
107, *466*

cyrman, *w.v.* (*1b*), [CHIRM]; cry
out. *p.t. pl.* **cyrmdon** 462

gecȳðan, *w.v.* (*1b*), [I-[1] + KITHE];
make known, reveal. *p.t. sg.* **ge-
cȳðde** 292, 406. *pp.* **gecȳðed** 420

D

dǣd, *f. i-stem,* DEED. *dat. pl.* **dǣdum**
542

*****dǣdlēan,**   *n.   a-stem,*   [DEED +
LEAN[1]]; recompense for actions;
acc. sg. 263

*****dǣdweorc,** *n. a-stem,* [DEED +
WORK]; action; *dat. sg.* **dǣd-
weorce** 576

dæg, *m. a-stem,* DAY 47, 542; *dat. sg.*
dæge in *to dæge þissum* today 263.
dat. pl. **dagum** by day 97. See
also **ǣrdæg, fyrndagas, lif-
dagas.** Cf. **āndæge**

*****dægsceld,**   *m.   a-stem,*   [DAY +
SHIELD]; day-shield   (cloud);
gen. sg. **dægsceldes** 79

dægweorc, *n. a-stem,* [DAYWORK];
day's work 519; *acc. sg.* 151;
gen. sg. **dægweorces** 315, 507

dægwōma,   *m.   n-stem,*   [DAY +];
dawn 344

dǣlan, *w.v.* (*1b*), DEAL; distribute
in shares 585. *pr. 3 pl.* **dǣlað**
share 539

gedǣlan, *w.v.* (*1b*), [I-[1] + DEAL];
divide, break off. *pp.* **gedǣled** 76,
207

dēad, *adj.,* DEAD. *acc. pl. m.* **dēade**
266; *gen. pl.* as *sb.* **dēadra** 41

dēað, *m. a-stem,* DEATH; *dat. sg.*
dēaðe 34, 448. See also **ǣrdēað,
meredēað**

*****dēaðdrepe,** *m. i-stem,* DEATH-
blow; *inst. sg.* 496

*****dēaðstede,** *m. i-stem,* [DEATH +
STEAD]; place of death; *dat. sg.*
590

dēawig, *adj.,* DEWY 344

dēawigfeðera,   *adj.,*   DEWY-
feathered. *nom. pl. m.* **dēawig-
feðere** 163

dēman, *w.v.* (*1b*) *w. dat.,* DEEM;
judge. *pr. 3 sg.* (*fut*) **dēmeð** 543

dēofolgyld, *n. a-stem,* [DEVIL +
YIELD]; idol. *nom. pl.* 47

dēop, *adj.,* DEEP; *nom. sg. n.* 507;

acc. sg. n. 315, 519. *superl. acc. sg. m.*
as *sb.* **dēopestan** 364

dēop, *n. a-stem,* DEEP; *acc. sg.* 281

dēor, *n.* *a-stem,* [DEER]; beast.
nom. pl. 166; *gen. pl.* **dēora** 322

dēore, *adj.,* DEAR¹; noble. *acc. pl. n.*
186

dēormōd, *adj.,* [DEAR² + MOOD¹];
brave. *gen. pl.* as *sb.* **dēormōdra**
97

dōm, *m. a-stem,* DOOM; ordinance;
dat. sg. **dōme** power 571. *acc. pl.*
dōmas 2; *gen. pl.* **dōma** 521. See
also **ealdordōm**

drēah, see **drēogan**

drēam, *m. a-stem,* [DREAM¹]; happi-
ness 532; *dat. sg.* **drēame** 547.
See also **seledrēam, woruld-
drēam**

gedrēas, see **gedrēosan**

gedreccan, *w.v.* (*1c*), [I-¹ +
DRETCH¹]; afflict. *p.t. pl.* **gedrecte**
501n. *pp.* **gedrecced** *34*

drenceflōd, *m. a-stem,* [DRENCH +
FLOOD]; deluge. *gen. pl.* **drence-
flōda** 364

drēogan, *v.* (*2*), [DREE]; endure.
p.t. sg. **drēah** 49

drēor, *m. a-stem,* blood; *dat. sg.*
drēore 151

drēosan, *v.* (*2*), [DRESE]; fall. *p.t. pl.*
druron 47

gedrēosan, *v.* (*2*), [I-¹ + DRESE];
perish. *p.t. sg.* **gedrēas** 500

-drepe, see **dēaðdrepe**

driht, *f. i-stem,* [DRIGHT¹] host. *nom.
pl.* **drihte** troops 496; *gen. pl.*
drihta 79

gedriht, *f. i-stem,* [I-¹ + DRIGHT¹];
troop 305. See also **sibgedriht**

Drihten, *m. a-stem,* [DRIGHTIN]; the
Lord, God 8, 25, 91 etc.; *acc. sg.*
547, 576

drihtfolc, *n. a-stem,* [DRIGHT¹ +
FOLK]; nation. *gen. pl.* **drihtfolca**
34, 322, 590

*drihtnēas, *m. pl. i-stem,* [DRIGHT¹

+]; dead troops; *dat.* **drihtnēum**
163n.

druron, see **drēosan**

drȳge, *adj.,* DRY. *nom. pl. m.* 283

gedrȳme, *adj.,* joyful. *superl.* **gedrȳ-
most** 79

dugoð, *f. ō-stem,* [DOUTH]; (troop of)
warriors 41, 91, 501, 547; *gen. sg.*
duguðe 228; *dat. sg.* **dugeðe** 183

E

ēac, *prep. w. dat.,* in addition to 245,
374, 381, etc.

ēad, *n. a-stem,* wealth; *acc. sg.* 339

ēadig, *adj.,* [EADI]; blessed. *acc. pl.
m.* **ēadige** 545; *gen. pl.* as *sb.*
ēadigra 4. See also **tirēadig**

eafera, *m. n-stem,* son; *acc. sg.*
eaferan 412

ēage, *n. n-stem,* EYE¹. *dat. pl.* **ēagan**
179, **ēagum** 278

eald, *adj.,* OLD, ancient; *acc. sg. f.*
ealde 408, *n. 186; dat. sg. m.* **alde**
495. *nom. pl. m.* **ealde** 285, as *sb.*
359; *acc. pl. m.* 586; *dat. pl.*
ealdum famous in history 33n.
compar. **yldra** ELDER; former 141

ealdordōm, *m. a-stem,* [ALDERDOM];
chief authority; *acc. sg.* 317, 335

*ealdwērig, *adj.,* [OLD +]; ac-
cursed/malicious as of old;
nom. sg. n. wk. **ealdwērige** 50n.

eall, *adj.,* ALL 88, 100, 214 etc.; *gen.
sg. m.* **ealles** 509, *n.* 144; *dat. sg.
n.* **eallum** 370; *inst. sg. m.* **ealle**
84, 437. *nom. pl. m.* **ealle** 190, 249
(as *sb.*), *n.* 573; *acc. pl. m.* 440;
dat. pl. m. **eallum** 261

*eallwundor, *n. a-stem,* [ALL +
WONDER]; miracle. *gen. pl.* **eall-
wundra** 579

earg, *adj.,* [ARGH]; cowardly *339*

earm, *adj.,* [ARM]; wretched. *gen. pl.*
as *sb.* **earmra** 534

ēca, *m. n-stem,* [EKE¹]; reinforce-
ment (of troops); *acc. sg.* **ēcan** 194

ēce, *adj.,* [ECHE]; everlasting 11,

538: *acc. sg. f.* 288. *nom. sg. m. wk.*
ēcea 273. *occ. pl. m.* **ēce** 474, 516, *f.* 370
ecg, *f. jō-stem,* cutting EDGE, blade 408. *dat. pl.* **ecgum** *413*
-edor, see **lyftedor**
efne, *adv.,* EVENly 76
***efngedǣlan,** *w.v.* (*1b*), [EVEN + DEAL]; divide equally. *p.t. sg.* **efngedǣlde** 95
eft, *adv.,* [EFT]; back 452, 508; later 389
***eftwyrd,** *f. i-stem,* [EFT + WEIRD]; Last Judgment 540
egesa, *m. n-stem,* fear. *nom. pl.* **eg(e)san** 136, 201, 491. See also **bēlegsa, blōdegesa, flōdegsa**
egesfull, *adj.,* [EISFUL]; terrifying 506
ellen, *n. a-stem,* [ELNE]; courage; *acc. sg.* 218
ende, *m. ja-stem,* END; *dat. sg.* 128, 267, 467
enge, *adj.,* narrow. *acc. pl. m.* 58
engel, *m. a-stem,* ANGEL 205. *gen. pl.* **engla** 380, 432, 559
ēode, see **gān**
***eoferholt,** *n. a-stem,* [EVER sb. + HOLT¹]; boar-spear. *acc. pl.* *157*n.
ēored, *n. a-stem,* cavalry; *acc. sg.* 157
eorl, *m. a-stem,* [EARL]; (noble) man, warrior 412. *nom. pl.* **eorlas** 293; *acc. pl.* 216; *gen. pl.* **eorla** 154, 261, 305, 353
eorp, *adj.,* dark; *acc. sg. n.* 194
eorðbūend, *m. nd-stem,* [EARTH¹ +]; dweller on earth, man. *nom. pl.* **eorðbūende** 84
eorðcyning, *m. a-stem,* [EARTH¹ + KING]; king on earth. *gen. pl.* **eorðcyninga** 392
eorðcynn, *n. ja-stem,* [EARTH¹ + KIN¹]; race of earth; *dat. sg.* **eorðcynne** 370
eorðe, *f. n-stem,* EARTH¹ 427; *acc. sg.* **eorðan** 76, 403, 437; *gen. sg.* 26, 430; *dat. sg.* 441

ēow, see **gē**
ēower, *poss. adj.,* YOUR 564
ēðel, *m. a-stem,* [ETHEL]; homeland; *gen. sg.* **ēðles** 18
ēðellēas, *adj.,* [ETHEL + -LESS]; lacking a homeland; *dat. sg.* **ēðellēasum** 139. *nom. pl. m.* **ēðellēase** 534
ēðelriht, *n. a-stem,* [ETHEL + RIGHT¹]; rightful homeland; *gen. sg.* **ēðelrihtes** 211
ēðfynde, *adj.,* [EATH +]; easy to find 580

F

fācn, *n. a-stem,* [FAKEN]; treachery; *dat. sg.* **fācne** 150
fāh, *adj.,* [FAW]; mottled. *nom. pl. m.* **fāge** 287n.
fāh, *adj.,* [FOE]; hostile 476, 542
fāmgian, *w.v.* (*2*), seethe. *p.t. sg.* **fāmgode** 482
***fāmigbōsma,** *adj.,* [FOAMY + BOSOM sb.]; foamy-breasted 494
fana, *m. n-stem,* [FANE¹]; standard, banner 248
-fara, see **nȳdfara**
faran, *v.* (*6*), FARE¹; go. *pr. 3 sg.* **fǣreð** mounts 282. *p.t. sg.* **fōr** 330, departed 48, marched 336, 347; *pl.* **fōran** proceeded 93, **fōron** 106, *340*
faru, *f. ō-stem,* [FARE¹]; journey; *acc. sg.* **fare** 555. See also **gārfaru, wǣgfaru**
fæder, *m. r-stem,* FATHER 353, 379, 415; *acc. sg.* 371; *gen. sg.* 446. *gen. pl.* **fædera** 29. See also **hēahfæder**
fæderæðelo, *n. pl. ja-stem,* [FATHER + ATHEL¹]; ancestry; *acc.* 361
fæderyncynn, *n. ja-stem,* [FATHER-KIN]; race of forefathers; *dat. sg.* **fæderyncynne** 560
fǣge, *adj.,* [FEY]; doomed to death 169n. *nom. pl. m. as sb.* 482; *acc. pl.*

m. 267; *dat. pl.* **fǣgum** 463.
compar. **fǣgra** 399. [See *SGG* iv (1962) 165–201]

fæger, *adj.,* FAIR; delightful; *acc. sg. m.* **fægerne** 567

fægre, *adv.,* FAIR; beautifully 297

fǣr, *m. a-stem,* [FEAR]; sudden disaster; *acc. sg.* 453

***fǣrbryne,** *m. i-stem,* [FEAR + BRUNE]; terrible heat; *dat. sg.* 72

fǣreð, see **faran**

fǣrspell, *n. a-stem,* [FEAR + SPELL[1]]; sudden terrifying news 135

***fǣrwundor,** *n. a-stem,* [FEAR + WONDER]; sudden awe-inspiring miracle. *gen. pl.* **fǣrwundra** 279

fæst, *adj.,* FAST, firm, fixed; *acc. sg. m.* (*predic.*) constant 140; *n.* 178, 537; *f.* **fæste** 423. *dat. pl.* **fæstum** 306. See also **ginfæst, sōðfæst, tirfæst, þrymfæst, wuldorfæst**

fæste, *adv.,* FAST; firmly 407, 470, closely 498

fæsten, *n. ja-stem,* (place of) confinement; *acc. sg.* 49n. *gen. pl.* **fæstena** (natural) strongholds 56. See also **sǣfæsten, weal(l)-fæsten**

-fæt, see **siðfæt**

fæðm, *m. a-stem,* [FATHOM]; embrace, grasp; *dat. sg.* **fæðme** 294, 527. *dat. pl.* **fæðmum** 75, 306. See also **heorufæðm, wælfæðm**

gefeallan, *v.* (*7*), [I-FALLE]; fall on. *p.t. sg.* **gefēol** 483, 492

fela, *n. u-stem indecl.,* [FELE]; much 29, *w. part. gen.* many 10, 21, 24 etc.

feld, *m. a-stem,* FIELD; open expanse of land. *nom. pl.* **feldas** 287

feldhūs, *n. a-stem,* [FIELD + HOUSE[1]]; tent. *gen. pl.* **feldhūsa** 85; *dat. pl.* **feldhūsum** 133, 223

feng, *m. i-stem,* [FENG]; grip 246

gefēon, *v.* (*5*), rejoice. *p.t. pl.* **gefēgon** *570*

fēond, *m. nd-stem,* FIEND; enemy *45,* 203; *acc. sg.* 32, 237. *gen. pl.* **fēonda** 22, 294, 562, 571; *dat. pl.* **fēondum** 64, 476

feor, *adv.,* FAR 1, 381

feorh, *n. a-stem,* life; *acc. sg.* (*coll.*) 17, 571; *gen. sg.* **fēores** 404; *dat. sg.* **feore** in *to widan feore* for evermore 548. *gen. pl.* **fēora** living beings 384, men 361; cf. **firas**

***feorhgebeorh,** *n. a-stem,* [+ I-[1] + BERGH]; saving of life; *acc. sg.* 369

***feorhlēan,** *n. a-stem,* [+ LEAN[1]]; reward for life saved; *acc. sg.* 150n.

fēorða, *adj.,* FOURTH; *nom. sg. n.* **fēorðe** 133, 310

fēran, *w.v.* (*1b*), [FERE[1]]; travel. *pr.p. acc. sg. n.* **fērende** 45

gefēran, *w.v.* (*1b*), [I-[1] + FERE[1]]; traverse 286

***fērclamm,** *m. a-stem,* [FEAR + CLAM[1]]; sudden terrifying clutch; *dat. sg.* **fērclamme** *119*. Cf. **fǣr(-)**

ferhð, *mn. a-stem; acc. sg.* life 119; *dat. sg.* **ferhðe** mind 355. Cf. **wideferð**

***ferhðbana,** *m. n-stem,* [+ BANE[1]]; soul-slayer, person who inflicts death 399n.

ferhðloca, *m. n-stem,* body. *acc. pl.* **ferhðlocan** 267

ferian, *w.v.* (*1a*), [FERRY]; convey. *p.t. pl.* **feredon** 375

gefeterian, *w.v.* (*2*), fetter. *pp.* **gefeterod** 470

fēða, *m. n-stem,* troop, tribe 312. *acc. pl.* **fēðan** 225, 266

***fēðegāst,** *m. a-stem,* [+ GHOST]; warlike spirit 476n.

-feðera, see **dēawigfeðera**

fiftig, *num.,* FIFTY *w. part. gen.* 229

findan, *v.* (*3*), FIND 189, seek out 454. *pr. 3 pl.* **findað** 520. *p.t. pl.* **fundon** 387

firas, *m. pl. ja-stem,* men; *gen.* **fira** 396. Cf. *pl.* of **feorh**

flāh, *adj.,* hostile, treacherous; *acc. sg. m.* **flāne** 237

flēon, *v.* (*2*), FLEE. *p.t. sg.* **flēah** 169; *pl.* **flugon** 203, 453

flōd, *m. a-stem,* FLOOD, mass of flowing water 482; *acc. sg.* 463. *acc. pl.* **flōdas** 362. See also **drenceflōd, mereflōd**

*****flōdblāc,** *adj.,* [FLOOD + BLOK(E)]; flood-pale 498n.

*****flōdegsa,** *m. n-stem,* [FLOOD +]; terror of the flood 447

*****flōdweard,** *m. a-stem,* [FLOOD + WARD[1]]; guardian of the flood (God) *494*

flōdweg, *m. a-stem,* [FLOOD+WAY[1]]; watery way, road of the sea; *dat. sg.* **flōdwege** 106n.

flota, *m. n-stem,* sailor 331. *nom. pl.* **flotan** 133, 223

flugon, see **flēon**

folc, *n. a-stem,* FOLK; people 50, 106, 169 etc.; *acc. sg.* 45, 72, 217; *dat. sg.* **folce** 88, 102, *inst.* 56. *nom. pl.* **folc** 350; *gen. pl.* **folca** 279, 340n., 446; *dat. pl.* **folcum** troops 502. See also **drihtfolc.** Cf. **ingefolc**

folccūð, *adj.,* [FOLK + COUTH]; famous 407

folcmægen, *n. a-stem,* [FOLK + MAIN[1]]; people's army (i.e. tribe) 347

folcriht, *n. a-stem,* [FOLKRIGHT]; authority; *acc. sg.* 22n.

*****folcswēot,** *n. a-stem,* [FOLK +]; host. *gen. pl.* **folcswēota** 578

*****folctalu,** *f. ō-stem,* [FOLK + TALE]; genealogy; *dat. sg.* **folctale** 379

*****folcgetæl,** *n. a-stem,* [FOLK + I-TEL]; number of the people; *acc. sg.* 229

folctoga, *m. n-stem,* [FOLK +]; commander 14. *acc. pl.* **folctogan** 254

folde, *f. n-stem,* [FOLD[1]]; earth, world; *gen. sg.* **foldan** 369, 429; *dat. sg.* 396, 537

folm, *f. ō-stem,* hand. *dat. pl.* **folmum** 237, 396, 407

for, *prep. w. dat.,* FOR; before 276, in front of 252, 314; because of 235, 576

fōr, fōran, sēe **faran**

foran, *prep. (in postponed position) w. dat.,* [FORNE]; in front of 172

forbærnan, *w.v.* (*1b*), [FORBURN]; consume (with fire). *p.t. sg.* (*subj.*) **forbærnde** 123. *pp. adj.* **forbærned** scorched 70

foregenga, *m. n-stem,* FORErunner (fire-pillar) 120

foreweall, *m. a-stem,* [FOREWALL]; bulwark. *nom. pl.* **foreweallas** 297

forgiefan, *v.* (*5*), [FORGIVE]; give. *p.t. sg.* **forgeaf** 11; *subj.* **forgēfe** 153

forgieldan, *v.* (*3*), [FORYIELD]; pay (for). *p.t. sg.* **forgeald** 315

forgietan, *v.* (*5*) *w. gen.,* FORGET. *p.t. pl.* **forgēton** 144

forhabban, *w.v.* (*3*), [FOR-[1] + HAVE]; restrain 488

forht, *adj.,* afraid. *compar. nom. pl.* **forhtran** 259. See also **unforht**

forhtian, *w.v.* (*2*), be terrified. *pr.p.* **forhtigende** 453

forma, *adj.,* [FORME]; first 22

forniman, *v.* (*4*), [FORNIM]; do away with. *p.t. sg.* **fornam** 289

fōron, see **faran**

*****forscūfan,** *v.* (*2*), [FOR-[1]+SHOVE]; head off. *p.t. sg.* **forscēaf** 204

forstandan, *v.* (*6*) *w. dat.,* [FORSTAND[1]]; stand in the way of. *p.t. sg.* **forstōd** 128

forð, *adv.,* FORTH (of space) 41, 156, 346, in front 103, into view 526; (of time) long 404, henceforth 562 and in *forð heonon* 287

forðgang, *m. a-stem,* [FORTHGANG]; advance; *gen. sg.* **forðganges** 470n.

*****forðhere,** *m. ja-stem,* [FORTH +

HERE]; advancing army; *dat. sg.*
forðherge 225

forþon, *adv.,* [FOR-THON]; accordingly 187, 367, consequently 200. *conj.* **forþām** for 508

forðweg, *m. a-stem,* [FORTH + WAY[1]]; onward journey; *acc. sg.* 129; *gen. sg.* **forðwegas** 248. *acc. pl.* **forðwegas** 32, 350

gefrǣge, *adj.,* famous. *superl. acc. sg. n.* **gefrǣgost** 394

gefrǣge, *n. ja-stem,* information; *dat. sg.* in **mine gefræge** as I have heard say *368*

gefrægn, see **gefrignan**

frǣton, see **fretan**

Frēa, *m. n-stem,* the Lord 19, 274

freca, *m. n-stem,* warrior. *acc. pl.* **frecan** 217

frēcne, *adj.,* bold. *nom. pl. n.* 203

frēcne, *adv.,* severely 38, daringly 571

fremman, *w.v.* (*1a*), [FREME]; commit. *p.t. pl.* **fremedon** 146

frēobearn, *n. a-stem,* [FREE + BAIRN]; noble son. *nom. pl.* 446

***frēobrōðor,** *m. r-stem,* [FREE + BROTHER]; own brother 338

frēod, *f. ō-stem,* goodwill; *dat. sg.* **frēode** *423*

freom, see **from**

frēomǣg, *m. a-stem,* [FREE+MAY[2]]; noble kinsman. *dat. pl.* **frēomāgum** 355

frēond, *m. nd-stem,* FRIEND. *nom. pl.* 178

freoðowǣr, *f. ō-stem,* [FRITH[1] +]; treaty of protection, covenant; *acc. sg.* **freoðowǣre** 306

fretan, *v.* (*5*) [FRET[1]]; devour, destroy. *p.t. pl.* **frǣton** 147

gefrignan, *v.* (*3*), [I-[1] + FRAYNE]; hear tell. *p.t. sg.* **gefrægn** 98, 285; *pl.* **gefrūnon** 360, 388. *pp.* **gefrigen** 1

frōd, *adj.,* experienced 29, 355

frōfor, *f. ō-stem,* [FROVER]; comfort;

acc. sg. **frōfre** 404; *dat. sg.* 88

from, freom, *adj.,* valiant 14, 54

from, *prep. w. dat.,* FROM 378

-fruma, see **lēodfruma**

frumbearn, *n. a-stem,* [+ BAIRN]; first-born child; *gen. sg.* **frumbearnes** 338. *gen. pl.* **frumbearna** 38

***frumcnēow,** *m. wa-stem,* first generation; *acc. sg.* 371

frumcyn, *n. ja-stem,* [+ KIN[1]]; origin; *acc. sg.* 361

frumsceaft, *f. ō-stem,* [FRUMSCHAFT]; created being. *gen. pl.* **frumsceafta** 274

gefrūnon, see **gefrignan**

-fugol, see **herefugol**

ful, *adj.,* FULL 451

fullēst, *m. i-stem,* [FILST]; help. *gen. pl.* **fullēsta** 555

fundon, see **findan**

fūs, *adj.,* [FOUS]; eager, ready 103, 248; *dat. sg. n.* (*uninflect.*) 129. *nom. pl. m.* **fūse** 196

fyl, *m. i-stem,* FALL[1], death (in battle); *acc. sg. 167*

gefyllan, *w.v.* (*1b*), [YFELL]; strike down. *pp.* **gefylled** 38

-fynde, see **ēðfynde**

fȳr, *n. a-stem,* FIRE 93, 537. See also **adfȳr, ligfȳr**

fyrd, *f. i-stem,* [FERI[1]]; army 54, 88, 223; *acc. sg.* 135, 156, 274, **fyrde** 62, 254; *dat. sg.* **fyrde** 331

fyrdlēoð, *n. a-stem,* [FERD[1] + LEOTH]; martial song; *acc. sg.* 578

***fyrdgetrum,** *n. a-stem,* [FERD[1] +]; troop of warriors 103; *acc. sg. 178*

fyrdwīc, *n. a-stem,* [FERD[1]+WICK[2]]; camp 129

fȳren, *adj.,* [FIREN]; fiery. *acc. pl. m.* **fȳrene** 120

fyrmest, *adv.,* [FOREMOST]; first 310

fyrndagas, *m. pl. a-stem,* [FERN a. + DAY]; days of old; *dat.* **fyrndagum** 560 fyrst, *adj.*, FIRST, foremost 399

fyrst, *m. i-stem*, [*FRIST*]; period, (space of) time 267; *acc. sg.* 208, 304; *dat. sg.* fyrste 189

gefȳsan, *w.v.* (*1b*), [I-FUSE]; make ready. *pp.* gefȳsed 54, 221

G

galan, *v.* (*6*), [GALE¹]; sing. *p.t. pl.* gōlan *578*

gamol, *adj.*, old. *nom. pl. m.* as *sb.* gamele 240

gān, *anom. v.*, GO. *pr. 3 sg.* (*fut.*) gǣð 526. *p.t. sg.* ēode 310, 335

-gang, see forðgang

gār, *m. a-stem*, [GARE¹]; spear; *gen. sg.* gāres 240. *nom. pl.* gāras 158

*gārbēam, *m. a-stem*, [GARE¹ + BEAM¹]; spear; *gen. sg.* gārbēames 246

gārberend, *m. nd-stem*, [GARE¹ +]; warrior. *gen. pl.* gārberendra 231

gārfaru, *f. ō-stem*, [GARE¹ + FARE¹]; martial company; *dat. sg.* gārfare 343

*gārhēap, *m. a-stem*, [GARE¹ + HEAP]; band of armed warriors; *dat. sg.* gārhēape 321

gārsecg, *m. ja-stem*, sea 490n.; *gen. sg.* gārsecges 281, 431; *dat. sg.* gārsecge *345*

*gārwudu, *m. u-stem*, [GARE¹ + WOOD¹]; spear; *acc. sg.* 325

gāst, *m. a-stem*, [GHOST]; spirit 169. *acc. pl.* gāstas 448, 545. See also fēðegāst and *Index* Hālig Gāst

gǣð, see gān

gē, *pron. pl.*, YE 259, 270, 272 etc.; *dat.* ēow YOU 266, 268, 271, 292

-geard, see lēodgeard, middangeard

gearwe, *f. pl. wō-stem*, *GEAR*, arms; *acc.* 59, 193

gēn, *adv.*, yet; in *þa gen* still 249

-genga, see foregenga

geofon, *n. a-stem*, sea 448; *gen. sg.* geofones 581

geoguð, *f. ō-stem*, YOUTH; *dat. sg.* geoguðe 235

gēomor, *adj.*, [YOMER]; sorrowful; *nom. sg. f. wk.* gēomre 431. *acc. pl. m.* gēomre 448

georne, *adv.*, [YERNE]; diligently 177

gere, *adv.*, [*YARE*]; very well 291

gēsne, *adj. w. gen.*, [GEASON]; lacking. *nom. pl. m.* 529

gif, *conj.*, IF 52, 242, 414 etc.

gihðu, *f. ō-stem*, sorrow. *dat. pl.* gihðum 535

*gin, *n. a-stem*, vastness 431

ginfæst, *adj.*, [+ FAST]; ample. *acc. pl. n. wk.* ginfæsten 525

-glæd, see ǣrglæd

-glēaw, see hreðerglēaw

gnorn, *adj.*, sad. *compar.* gnornra less optimistic 455

gōlan, see galan

gōd, *n. a-stem*, GOOD, benefit. *acc. pl.* 525

godweb, *n. ja-stem*, [GOD + WEB]; fine purple cloth; *acc. sg.* 588

gold, *n. a-stem*, GOLD; *acc. sg.* 588; *dat. sg.* golde 581

gram, *adj.*, [GRAME]; hostile. *nom. pl. m.* grame 144

grǣdig, *adj.*, GREEDY. *nom. pl. m.* grǣdige 162

grēne, *adj.*, GREEN; *acc. sg. m.* grēnne 312; *dat. sg.* grēne 281

grētan, *w.v.* (*1b*), GREET¹ 44n., match up to *246*. *p.t. pl.* grētton sought after 181, 233

grimhelm, *m. a-stem*, [+ HELM¹]; helmet (with visor); *acc. sg.* 174. *gen. pl.* grimhelma 330

gegrind, *n. a-stem*, [I-¹ +]; clash 330

grund, *m. a-stem*, GROUND, bottom (of the sea); *acc. sg.* 312, *503*. See also sǣgrund. Cf. ungrund

grymetian, *w.v.* (*2*), roar. *p.t. sg.* grymetode 408

gryre, *m. i-stem*, terror; *dat. sg.* 20,

490. See also **wælgryre, wēsten-gryre**

guma, *m. n-stem,* [GOME[1]]; man. *gen. pl.* **gumena** 174, 193

gūð, *f. ō-stem,* battle 158; *dat. sg.* **gūðe** 325

***gūðcyst,** *f. i-stem,* troop; *dat. sg.* **gūðcyste** 343

gūðfremmend, *m. nd-stem,* [+ *pr. p.* of *FREME v.*]; fighting man. *gen. pl.* **gūðfremmendra** 231

***gūðmyrce,** *m. pl. i-stem,* warlike border-dwellers; *acc.* 59

***gūðþrēat,** *m. a-stem,* [+ THREAT]; troop 193

gūðweard, *m. a-stem,* [+ WARD[1]]; leader 174

gyfan, *v.* (*5*), *GIVE* 263

-gyld, see **brōðorgyld, deofolgyld**

gyldan, *v.* (*3*), YIELD; repay 150

gylden, *adj.,* [GILDEN]; golden; *acc. sg. m.* **gyldenne** 321

gyllan, *v.* (*3*), YELL. *pr.p. adj.* **gyllende** *YELLING;* character-ised by shrieks 490n.

gylp, *mn. a-stem,* [YELP]; vow 455n.; *acc. sg.* 515

***gylpplega,** *m. n-stem,* [YELP + PLAY]; valorous combat; *acc. sg.* **gylpplegan** 240n.

gȳman, *w.v.* (*1b*), [YEME]; pay attention to, keep. *p.t. pl.* **gȳmdon** 140

***gyrdwite,** *n. ja-stem,* [YARD[2] + WITE[2]]; punishment inflicted through (Moses's) rod; *dat. sg.* 15n.

gystsele, *m. i-stem,* [*GUEST* +]; hall of visitors (the world); *acc. sg.* 535

gȳt, *adv.,* YET 235, still 520

H

habban, *w.v.* (*3*), *HAVE,* take hold of 218. *pr. 3 sg.* **hafað** 527. *p.t. sg.* **hæfde** 120, 208, 366. *Auxil. of p.t., pr. 3. sg.* **hafað** 556; *1 pl.*

habbað *1. p.t. sg.* **hæfde** 30, 37, 75 etc.; *pl.* **hæfdon** 64, 197, 238 etc.

hālig, *adj.,* HOLY 71; *acc. sg. m.* **hāligne** 392, *f.* **hālige** 357, 366, 388 etc., *n.* **hālig** 416; *gen. sg. m.* **hāliges** 96, as *sb.* 307, 385 (God). *dat. sg. f. wk.* **hālgan** 257, *n.* 74. *nom. pl. m.* **hālige** 89; *acc. pl. m.* 382, 569. *superl. acc. sg. n.* **hāligost** 394

***halswurðung,** *f. ō-stem,* [HALSE + WORTHING[1]]; necklace, torque. *acc. pl.* **halswurðunge** 582

hām, *adv.,* HOME 508

hām, *m. a-stem,* HOME[1]; *dat. sg.* **hāme** 457. *acc. pl.* **hāmas** 454

hand, *f. u-stem,* HAND 280; *acc. sg.* 262, 480, 486; *dat. sg.* 275, **handa** *582. nom. pl.* **handa** 43; *acc. pl.* 416

handlēan, *n. a-stem,* [HAND + LEAN[1]]; reward 19n.

handplega, *m. n-stem,* [HAND + PLAY]; fighting 327

***handrōf,** *adj.,* [HAND +]; strong-armed. *gen. pl.* as *sb.* **handrōfra** 247

handweorc, *n. a-stem,* [HAND-WORK]; handiwork 493

hār, *adj.,* [HOAR]; grey 118. *nom. pl. m.* **hāre** experienced 181, vener-able 241

hasu, *adj.,* silvery. *nom. pl. f.* **haswe** 284n.

hāt, *adj.,* HOT. *dat. sg. m. wk.* **hātan** 122. *dat. pl.* **hātum** 71

hāt, *n. a-stem,* heat; *dat. sg.* **hāte** 78

-hata, see **lēodhata**

-hāta, see **beodohāta**

hātan, *v.* (*7*), [HIGHT[1]]; com-mand. *p.t. sg.* **heht** *63,* 254, **hēt** 177

gehātan, *v.* (*7*), [I-[1] + HIGHT[1]]; promise. *p.t. sg.* **gehēt** 558

***hātwende,** *adj.,* [HOT +]; torrid; *acc. sg. m.* **hātwendne** 74

hæfde, hæfdon, see **habban**

hæft, *m. a-stem,* captivity 584

hægsteald, *mn. a-stem,* [*HAW*[1] +]; young warrior. *nom. pl.* 327n.

hægstealdman, *m. monos. stem,* [*HAW*[1] + + MAN[1]]; young warrior. *nom. pl.* **hægstealdmen** 192 -**hæl,** see **mūðhæl**

hæle(ð), *m. þ-stem,* [*HELETH*]; warrior. *nom. nom. pl.* 78, 376, 388; *acc. pl.* 63; *gen. pl.* **hæleða** 512; *dat. pl.* **hæleðum** 7, 252, 394, 468

hæs, *f. i-stem,* [*HEST*]; command, injunction. *dat. pl.* **hæsum** 385

*****hæðbrōga,** *m. n-stem,* HEATH-terror *118*n.

hæwen, *adj.,* [*HAW*]; blue; *nom. sg. f.* **hæwene** 477

hē, *pron. m.,* HE 12, 24, 30 etc., it 123n.; *acc.* **hine** 23, 180, 414; *gen.* **his** 9, 17, 27 etc.; *dat.* **him** 10, 16, 24 etc., *refl.* 183, 366, 409, 415. See also **hīe, hit**

hēaf, *m. a-stem,* lamentation 35

hēah, *adj.,* HIGH, lofty 468, 493, significant 19. *superl. acc. sg. n.* **hēahst** 394

hēah, *adv.,* on HIGH 461

hēahfæder, *m. r-stem,* [HIGH *a.* + FATHER]; patriarch. *gen. pl.* **hēahfædera** 357

*****hēahlond,** *n. a-stem,* [HIGH *a.* + LAND]; hill; *acc. sg.* 385

*****hēahtrēow,** *f. wō-stem,* [HIGH *a.* + TRUCE]; pledge, covenant; *acc. sg.* **hēahtrēowe** 388

*****hēahþegnung,** *f. ō-stem,*[HIGH *a.*+ THEINING]; high service; *dat. sg.* **hēahþegnunga** 96

hēahþungen, *adj.,* [HIGH *a.* + *pp.* of THEE[1]]; illustrious, noble 518

healdan, *v.* (*7*), *HOLD,* keep 177. *pr. 3. pl.* **healdeð** occupy 535. *p.t. 2 sg.* **hēolde** 422; *3 sg.* **hēold** 306, **hēald** contained 61n.

gehealdan, *v.* (*7*), [1-*HALD*]; keep,

observe. *pr. 2 pl.* **gehealdað** 561

healf, *f. ō-stem,* HALF; side. *gen. pl.* **healfa** 209

hēap, *m. a-stem,* HEAP; troop, band; *dat. sg.* **hēape** 192, 311. *acc. pl.* **hēapas** 382, 569. See also **gārhēap, mægenhēap, mōdhēap, wighēap**

heard, *adj.,* HARD; cruel 327

heaðorinc, *m. a-stem,* [+ RINK[1]]; warrior. *nom. pl.* **heaðorincas** 241

heaðowylm, *m. i-stem,* [+ *WALM*[1]]; battle-fervour, warlike feeling. *nom. pl.* **heaðowylmas** 148

hebban, *v.* (*6*), *HEAVE;* raise, lift up 99. *p.t. sg.* **hōf** 276; *pl.* **hōfon** 301, 575, *582*

hēdan, *w.v.* (*1b*) *w. gen.,* HEED; take charge of. *p.t. pl.* **hēddon** 584

heht, see **hātan**

hell, *f. jō-stem,* HELL; *dat. sg.* **helle** in *on helle* hellish 46n.

-**helm,** see **grimhelm, lyfthelm**

helpend, *m. nd-stem,* [HELPEND]; helper. *gen. pl.* **helpendra** 488n.

hēo, see **hīe**

heofon, *m. a-stem,* HEAVEN 427, divine power 46n.; *acc. sg.* sky 73. *dat. pl.* **heofonum** (w. sg. meaning) *161*, 376, 417 etc.

*****heofonbēacen,** *n. a-stem,* [HEAVEN + BEACON]; heavenly sign (fire-pillar) 107n.

heofoncandel, *f. jō-stem,* [HEAVEN +CANDLE]; heavenly candle (fire-pillar) 115n.

*****heofoncolu,** *n. pl. a-stem,* [HEAVEN + COAL]; scorching sun; *dat.* **heofoncolum** 71

Heofoncyning, *m. a-stem,* [HEAVEN-KING]; king of heaven (God); *dat. sg.* **Heofoncyninge** 410

heofonrice, *n. ja-stem,* [HEAVEN-RIC]; kingdom of heaven; *gen. sg.* **heofonrices** 486

heofontorht, *adj.*, [HEAVEN + TORHT]; bright in heaven 78
hēold(e), see **healdan**
heolfor, *mn. a-stem,* blood, gore; *dat. sg.* **heolfre** 450, 477
heolstor, *mn. a-stem,* [HOLSTER]; hiding-place; *acc. sg.* 115
heonon, *adv.*, [HEN]; henceforth 287
heora, see **hie**
*****heorawulf,** *m. a-stem,* [+ WOLF]; warrior. *nom. pl.* **heorawulfas** 181n.
heorte, *f. n-stem,* HEART. *dat. pl.* **heortan** 148
*****heorufæðm,** *m. a-stem,* [+ FATHOM]; hostile embrace, deadly clutch. *dat. pl.* **heorufæðmum** *505*
here, *m. ja-stem,* [HERE]; army, host 247, 498, 551; *gen. sg.* **her(i)ges** 13, 107, 234 etc.; *dat. sg.* **herge** *574. acc. pl.* **hergas** 260; *dat. pl.* **hergum** 276. See also **forðhere**
*****hereblēað,** *adj.*, [HERE+BLETHE]; cowardly. *nom. pl. m.* **hereblēaðe** 454
herebȳme, *f. n-stem,* [HERE + BEME]; trumpet. *acc. pl.* **herebȳman** 99
herecist, -cyst, *f. i-stem,* [HERE +]; troop. *nom. pl.* **herecyste** 301; *acc. pl.* **hereciste** 177, 257
*****herefugol,** *m. a-stem,* [HERE + FOWL]; bird of prey. *nom. pl.* **herefugolas** 162
hererēaf, *n. a-stem,* [HERE + REIF]; booty; *gen. sg.* **hererēafes** 584
herestrǣt, *f. ō-stem,* [HERE + STREET]; track, path. *nom. pl.* **herestrǣta** 284
hereþrēat, *m. a-stem,* [HERE + THREAT]; troop; *dat. sg.* **hereþrēate** 122. *nom. pl.* **hereþrēatas** 575
herewisa, *m. n-stem,* [HERE +]; leader of an army; *dat. sg.* **herewīsan** 323

*****herewōp,** *m. a-stem,* [HERE + WOP]; cry of an army. *gen. pl.* **herewōpa** 461
herg, *m. a-stem,* shrine. *nom. pl.* **hergas** 46n.
herian, *w.v.* (*1a*), [HERY]; praise. *pr. 3 pl.* (*fut.*) **herigað** 547. *p.t. pl.* **heredon** 576
her(i)ges, herge, hergas, hergum, see **here**
(ge)hēt, see **(ge)hātan**
-hete, see **tēonhete**
hettend, *m. nd-stem,* antagonist. *nom. pl.* 209
hīe, *pron. pl.*, they 29, 51, 59 etc., **hēo** 146, 587; *acc.* them 52, *refl.* 130; *gen.* **heora** 55, 60, 218n. etc., **hyra** 131, 135, 199; *dat.* **him** 19, 69, 93 etc., *refl.* 238
hiht, *m. i-stem,* [HIGHT³]; hope; *acc. sg.* 405
hild, *f. jō-stem,* battle; *acc. sg.* **hilde** 181, 505; *gen. sg.* 162; *dat. sg.* 241
hild, *m. i-stem,* protection; *acc. sg.* 569. Cf. **gehyld**
*****hildecalla,** *m. n-stem,* war-herald 252
*****hildespell,** *n. a-stem,* [+ SPELL¹]; song of battle; *dat. sg.* **hildespelle** 574
him, see **hē, hīe**
hine, his, see **hē**
hit, *pron. n.*, IT; *acc.* 571 (ref. to *feorh*)
*****hleahtorsmið,** *m. a-stem,* [LAUGHTER¹ + SMITH]; entertainer. *dat. pl.* **hleahtorsmiðum** 43
*****hlencan,** *f. pl. n-stem, LINK²*; coat of mail; *acc.* 218. See also **wælhlencan**
hlēo, *mn. wa-stem,* [LEE¹]; protection 79, *304*
hlēoðor, *n. a-stem,* voice 418
-hlēow, see **unhlēow**
hlifian, *w.v.* (*2*), tower. *p.t. pl.* **hlifedon** 89

-hliŏ, see **beorhhliŏ**

hlūd, *adj.*, LOUD 107; *acc. sg. f.* **hlūde** 276; *dat. sg. f. wk.* **hlūdan** 551. *acc. pl. f.* **hlūde** 575; *dat. pl. wk.* **hlūdan** 99

gehnēopan, *v.* (*2*) *w. dat.*, drag down, crush. *p.t. sg.* **gehnēop** *476*

-hof, see **mearchof**

hōf(on), see **hebban**

hold, *adj.*, [HOLD]; loyal, kind 19. See also **þeodenhold**

holm, *m. a-stem*, [HOLM¹]; sea 284, 450. See also **ȳŏholm**

holmig, *adj.*, [HOLM¹ + -Y¹]; of the sea. *dat. pl.* **holmegum** 118

holmweall, *m. a-stem*, [HOLM¹ + WALL¹]; wall of sea-water 468

-holt, see **eoferholt**

-hord, see **māŏmhord**

hordweard, *m. a-stem*, [HOARD¹ + WARD¹]; guardian of treasure, noble warrior. *gen. pl.* **hordwearda** 35, 512

horn, *m. a-stem*, HORN, trumpet 192

horsc, *adj.*, alert 13

hraŏe, *adv.*, [RATHE]; quickly 502

hrǣw, *n. a-stem*, corpse. *dat. pl.* **hrǣwum** 41

hrēam, *m. a-stem*, [REAM¹]; tumult 450

hrēopon, see **hrōpan**

-hrēoŏa, see **bordhrēoŏa, scyldhrēoŏa**

hrēŏ, *n. i-stem*, glory 316

hrēŏan, *w.v.* (*1b*), exult. *p.t. pl.* **hrēŏdon** 574

hreŏer, *m. a-stem*, heart; *dat. sg.* **hreŏre** 366

hreŏerglēaw, *adj.*, [+ GLEW]; prudent, wise 13

hrōf, *m. a-stem*, ROOF; *acc. sg.* 2̊98. *acc. pl.* **hrōfas** 572

hrōpan, *v.* (*7*), [ROPE²]; cry out, scream. *p.t. pl.* **hrēopon** *162*, 168

hryre, *m. i-stem*, [RURE]; death; *acc. sg.* 512; *dat. sg.* 35

hū, *adv.*, HOW 426; as *conj.* 25, 85, 89, 244

hund, *num.*, [HUND]; hundred. *acc. pl.* (*w. part. gen.*) 232

-hūs, see **feldhūs, mānhūs**

gehwā, *pron.* (*w. part. gen.*), [Y- + WHO]; each one; *acc.* **gehwone** 562; *gen.* **gehwæs** 361, *371*; *dat.* **gehwām** 4, 6, 108 etc.

hwæt, *pron. n.*, WHAT; *gen.* **hwæs** in *to hwæs* whither 192

hwæt, *interj.*, [WHAT]; listen! behold! 1, 278

-hwæt, see **mōdhwæt**

-hwearf, see **merehwearf**

hwearfian, *w.v.* (*2*), [WHARVE]; approach. *p.t. sg.* **hwearfode** 158

hwēop, see **hwōpan**

gehwilc, *pron. w. part. gen.*, EACH one 187, 230; *acc. m.* **gehwilcne** 521, *acc. n.* **gehwilc** 374; *gen.* **gehwylces** *538*. Cf. **hwylc**

hwilum, *adv.*, [WHILOM]; from time to time 170

hwīt, *adj.*, WHITE, gleaming. *acc. pl. f.* **hwīte** 301

gehwone, see **gehwā**

hwonne, *conj.*, WHEN 250, until the time when 472

hwōpan, *v.* (*7*), threaten. *p.t. sg.* **hwēop** 121, 448, 478

hwylc, *pron.*, [WHICH]; anyone 439. Cf. **gehwilc**

hwyrft, *m. i-stem*, course, way (of escape); *acc. sg.* 210. See also **ymbhwyrft**

hycgan, *w.v.* (*3*), be intent (on) 218

gehyld, *n. i-stem*, (I-¹ +]; keeping, protection; *acc. sg.* 382. Cf. **hild** *m.*

hȳnŏo, *f. ō-stem*, humiliation; *acc. sg.* 323

hyra, see **hīe**

hȳran, *w.v.* (*1b*) *w. dat.*, HEAR; obey. *p.t. sg.* (*prob.*) *subj.* **hȳrde** 410, *pl. subj.* 124

gehȳran, *w.v.* (*1b*), [YHERE]; HEAR, listen (to). *pr. 3 sg. subj.*

gehȳre 7. *p.t. pl.* **gehȳrdon** 222, 255

hyrde, *m. ja-stem,* [HERD²]; guardian 256

hyrnednebba, *m.n-stem,* [*HORNED* +]; horn-beaked one, raven *161*

gehyrwan, *w.v.* (*1b*), [I-¹ +]; despise. *p.t. pl.* **gehyrdon** 307

I

ic, *pron.,* I 98, 269, 280 etc.

in, *prep.,* IN, *w. acc.* 94, INTO 11, 234, 296 etc., going into 4, for 288; *w. dat.* 212, 439, 524, 560, among 122, 200, 244, 321, for 424

*ingefolc, *n. a-stem,* [IN-¹ + I-¹ + FOLK]; native people. *gen. pl.* **ingefolca** 142n.

*ingemen, *m. pl. monos. stem,* [IN-¹ + I-¹ + MAN¹]; native warriors, land-men 190n.

ingeþēod, *f. ō-stem,* [IN-¹ + I-¹ + THEDE]; native people. *acc. pl.* **ingeþēode** *444*n.

inlende, *adj.,* [IN-¹ +]; from within the land 136n.

is, see **bēon**

*īsernhere, *m. ja-stem,* [+ HERE]; mail-clad army. *dat. pl.* **īsern-hergum** 348

lūdisc, *adj.,* of Judah 312

L

gelād, *n. a-stem,* [I-¹ +]; path; *acc. sg.* 313. (*prob.*) *acc. pl.* 58

lāf, *f. ō-stem,* [LAVE¹]; what is left; *acc. sg.* **lāfe** heirloom (sword) 408; *dat. sg.* bequest 405, survivor 509. *acc. pl.* survivors 370. See also **sǣlāf, yrfelāf, ȳðlāf**

lāgon, see **licgan**

lagu, *m. u-stem,* [LAY¹]; sea-water 483

lagustrēam, *m. a-stem,* [LAY¹ + STREAM]; water. *acc. pl.* **lagu-strēamas** 367

land, *n. a-stem,* LAND; *acc. sg.* 40, 69,

445, 483; *gen. sg.* **landes** 128; *dat. sg.* **lande** 567. *nom. pl.* **land** 60; *acc. pl.* 57. See also **hēahlond, mearcland**

landmann, *m. monos. stem,* [LAND-MAN]; native inhabitant. *gen. pl.* **landmanna** 179n.

landriht, *n. a-stem,* [LAND-RIGHT]; right to the land (of Canaan); *acc. sg.* 354

lang, *adj.,* LONG¹-lasting; *acc. sg. m.* **langne** 53. *compar. acc. pl.* **len-gran** 532. See also **nihtlang, uplang**

lange, *adv.,* LONG 138, 558, for a long time 324. *compar.* **leng** 206, 264. *superl.* **lengest** for the longest time 424

langsum, *adj.,* [LONGSOME]; long-enduring; *acc. sg. m.* **langsumne** 6, 405

lār, *f. ō-stem,* LORE¹, teaching 268; *acc. sg.* **lāre** instruction 561, counsel 307. *dat. pl.* **lārum** 390

lāst, *m. a-stem,* [LAST¹]; track; *acc. sg.* in *on . . . last* behind 167, 337. See also **æflāst**

lāstweard, *m. a-stem,* [LAST¹ + WARD¹]; follower; *acc. sg.* pursuer 138, heir 400

lātþēow, *m. wa-stem,* [LATTEW]; guide; *acc. sg.* 104

lāð, *adj.,* [LOATH]; hateful 40, as *sb.* enemy 195; *acc. sg. m.* **lāðne** 138; *dat. sg. m.* as *sb.* **lāðum** enemy 195. *nom. pl. m.* as *sb.* **lāðe** 462; *gen. pl.* **lāðra** 57, as *sb.* 167; *dat. pl.* **lāðum** 179

gelāð, *adj.,* [I-¹ + LOATH]; hostile. *nom. pl. m.* as *sb.* **gelāðe** enemies 206

*lāðsīð, *m. a-stem,* [LOATH *a.* + SITHE¹]; hateful journey 44

lǣdan, *w.v.* (*1b*), LEAD¹. *pr. 3 sg.* **lǣdeð** 555, (*fut.*) 544. *p.t. sg.* **lǣdde** 54, 77; *pl.* **lǣddon** 194

gelǣdan, *w.v.* (*1b*), [I-¹ + LEAD¹];

lead. *p.t. sg.* **gelædde** 62, 367, 397, led out 384. *pp.* **gelæded** 568

læne, *adj.*, transitory 532; *gen. sg. n.* **længes** 268

lærig, *m. a-stem,* rim (of shield); *acc. sg.* 239n.

læs, *compar. adv.,* LESS; in **þȳ læs** *conj.* LEST 117

*****læst,** *f. i-stem,* performance; *dat. sg.* **læste** 308

læstan, *w.v.* (*1b*), LAST[1]; fare 244

gelæstan, *w.v.* (*1b*), [YLAST]; carry out 558

lætan, *v.* (*7*), LET[1]. *p.t. sg. subj.* **lēte** 52, 414

lēan, *n. a-stem,* [LEAN[1]]; requital 507; *acc. sg.* reward 315. See also **dædlēan, feorhlēan, handlēan**

-lende, see **inlende**

leng(est), see **lange**

lengran, see **lang**

lēo, *m. n-stem, LION*; *acc. sg.* **lēon** *321*

-leoda, see **sǣleoda**

lēode, *m. pl. i-stem,* [LEDE]; people 90, 152, 445; *acc.* 44, 70; *gen.* **lēoda** 12, 183, 228; *dat.* **lēodum** 277, 405

lēodfruma, *m. n-stem,* [LEDE + FRUME]; founder of the people, leader 354

lēodgeard, *m. a-stem,* [LEDE + YARD[1]]; territory; *acc. sg.* 57

lēodhata, *m. n-stem,* [LEDE +]; persecutor of the people 40

lēodmægen, *n. a-stem,* [LEDE + MAIN[1]]; people's army; *gen. sg.* **lēodmægnes** 167, 195; *dat. sg.* **lēodmægne** *128*

*****lēodscearu,** *f. ō-stem,* [LEDE + SHARE[3]]; nation; *dat. sg.* **lēodsceare** 337

lēodscipe, *m. i-stem,* [LEDE + -SHIP]; nation; *dat. sg.* 244

lēodweras, *m. pl. a-stem,* [LEDE + WERE[1]]; people; *dat.* **lēodwerum** 110

*****lēodwerod,** *n. a-stem,* [LEDE + WERED]; people; *acc. sg.* 77

lēof, *adj.,* [LIEF]; beloved 12, 354, 355; *gen. sg. m.* **lēofes** 53, as *sb.* loved one 308, 337. *compar. acc. pl. m.* **lēofran** 409. *superl.* **lēofost** 279; *acc. sg. n.* 384

lēoht, *adj.,* LIGHT[2], bright 251. *nom. pl. n.* 90

lēoht, *n. a-stem,* LIGHT 546

lēoma, *m. n-stem,* [LEAM[1]]; ray of light, flame. *nom. pl.* **lēoman** 112

lēoð, *n. a-stem,* [LEOTH]; song 308. See also **æfenlēoð, fyrdlēoð, wīglēoð**

-lēst, see **fullēst**

lēte, see **lætan**

licgan, *v.* (*5*), LIE[1]. *p.t. pl.* **lāgon** 458, 589

*****licwund,** *f. ō-stem,* [LICH + WOUND]; wound; *gen. sg.* **licwunde** 239

līf, *n. a-stem,* LIFE 546; *acc. sg.* 434; *gen. sg.* **līfes** 5, 104, 268, 523; *dat. sg.,* **līfe** 570

līfdagas, *m. pl. a-stem,* [LIFE-DAY]; life; *acc.* 409; *dat.* **līfdagum** 424

Liffrēa, *m. n-stem,* [LIFE +]; the Lord; *acc. sg.* **Liffrēan** 271

lifian, *w.v.* (*orig. 3*), LIVE[1]. *pr.p., dat. sg. m.* **lifigendum** 324; *nom. pl. m.* **lifigende** 264; *gen. pl. as sb.* **lifigendra** 6, 277. *p.t. sg.* **lifde** 383

līfweg, *m. a-stem,* [LIFE + WAY[1]]; way of life; *acc. sg.* 104n.

līg, *m. i-stem,* [LEYE]; fire, flame; *dat. sg.* **līge** 110, 122, 400

*****līgfȳr,** *n. a-stem,* [LEYE + FIRE]; flaming fire (of the sun) 77

lind, *f. ō-stem,* [LIND]; (wooden) shield; *gen. sg.* **linde** 239. *acc. pl.* **linde** 301; *dat. pl.* **lindum** 251, in *under lindum* bearing shields 228

lindwiga, *m. n-stem,* [LIND + WYE[1]]; warrior. *nom. pl.* **lindwigan** *570*

linnan, *v. (3) w. dat.,* [LIN]; part
from. *p.t. pl.* **lunnon** 497
liss, *f. jō-stem,* [LISS]; kindness.
gen pl. **lissa** grace 271, 546
lixan, *w.v. (1b),* gleam 157. *p.t. pl.*
lixton 125, 175
-loca, see **ferhŏloca**
locc, *m. a-stem,* LOCK[1] (of hair), tress.
acc. pl. **loccas** 120
lōcian, *w.v. (2),* LOOK. *pr. 2 pl.*
lōciaŏ 278
lunnon, see **linnan**
lust, *m. a-stem,* LUST; desire; *acc. sg.*
53
gelȳfan, *w.v. (1b),* [I-[1] + LEVE[1]];
grant. *pp.* **gelȳfed** 556
lyft, *mf. i-stem,* [LIFT[1]]; air, sky 431,
462, 477, 483; *acc. sg.* 74
*****lyftedor,** *m. a-stem,* [LIFT[1] +
EDDER]; air-rcof. *acc. pl.* **lyft-
edoras** clouds 251n.
lyfthelm, *m. a-stem,* [LIFT[1]+HELM[1]];
cloud; *dat. sg.* **lyfthelme** 60n.
*****lyftwundor,** *n. a-stem,* [LIFT[1] +
WONDER]; miracle of the air.
nom. pl. 90
lyftwynn, *f. jō-stem,* [LIFT[1] + WIN[2]];
joy in heaven. *acc. pl.* **lyftwynna**
532
lȳt, *n. i-stem indecl. w. part. gen.,*
[LITE[4]]; few 42

M

mā, *sb. indecl.,* [MO]; more; *acc.* 530
mādmas, see **māŏm**
maga, *m. n-stem,* son; *acc. sg.* **magan**
397, 414
māga, māgum, see **mǣg**
magan, *pret. pr.,* MAY[1]; can. *pr. 3
sg.* **mæg** 427, *subj.* **mæge** 440; *pl.*
429. *p.t. sg.* **mihte** 189, *246; pl.*
mihton 114, 206, 235, 488,
meahton 83
magorǣswa, *m. n-stem,* leader *55,*
102; *dat. sg.* **magorǣswum** 17
mān, *adj.,* [MAN[2]]; false. *dat. pl.*
mānum 149

*****mānhūs,** *n. a-stem,* [MAN[2] +
HOUSE[1]]; place of wickedness
(hell); *acc. sg.* 536
manig, *adj.* as *sb.* MANY. *nom. pl. m.*
monige 255; *dat. pl.* **manegum**
489, 543, **mænegum** 553
mann, *m. monos. stem,* MAN[1]; *gen. sg.*
mannes 426. *nom. pl.* **men** 82,
373, 377; *acc. pl.* 286; *gen. pl.*
manna 57, 143, 173 etc. See also
**hægstealdman, landmann, sǣ-
mann, wrǣcmon.** Cf. **ingemen**
mānsceaŏa, *m. n-stem,* [MAN[2] +
SCATHE]; persecutor. *acc. pl.*
mānsceaŏan 37n.
māra, *compar. adj.,* MORE; greater;
acc. sg. m. **māran** further 210;
gen. sg. f. 426, *n.* 215
māŏ, see **miŏan**
māŏm, *m. a-stem,* [MADME]; treas-
ure. *acc. pl.* **madmas** 586; *dat. pl.*
māŏmum 143
*****māŏmhord,** *mn. a-stem,* [MADME +
HOARD[1]]; treasure-hoard. *gen. pl.*
māŏmhorda 368
mǣg, *m. a-stem,* [MAY[2]]; kinsman.
gen. pl. **māga** 17; *dat. pl.* **māgum**
52. See also **cnēowmǣg, frēo-
mǣg.** Cf. **sibgemǣg**
mǣgburh, *f. monos. stem,* [MAY[2] +
BOROUGH]; family; *acc. sg.* people
55. *acc. pl.* **mǣgburge** genealogy
360; *gen. pl.* **mǣgburga** tribes
352
mǣg(e), see **magan**
mǣgen, *n. a-stem,* MAIN[1]; (1)
strength 242; *acc. sg.* 131; *gen. sg.*
mǣgnes 67n., 245. (2) troop,
army 101, 210, 226 etc.; *gen. sg.*
mǣgenes 215. See also **beadu-
mǣgen, folcmǣgen, lēodmǣ-
gen, þēodmǣgen**
*****mǣgenhēap,** *m. a-stem,* [MAIN[1] +
HEAP]; powerful troop. *dat. pl.*
mǣgenhēapum 197
mǣgenrōf, *adj.,* [MAIN[1] +]; power-
ful 275

mægenþrēat, *m. a-stem*, [MAIN[1] + THREAT]; powerful troop. *acc. pl.* **mægenþrēatas** 513

mægenþrymm, *m. ja-stem*, [MAIN[1] + THRUM[1]]; power. *gen. pl.* **mægenþrymma** 541; *dat. pl.* **mægenþrymmum** 349

mægenwīsa, *m. n-stem*, [MAIN[1]+]; leader (God) 554

mǣgwine, *m. i-stem*, [MAY[2] + WINE[2]]; kinsman. *dat. pl.* **mǣgwinum** 146, 314

mǣnegum, see **manig**

mǣre, *adj.*, [MERE[1]]; famous, renowned 47, 102, 349. *superl. acc. sg. n.* **mǣrost** 395

mǣst, *adj. superl.*, *MOST*; greatest *nom. sg. m.* 349, 461, 541, 555, as *sb.* 465, *n. as sb.* 34, 85, 322 etc.; *acc. sg. n.* 395, *as sb.* 368, 511; *dat. sg. m. (uninflect.)* 500, *n. as sb.* **mǣste** 67

mǣst, *adv. superl.*, *MOST*; best 360

mǣstrāp, *m. a-stem*, [MAST[1] + ROPE[1]]; halyard. *acc. pl.* **mǣstrāpas** 82

mǣton, see **metan**

mēagollice, *adv.*, [+ -LY[2]]; earnestly 528

meahton, see **magan**

mearc, *f. ō-stem*, [MARK[1]]; borderland; *acc. sg.* 160

mearchof, *n. a-stem*, [MARK[1] +]; borderland dwelling. *acc. pl.* **mearchofu** 61

mearcland, *n. a-stem*, [MARK[1] + LAND]; borderland. *dat. pl.* **mearclandum** 67

mearcweard, *m. a-stem*, [MARK[1] + WARD[1]]; guardian of the (border)-land. *nom. pl.* **mearcweardas** 168n.

mearcþrēat, *m. a-stem*, [MARK[1] + THREAT]; army; *dat. sg.* **mearcþrēate** 173

mearh, *m. a-stem*, horse. *gen. pl.* **mēara** 171

mēce, *m. ja-stem*, sword; *dat. sg.* 414, 495

meltan, *v. (3)*, MELT[1], dissolve. *p.t. pl.* **multon** 485

men, see **mann**

men(i)geo, menio, *f. ō-stem*, multitude 48, 334, 554; *acc. sg.* 205

mēowle, *f. n-stem*, woman 580

mere, *m. i-stem*, MERE[1]; sea 300, 459

meredēað, *m. a-stem*, [MERE *sb.*[1] + DEATH]; death at sea 513. *gen. pl.* **meredēaða** 465

mereflōd, *m. a-stem*, [MERE *sb.*[1] + FLOOD]; surging sea; *gen. sg.* **mereflōdes** 504

merehwearf, *m. a-stem*, [MERE *sb.*[1] + WHARF[1]]; sea-shore; *dat. sg.* **merehwearfe** 517

merestrēam, *m. a-stem*, [MERE *sb.*[1] + STREAM]; sea 210, waters of the sea 469; *gen. sg.* **merestrēames** 489

meretorht, *adj.*, [MERE *sb.*[1] + TORHT]; bright from the sea *346*

meretorr, *m. a-stem*, [MERE *sb.*[1] + TOWER[1]]; tower of sea-water. *nom. pl.* **meretorras** 485

mēring, *f. ō-stem*, [MERING]; borderland. *gen. pl.* **mēringa** *62*

mersc, *m. a-stem*, MARSH; *acc. sg.* 333

metan, *v. (5)*, [METE[1]]; mark out 92, 104. *p.t. pl.* **mǣton** traversed 171

meteþegn, *m. a-stem*, [MEAT + THANE[1]]; steward. *nom. pl.* **meteþegnas** 131

Metod, *m. a-stem*, God 52, *414*, 479; *gen. sg.* **Metodes** 102, 530

meðel, *n. a-stem*, speech; *acc. sg.* 255

meðelstede, *m. i-stem*, [+ STEAD]; meeting-place; *dat. sg.* 397, 543

micel, *adj.*, [MICKLE]; great *nom. sg. m.* 564, *f.* 554, *n.* 334; *gen. sg. (adv.)* **miceles** MUCH 143. *dat. sg. f. wk.* **miclan** 275

mid, *prep.*, [MID[1]]; *w. acc.* with 9, 416, 486; *w. dat.* with 66, 86, 206 etc., together with 56, 363, 502, through 21

midd, *adj.*, MID; middle of; *dat. sg. f.* **middere** 37. *dat. pl.* **middum** 168

middangeard, *m. a-stem*, [MIDDEN-ERD]; world; *acc. sg.* 2, 48, 286, 541

miht, *f. i-stem*, MIGHT; power; *acc. sg.* 9. *dat. pl.* **mihtum** 550

mihte, mihton, see **magan**

mihtig, *adj.*, MIGHTY 152, 205, 262 etc. *nom. sg. m.* as *sb.* **Mihtiga** 485. *compar.* **mihtigra** 504

****mihtmōd**, *n. a-stem*, [MIGHT *sb.* + MOOD[1]]; strong passion. *nom. pl.* 149

milde, *adj.*, MILD; kind. *superl.* **mildost** 550

milpæð, *m. a-stem*, [MILE[1] + PATH]; track. *acc. pl.* **milpaðas** 171

milts, *f. jō-stem*, [MILCE]; kindness, favour; *acc. sg.* **miltse** 292. *gen. pl.* **miltsa** 530

min, *poss. adj.*, MY; *acc. sg. f.* **mine** 262; *dat. sg. n.* 368

missenlic, *adj.*, [+ -LY[1]]; diverse. *compar. gen. pl.* **missenlicra** 373

missēre, *n.* ? *ja-stem*, half-year. *gen. pl.* **missēra** 49

-mist, see **wælmist**

miðan, *v.* (1), [MITHE]; remain concealed. *p.t. sg.* **māð** 519

mōd, *n. a-stem*, [MOOD[1]]; spirit 154, 245; *acc. sg.* will 480, 489; *gen. sg.* **mōdes** resolve 305; heart 98; *dat. sg.* **mōde** 226, 536. *dat. pl.* **mōdum** minds, souls 528. See also **mihtmōd**. Cf. **anmōd, dēormōd**

mōder, *f. r-stem*, MOTHER; *acc. sg.* 371

mōdgian, *w.v.* (2), rage. *p.t. sg.* **mōdgode** 459n., **mōdgade** in *mōdgade æfter* followed boldly 331

****mōdhēap**, *m. a-stem*, [MOOD[1] +

HEAP]; bold troop. *dat. pl.* **mōd-hēapum** 242

mōdhwæt, *adj.*, [MOOD[1] + WHAT[2]]; brave-hearted. *nom. pl. m.* **mōd-hwate** 124

mōdig, *adj.*, [MOODY]; high-spirited, valiant, noble 55, 275, raging (of sea) 469n.; *gen. sg. m.* as *sb.* **mōdiges** 255, 553; *dat. sg. m.* **mōdgum** 17. *nom. pl. m.* **mōdige** 131, 327, as *sb.* 465n.; *gen. pl.* as *sb.* **mōdigra** 101, 300

****mōdwǣg**, *m. i-stem*, [MOOD[1] + WAW[1]]; wave (representing God's will). *gen. pl.* **mōdwǣga** 500n.

monige, see **manig**

mōr, *m. a-stem*, MOOR[1], wilderness 61

morgen, *m. a-stem*, MORNing 346; *loc. sg.* in *on morgen* early one morning 98

morðor, *n. a-stem*, MURDER; *acc. sg.* 146

mōtan, *pret. pr.* (6), [MOTE[1]]; be able (to). *pr. 3 pl.* (*fut.*) **mōton** 264. *p.t. sg.* **mōste** 510; *pl.* **mōston** 240

multon, see **meltan**

gemunan, *pret. pr.* (4), [I-MUNE]; heed. *p.t. pl.* **gemundon** 220

murnan, *v.* (3), MOURN[1], be anxious. *pr. 3 pl.* **murnað** 536

****mūðhǣl**, *f. ō-stem*, [MOUTH + HEAL]; salvation by word of mouth; *acc. sg.* 553

-mynd, see **wurðmynd**

gemyndig, *adj.*, [I-[1] + MINDY]; mindful (of) 549

gemyntan, *w.v.* (1b), [I-MUNTE]; resolve. *pp.* **gemynted** 197

-myrce, see **gūðmyrce**

N

nacud, *adj.*, NAKED 475n.

nāhton, see **āgan**

nalles, *adv.*, NOT at ALL 307

genam, see **geniman**

nama, *m. n-stem,* NAME; *acc. sg.*
naman 27, 381
genāp, see **genipan**
nǣgan, *w.v.* (*1b*), address. *p.t. sg.*
nǣgde 23
genǣgan, *w.v.* (*1b*), approach. *p.t.*
pl. **genǣgdon** 130. *pp.* **genǣged**
attacked *169*
nǣs, see **bēon**
ne, *neg. adv.,* [NE]; not 28, 82, 114
etc.
nē, *conj.,* [NE[1]]; nor 83, 238, 456
nēah, *adv.,* NIGH; near(by) 1, 114,
381. *compar.* **nēar** NEAR[1]; nearer
220, 308
nēah, *prep. w. dat.,* NIGH; near 250
nearu, *f. wō-stem,* difficulty. *nom. pl.*
nearwe 68
-nebba, see **hyrnednebba**
nēosan, *?s.v.* (*2*), seek out 475
neowol, *adj.,* [NUEL]; prone, low-
lying. *nom. pl. m.* **neowle** 114
*****nēp,** *adj.,* [NEAP]; without power
(of) 470n.
nett, *n. ja-stem,* NET[1]; *dat. sg.* **nette**
74. See also **brēostnet, wælnet**
genēðan, *w.v.* (*1b*), risk. *p.t. pl.*
genēðdon 571
nigoða, *adj., NINTH* 378
niht, *f. monos. stem,* NIGHT; *dat. sg.*
37. *occ. pl.* 63; *dat. pl.* **nihtum**
97, 168
nihtlang, *adj.,* NIGHT-LONG; lasting
all night; *acc. sg. m.* **nihtlangne**
208
nihtscua, *m. n-stem,* [NIGHT +];
shadow at night. *nom. pl.* **niht-
scuwan** 114
*****nihtweard,** *m. a-stem,* [NIGHT +
WARD[1]]; night guardian (fire-
pillar) 116
geniman, *v.* (*4*), [I-[1] + NIM]; take.
p.t. sg. **genam** 406
genipan, *v.* (*1*), grow dark. *p.t. sg.*
genāp 455
niwe, *adj.,* NEW 116n. *acc. sg. m. wk.*
niwan 381. *acc. pl. m.* **niwe** 362

geniwian, *w.v.* (*2*), (I-[1] + NEW];
renew. *pp.* **geniwad** 35
nō, *adv.,* by *NO*[2] means 399
*****norðweg,** *m. a-stem,* [NORTH +
WAY[1]]; northerly track. *acc. pl.*
norðwegas 68
nū, *adv.,* NOW 539, 558. *conj.* NOW
(that) 295, 421, 531. *correl.* now . . .
now that 278/*280*
nȳd, *f. i-stem,* NEED; necessity; *dat.
sg.* as *adv.* **nȳde** 116. See also
onnied
genȳdan, *w.v.* (*1b*), [I-[1] + NEED[1]];
force. *p.t. pl.* **genȳddon** 68
*****nȳdboda,** *m. n-stem,* [NEED +
BODE[1]]; messenger of unavoidable
distress 475
*****nȳdfara,** *m. n-stem,* [NEED +];
fugitive, exile 208
nymðe, *conj.,* if . . . not 124, unless
439

O

of, *prep. w. dat.,* OF; from 155, 269,
294 etc., from among 170
ofer, *prep.,* OVER *w. acc.* 312, 318,
333, etc., past 239, through 61,
throughout 2, 48, 286 etc., to
257; *w. dat.* 112, 222, 345, above
110, 117, 127 etc., through 80,
concerning 163
oferbrǣdan, *w.v.* (*1b*), [OVER-
BREDE]; cover over. *p.t. sg.* **ofer-
brǣdde** 73
ofercuman, *v.* (*4*), OVERCOME, sub-
due. *p.t. sg.* **ofercōm** 21
oferfaran, *v.* (*6*), [OVERFARE]; pass
by. *p.t. sg.* **oferfōr** 56
ofergangan, *v.* (*7*), [OVERGANG];
subdue. *pr. 2 pl.* (*fut.*) **ofer-
gangað** 562
oferlīðan, *v.* (*1*), [OVER- + LITHE[1]];
travel over. *p.t. sg.* **oferlāð** 362
*****oferteldan,** *v.* (*3*), [OVER- +];
cover. *pp.* **ofertolden** 81n.
ofest, *f. ō-stem,* haste 293; *dat. sg.*

ofste 223. *dat. pl.* as *adv.* **ofstum** quickly 282

oft, *adv.*, OFTEN 191

ōht, *f. ō-stem*, hostile pursuit 136

on, *adv.*, ON down 491

on, *prep.*, ON, *w. acc.* 32, 129, 218, 350, onto 68, 386, to 59, 135, in 167, 199, 337 (1st) etc., into *283*, 311 (1st), 319 etc., along 313 (displaced), under 569, from 229, at 216, 278 (displaced), with 53, in accordance with 186, 587; *w. dat.* 209, 302, 441 (1st) etc., to 556 (postposited), in 8, 46, 67 etc., among 192, 450, 577, at 189, 543

on *pr. 1 sg.*, see **unnan**

onbrinnan, *v.* (*3*), [ON-1 + BURN1]; kindle. *p.t. sg.* **onbran** 398

onbūgan, *v.* (*2*) *w. dat.*, [ONBOW]; bow down (to). *p.t. pl.* **onbugon** *499*

oncyrran, *w.v.* (*1b*), [ON-1 + CHARE]; turn. *pp. nom. pl. m.* **oncyrde** 452

ond, *conj.*, AND 1, 10, 13 etc.

ōnettan, *w.v.* (*1b*), hasten. *p.t. sg.* **ōnette** *313*

onfindan, *v.* (*3*), [ON-1 + FIND]; discover. *p.t. sg.* **onfond** *502*

ongangan, *v.* (*7*), [ON-1 + GANG1]; move 156

ongēn, *prep. w. dat.*, AGAINST (postposited) 455

ongetan, *v.* (*5*), [*ANGET*]; perceive. *p.t. pl.* **ongēton** 90, recognized 552, experienced 453

onginnan, *v.* (*3*), [ONGIN]; proceed (to). *p.t. pl.* **ongunnon** 585

onhrēran, *w.v.* (*1b*), [ON-1 +]; arouse. *pp.* **onhrēred** 226, disturbed 483

onhwelan, *v.* (*4*), cry out (in anticipation). *p.t. sg.* **onhwæl** 161

onlēon, *v.* (*1*), [ON-1 +]; grant. *pr. 3 sg.* **onlȳhð** 530

onlūcan, *v.* (*2*), [UNLOUK]; *UNLOCK* 523

*onnīed, *f. i-stem*, [ON-2 + NEED]; oppression; *acc. sg.* 139

onriht, *adj.*, [ON-1 + RIGHT]; befitting; *acc. sg. n.* 358n.

onsǣlan, *w.v.* (*1b*), [ON-3 + SEAL2]; unloose. *pp.* **onsǣled** 584

onsēon, *v.* (*5*), [ON-1 + SEE]; see. *p.t. pl.* **onsēgon** *178*

onþēon, *v.* (*1*), [ON-1 + THEE1]; be successful 241

onþringan, *v.* (*3*), [ON-1+THRING]; press forward. *p.t. sg.* **onþrang** 343

*onwist, *f. i-stem*, [ON-1 +]; inhabitation; *acc. sg.* 18

open, *adj.*, OPEN 538

ōr, *n. a-stem*, [ORE3]; front; *dat. sg.* **ōre** 326

ortrȳwe, *adj.*, [*ORTROW*]; distrustful 154

orþanc, *m. a-stem*, [OR- + THANK]; skill. *dat. pl.* as *adv.* **orþancum** 359

orwēne, *adj. w. gen.*, [OR- +]; despairing (of). *nom. pl. m. wk.* **orwēnan** 211

oð, *conj.*, until 215. See also **oðþæt**

oð, *prep. w. acc.*, up to 298, as far as 444

ōðer, *adj.*, ANOTHER, second 108. *dat. pl.* as *sb.* **ōðrum** others 347, 577

*oðfaran, *v.* (*6*) *w. dat.*, [*ATFARE*]; escape (from). *pp.* **oðfaren** 64

oðlǣdan, *w.v.* (*1b*), [*ATLEAD*]; bring away. *pp.* **oðlǣded** 570

oðþæt, *conj.*, until 59, 127, 204, 479

oððe, *conj.*, [*OTHER*]; or 210, 540

*oðþicgan, *v.* (*5*), [+ THIG]; take away. *p.t. sg.* **oðþāh** 338

P

pað, *m. a-stem*, PATH; course; *acc. sg.* 488n. See also **ānpæð, milpæð**

-plega, see **gylpplega, handplega**

R

-rād, see **setlrād**

(ge)rād, see **(ge)ridan**

rand, *m. a-stem,* [RAND]; shield. *acc. pl.* **randas** 332, 587

***randgebeorh,** *n. a-stem,* [RAND + I-[1] + BERGH]; rampart; *acc. sg.* 296

randburh, *f. monos. stem,* [RAND + BOROUGH]; rampart (of water). *nom. pl.* **randbyrig** 464

randwiga, *m. n-stem,* [RAND + WYE[1]]; warrior. *nom. pl.* **randwigan** 126; *gen. pl.* **randwigena** 134

randwigend, *m. nd-stem,* [RAND +]; warrior. *gen. pl.* **randwiggendra** 436

-rāp, see **mæstrāp**

rǣd, *m. a-stem,* [REDE[1]]; wisdom 526, counsel; *acc. sg.* 6, 269. *acc. pl.* **rǣdas** 516; *gen. pl.* **rǣda** 549

rǣran, *w.v.* (*1b*), [REAR[1]]; raise. *p.t. pl.* **rǣrdon** 325

rǣs, *m. a-stem,* [RESE]; onslaught 329

rǣst, *f. jō-stem,* place of REST[1] 134

rǣswa, *m. n-stem,* leader. *nom. pl.* **rǣswan** 234. See also **mago-rǣswa**

rēad, *adj.,* RED; *inst. sg. m. wk.* **rēadan** 134. *acc. pl. m.* **rēade** 296; *dat. pl. wk.* **rēodan** 413

rēaf, *n. a-stem,* [REAF]; spoil, clothing. *acc. pl.* 587; *dat. pl.* **rēafum** 212. See also **hererēaf**

reccan, *w.v.* (*1c*), [RECCHE]; tell, explain. *pr. pl.* **reccað** 359

gerecenian, *w.v.* (*2*), [I-[1] + RECKON]; explain. *pp.* **gerecenod** 526

regnþēof, *m. a-stem,* arch-THIEF. *nom. pl.* **regnþēofas** 539

rēodan, see **rēad**

***rēofan,** *v.* (*2*), break. *pp. nom. pl. f.* **rofene** 464

reordigean, *w.v.* (*2*), [RERD(E)]; w. *ofer* address 256. *p.t. sg.* **reordode** spoke 549

rice, *n. ja-stem,* [RICHE]; power; *acc. sg.* 539, 557; *gen. sg.* **rices** kingdom 256. See also **cynerice, heofonrice, sigerice, woruldrice**

ridan, *v.* (*1*), RIDE. *p.t. sg.* **rād** 173

geridan, *v.* (*1*), [I-[1] + RIDE]; move along. *p.t. sg.* **gerād** *248*

riht, *adj.,* [RIGHT]; straight; *acc. sg. f.* **rihte** 126

riht, *n. a-stem,* RIGHT[1], what is due (to); *acc. sg.* 338, 352; custom 186; equity, in *on riht* in a proper manner 587. See also **ēðelriht, folcriht, landriht, wordriht.** Cf. **onriht**

rim, *n. a-stem,* [RIME[3]]; number; *acc. sg.* 436; *dat. sg.* **rime** 372. See also **unrim**

geriman, *w.v.* (*1b*), [I-[1] + RIME[3]]; count 440

-rinc, see **heaðorinc**

***rincgetæl,** *n. a-stem,* [RINK[1] + I-TEL]; company of warriors; *acc. sg.* 234

-rōd, see **seglrōd**

rodor, *m. a-stem,* sky; *acc. sg.* 464. See also **beorhtrodor, uprodor**

rōf, *adj.,* courageous, strong. as *sb., acc. pl. wk.* **rōfan** 98; *gen. pl.* **rōfra** *226*. See also **cwyldrōf, handrōf, mægenrōf**

rofene, see **rēofan**

rūn, *f. ō-stem,* [ROUN]; mystery 526

gerȳman, *w.v.* (*1b*), [I-[1] + RIME[4]]; open. *p.t. sg.* **gerȳmde** manifested 480n. *pp.* **gerȳmed** opened up 284

S

sālum, see **sǣl**

sand, *n. a-stem,* SAND[2]; *acc. sg.* 291; *dat. sg.* **sande** 220, 302. *nom. pl.* **sand** 471; *acc. pl.* *442*

sang, *m. a-stem,* SONG; *acc. sg.* 577; *gen. sg.* **sances** pitch 309

sang *p.t. sg.*, see **singan**

sāwol, *f. ō-stem*, SOUL. *acc. pl.* **sāwla** 544; *dat. pl.* **sāwlum** 497

gesāwon, see **gesēon**

sǣ, *m. i-stem*, SEA 473; *inst. sg.* 134. *dat. pl.* **sǣm** 443, 563

sǣbeorh, *m. a-stem*, [SEA + BAR-ROW[1]]; cliff. *gen. pl.* **sǣbeorga** 442

*****sǣcir,** *m. i-stem*, [SEA + CHARE[3]]; undertow 291

sǣd, *n. i-stem*, SEED: *gen. pl.* **sǣda** 374

*****sǣfæsten,** *n. ja-stem*, [SEA +]; barrier of the sea 127

(ge)sægde, see **(ge)secgan**

sǣgrund, *m. a-stem*, [SEA + GROUND]; (in *pl.*) depths of the sea. *acc. pl.* **sǣgrundas** 289

sǣl, *mf. i-stem*, [SELE]; joy. *dat. pl.* **sālum** in *on salum* joyful 106, 565

*****sǣlāf,** *f. ō-stem*, [SEA + LAVE[1]]; sea-survivor. *nom. pl.* **sǣlāfe** 585n.

sǣlan, *w.v.* (*1b*), [SEAL[2]]; confine. *pp. adj. acc. pl. m.* **sǣlde** 289

gesǣlan, *w.v.* (*1b*) *w. dat.*, befall. *p.t. sg.* **gesǣlde** 316

sǣleoda, *m. n-stem*, [SEA +]; sailor 374

sǣmann, *m. monos. stem*, SEAMAN. *nom. pl.* **sǣmen** 105; *gen. pl.* **sǣmanna** 479

sǣstrēam, *m. a-stem*, [SEA-STREAM]; (in *pl.*) sea. *dat. pl.* **sǣstrēamum** 250

sǣton, see **sittan**

sǣweall, *m. a-stem*, [SEA-WALL]; wall of sea-water 302

*****sǣwicing,** *m. a-stem*, [SEA + VIKING]; sailor. *nom. pl.* **sǣwicingas** 333

sceacan, *v.* (*6*), SHAKE; rattle. *p.t. sg.* **sceōc** 176

scead, *n. a-stem*, SHADE; shadow. *nom. pl.* **sceado** *113*

sceādan, *v.* (*7*), [SHED[1]]; divide. *p.t. pl.* **sceodon** *587*

gesceādan, *v.* (*7*), [I-[1] + SHED[1]]; decide 505

sceaft, *m. a-stem*, SHAFT[2]; spear. *dat. pl.* **sceaftum** 344

-sceaft *f.*, see **frumsceaft**

sceal, see **sculan**

sceān, see **scinan**

-scearu, see **lēodscearu**

sceat, *m. a-stem*, [SHEET[1]]; corner. *nom. pl.* **sceattas** expanse 429

sceōc, see **sceacan**

gesceōd *p.t. sg.*, see **gesceððan**

sceodon, see **sceādan**

sceolde, see **sculan**

gescēon, *w.v.* (*1b*) (*orig. s.v.* 5), happen. *pp.* **gesceod** (*used predicatively w. dat.*) in *weard gesceod* befell 507

sceotend, *m. nd-stem*, warrior. *dat. pl.* **sceotendum** 112

gesceððan, *v.* (*6*) *w. dat.*, [I-[1] + SCATHE]; harm, destroy. *p.t. sg.* **gesceōd** 489

scinan, *v.* (*1*), SHINE, glitter 110. *p.t. sg.* **sceān** 125; *pl.* **scinon** 113, 467

scip, *n. a-stem*, SHIP[1]; *gen. sg.* **scipes** 375

-scipe, see **lēodscipe, þeodscipe**

scir, *adj.*, [SHIRE]; gleaming. *nom. pl. m.* **scire** 112

scirwerod, *adj.*, [SHIRE + pp. of WEAR[1]]; enveloped in brightness 125

scræf, *n. a-stem*, pit 538

gescrifan, *v.* (*1*), [I-[1] + SHRIVE]; assign. *p.t. sg.* **gescrāf** 139

scriðan, *v.* (*1*), [SCRITHE]; range. *p.t. sg.* **scrāð** 39

-scua, see **nihtscua**

sculan, *pret. pr.* (*4*), SHALL. *pr. 3 sg.* **sceal** is to 423. *p.t. sg.* **sceolde** was to 317, had to 116

scyld, *m. a-stem*, SHIELD. *nom. pl.* **scyldas** 125. See also **dægsceld**

gescyldan, *w.v.* (*1b*), [I-SCHIELD]; protect. *p.t. sg.* **gescylde** 72

scyldhrēoða, *m. n-stem,* [SHIELD+]; shield. *nom. pl.* **scyldhrēoðan** 113

se, *dem. adj. (def. art.) m., THE* 141, 202, 273 etc., that 412, *f.* **sēo** 48, 214, 305, 477, *n.* **þæt** 19, 310; *acc. sg. m.* **þone** 172, 364, 400, 406, *f.* **þā** 83, 205, *n.* **þæt** 150, 151, 186, 234; *gen. sg. m.* **þæs** 508, *n.* 315, 507; *dat. sg. m.* **þām** 122, 153, 189 etc., *f.* **þǣre** 331, this 275, *n.* **þām** 170, that 576; *inst. sg. m.* **þan** 134, **þȳ** 21, 496, *n.* 56. *nom. pl.* **þā** 297; *acc. pl.* 82, 254, 513; *dat. pl.* **þām** 197, these 299, 565

sē, *dem. pron. m.,* [THE]; *n.* **þæt** 185n., THAT 233, 380; *acc. sg. m.* **þone** him 8, *n.* **þæt** it 359, (*anticipating clause*) 377, 406; *gen. sg. n.* **þæs** 144; *inst. sg. n.* **þon** 374, 381, *514,* 546, **þan** 245, **þȳ** *w. compar.* 117, 259, than that 399; *acc. pl.* **þā** these 61. *W. rel. part., dem. in case of principal clause*: *gen. pl.* **þāra þe** that 365, 376, 521, of those whom 189, of those which 395. See also **þæs**

sē, *rel. pron. m.,* [THE]; who 205, 274, 555, *w. pers. pron. in se* him to whom 380; *acc. sg. m.* **þone** which 28, *f.* **þā** which 404, *n.* **þæt** what 558; *inst. sg. n.* **þȳ** for which 349; *nom. pl.* **þā** which 287; *acc. pl.* 285, 573; *gen. pl.* **þāra** of which 95. *W. rel. part., rel. pron. in case of subord. clause.*: **sē þe** who 138, he who, the one who 7, 54, 476, 514, *f.* **sēo þe** which 423; *nom. pl.* **þā þe** who 235, those who 360, 501

geseah, see **gesēon**

gesealde, see **gesyllan**

sealt, *adj.,* SALT[1]; *acc. sg. m.* **sealtne** 333. *acc. pl. f.* **sealte** 442; *dat. pl.* **sealtum** 473

searo, *n. wa-stem,* armour; *acc. sg.*

219. *dat. pl.* **searwum** 471. See also **beadosearo**

-secg, see **gārsecg**

secgan, *w.v.* (*3*), SAY[1]; declare 7, report 510. *pr. 3 pl.* **secgað** relate 377, announce 531. *p.t. sg.* **sægde** spoke 517

gesecgan, *w.v.* (*3*), [I-SEGGEN]; tell; *inflected inf.* **gesecgenne** 438. *p.t. sg.* **gesægde** 24

sefa, *m. n-stem,* heart; *dat. sg.* **sefan** 439

segl, *m. a-stem,* SAIL[1], (also 'veil', 'banner') *105*; *dat. sg.* **segle** *81*n. *nom. pl.* **seglas** 89

***seglrōd,** *f. ō-stem,* [SAIL[1] + ROOD]; sailyard; *acc. sg.* **seglrōde** 83n.

segn, *m. a-stem,* [SENYE]; banner, battle-standard; *acc. sg.* 127n., 172; *dat. sg.* **segne** 319. *nom. pl.* **segnas** 566; *acc. pl.* 302; *dat. pl.* **segnum** (i.e. 'tribes') 585

***segncyning,** *m. a-stem,* [SENYE + KING]; king 172

-sele, see **bēorsele, gystsele**

seledrēam, *m. a-stem,* [+ DREAM[1]]; hall-joy. *nom. pl.* **seledrēamas** 36n.

sēlost, *superl. adj.,* [SELE + -EST] best 293, 446; *acc. sg. m.* 401

seomian, *w.v.* (*2*), lie in wait. *p.t. pl.* **seomedon** 209

gesēon, *v.* (*5*), [I-SEE]; see 83, 207. *p.t. sg.* **geseah** 88; *pl.* **gesāwon** 103, 126, 155, 572, perceived 387, 583

sēo þe, see **sē** *rel.*

***setlrād,** *f. ō-stem,* [SETTLE[1] + ROAD]; course; *acc. sg.* **setlrāde** 109

gesettan, *w.v.* (*1a*), [I-SET]; establish. *p.t. sg.* **gesette** 27

-sibb, see **cnēowsibb**

sibgedriht, *f. i-stem,* [SIB[1] + I-[1] + DRIGHT[1]]; host of kinsmen 214

***sibgemǣg,** *m. a-stem,* [SIB[1] + I-[1] +

MAY²]; kinsman. *nom. pl.* **sib-gemāgas** 386

sid, *adj.,* [SIDE]; vast. *acc. pl. m.* **sīde** 260. *compar. acc. pl. n. (uninflected)* **siddra** ampler 428

*****sigebȳme,** *f. n-stem,* [SIƷE+BEME]; trumpet of victory. *nom. pl.* **sige-bȳman** 566

sigerice, *n. ja-stem,* [SIƷE + RICHE]; victorious kingdom; *acc. sg.* 27, 563.

*****sigetiber,** *n. a-stem,* [SIƷE +]; sacrifice for victory; *dat. sg.* **sige-tibre** 402

sigor, *m. a-stem,* [SIƷE]; victory. *gen. pl.* **sigora** 16, 272, 434

*****sigorweorc,** *n. a-stem,* [SIƷE + WORK]; victorious deed. *gen. pl.* **sigorworca** 316

sin, *poss. pron.,* his; *acc. sg. m.* **sinne** 412

sinc, *n. a-stem,* wealth; *dat. sg.* **since** 36

*****sincald,** *adj.,* perpetually COLD; *nom. sg. m. wk.* **sincalda** 473

singan, *v. (3),* SING¹, resound. *p.t. sg.* **sang** 132; *pl.* **sungon** 159, 164, 566

sittan, *v. (5),* SIT: *p.t. pl.* **sǣton** 212

gesittan, *v. (5),* [I-¹ + SIT]; occupy. *pr. 2 pl.* **gesittaƥ** 563, *3 pl.* 443

sīƥ, *m. a-stem,* [SITHE¹]; advance 207, time 22; *acc. sg.* journey 97, 479, misfortune, death 510; *gen. sg.* **sīƥes** journey 53; *dat. sg.* **sīƥe** 105. See also **bealusīƥ, lāƥsīƥ, spildsīƥ**

*****sīƥboda,** *m. n-stem,* [SITHE¹ + BODE¹]; herald of the journey 250n.

sīƥfæt, *m. a-stem,* [SITHE¹ +]; course; *acc. sg.* 81; *dat. sg.* **sīƥfate** journey 522

sīƥian, *w.v. (2),* [SITHE¹]; go. *pr. 2 pl. subj.* **sīƥien** 272

sīƥor, *compar. adv.,* [SITHRE]; later 336

siƥƥan, *adv.,* [SITHEN]; then 224, later 384. *conj.* when 64, 86, 132 etc.

slēan, *v. (6),* SLAY¹, kill 412, *imper. sg.* **sleh** 419. *p.t. sg.* **slōh** have struck 280, struck down 485

geslēan, *v. (6),* [I-¹ + SLAY¹]; strike. *p.t. sg.* **geslōh** 494

-sliht, see **wælsliht**

slūpan, *v. (2),* glide. *p.t. sg.* **slēap** 491

-smiƥ, see **hleahtorsmiƥ**

snelle, *adv.,* [SNELL]; quickly 220

snottor, *adj.,* [SNOTER]; wise 374, 439; *nom. sg. m. wk.* **snottra** 389

somnigean, *w.v. (2),* [SOMNE¹]; gather together 217

somod, *adv.,* [SAMED]; together 214

sōƥ, *adj.,* [SOOTH]; true 479. *dat. pl.* **sōƥum** 30, 438, 522

sōƥ, *n. a-stem,* [SOOTH]; truth 420; *acc. sg.* 291

sōƥfæst, *adj.,* [SOOTHFAST]; trustworthy 434, righteous 9. *gen. pl.* as *sb.* **sōƥfæstra** 544

sōƥwundor, *n. a-stem,* [SOOTH *sb.* + WONDER]; true marvel. *gen. pl.* **sōƥwundra** 24

gespannan, *v. (7),* [I-¹ + SPAN²]; fasten. *p.t. sg.* **gespēon** 174

spāw, see **spiwan**

spēd, *f. i-stem,* [SPEED]; power; *acc. sg.* 514, **spēde** success 153

spel, *n. a-stem,* [SPELL¹]; speech. *nom. pl.* 203. See also **bealospell, fǣrspell, hildespell**

spelboda, *m. n-stem,* [SPELL¹ + BODE¹]; messenger. *acc. pl.* **spelbodan** 514

gespēon, see **gespannan**

*****spildsīƥ,** *m. a-stem,* [+ SITHE¹]; journey of destruction; *dat. sg.* **spildsīƥe** 153

spiwan, *v. (1),* SPEW. *p.t. sg.* **spāw** 291, *(w. dat.)* 450

spor, *n. a-stem,* [cf. SPOOR¹]; mark; *acc. sg. 239*

spræc, *f. jō-stem, SPEECH*[1]. *acc. .pl*
spræce words 518

sprecan, *v.* (*5*), *SPEAK. p.t. sg.*
spræc 258, 277, 418, 553

gestāh, see **gestigan**

stān, *m. a-stem,* STONE. *acc. pl.*
stānas 441

standan, *v.* (*6*), STAND 572. *p.t. pl.*
stōdon mounted up 460, rose up
566, shone 111, arose 201, 491,
stōdan 136

gestandan, *v.* (*6*), [I-STAND]; stand.
p.t. sg. **gestōd** 303

staðol, *m. a-stem,* [STADDLE]; foun-
dation. *nom. pl.* **staðolas** 285;
acc. pl. **staðulas** 474

stæð, *n. a-stem,* [*STAITHE*]; shore;
dat. sg. **staðe** 581

-steal, see **wicsteal**

-steald, see **hægsteald**

-gesteald, see **wuldorgesteald**

-stede, see **dēaðstede, meðel-
stede**

stefn, *f. ō-stem,* [STEVEN[1]]; voice
417; *acc. sg.* **stefne** 276; *dat. sg.*
257, 551. *acc. pl.* **stefne** 575; *dat.
pl.* **stæfnum** 463, **stefnum** 579,
notes 99

steorra, *m. n-stem,* STAR[1]. *acc. pl.*
steorran 441

gestēpan, *w.v.* (*1b*), build up.
pp. nom. pl. m. **gestēpte** 297

stigan, *v.* (*1*), [STY[1]]; climb. *p.t. pl.*
stigon 385, moved through
319

gestigan, *v.* (*1*), [I-[1] + STY[1]]; reach.
p.t. sg. **gestāh** 503

gestillan, *w.v.* (*1b*), [I-STILL];
quieten 254

stille, *adv.,* STILL; quietly 551, calm
300

-stod, see **wealhstod**

gestōd, see **gestandan**

stōdon, -an, see **standan**

storm, *m. a-stem,* STORM; tumult
460

strǣt, *f. ō-stem,* STREET; road; *acc.*

sg. **strǣte** 126. See also **here-
strǣt**

strēam, *m. a-stem,* STREAM; surge
472. *nom. pl.* **strēamas** waters
460; *acc. pl.* 296. See also **lagu-
strēam, merestrēam, sǣ-
stream, wǣgstrēam**

gestrēon, *n. a-stem,* [I-STREON];
treasure; *acc. sg.* 588

stȳran, *w.v.* (*1b*) *w. dat.,* [STEER[1]];
restrain 417

sum, *pron.* (*w. gen.*), [SOME]; one
345, 357; *acc. sg. n.* 279

sund, *n. a-stem,* SOUND[1]; sea; *acc. sg.*
319

sungon, see **singan**

sunne, *f. n-stem,* SUN; *gen. sg.* **sun-
nan** 81; *dat. sg.* 109

sunu, *m. u-stem,* SON 389, 426; *acc.
sg.* 402, 420. *nom. pl.* 332, 341;
dat. pl. **sunum** 18, 363

sūðan, *adv.,* [SOUTHEN]; from the
south; in *be sūðan* to the south 69

*****sūðweg,** *m. a-stem,* [SOUTH +
WAY[1]]; road to the south. *dat. pl.*
sūðwegum 155

*****sūðwind,** *m. a-stem,* SOUTH WIND
289

swā, *adv.,* so 404, and so 377, thus
194, 549, accordingly 49, 314, to
that extent 143, in *swa þeah* never-
theless 339

swā, *conj.,* so, as 101, 352, 359 etc.,
just as 520, 539, so that 82

swāpan, *v.* (*7*), [SWOPE[1]]; rush.
p.t. sg. **swēop** 481

-swaru, see **āðswaru**

swǣfon, see **swefan**

swǣs, *adj.,* beloved; *acc. sg. m.*
swǣsne 402

-swæð, see **bilswæð**

geswealh, see **geswelgan**

geswearc, see **gesweorcan**

swefan, *v.* (*5*), [SWEVE]; pass away.
p.t. pl. **swǣfon** 36, 496

swēg, *m. i-stem,* voice 309; *acc. sg.*
sound 567

*geswelgan, v. (3), [I-¹ + SWAL-LOW]; devour. p.t. sg. geswealh 513

sweltan, v. (3), [SWELT]; perish. p.t. pl. swulton 465

swēop, see swāpan

gesweorcan, v. (3), [I-¹ + SWERK]; grow dark. p.t. sg. geswearc 462

sweord, n. a-stem, SWORD; dat. sg. sweorde 420

*sweordwigend, m. nd-stem, [SWORD +]; warrior. gen. pl. sweordwigendra 260

swēot, n. a-stem, troop, band; acc. sg. 220. nom. pl. 497; dat. pl. swēotum 341, -on 127. See also folcswēot

swerian, v. (6), SWEAR. pr. 3 sg. swereð 432

-swiciende, see unswiciende

swipian, w.v. (2), [SWIP]; lash. p.t. sg. swipode 464

swiðan, w.v. (1b), strengthen. pp. swiðed 550

geswiðan, w.v. (1b), strengthen. pp. geswiðed 30

swiðra, compar. adj., [SWITHER]; stronger, right (hand); nom. sg. f. swiðre 280

swiðrian, w.v. (2), [cf. SWITHER¹]; diminish. p.t. sg. swiðrade 242, swiðrode subsided 309, abated 466; pl. swiðredon melted away 113

swulton, see sweltan

sylf, pron. as adj., SELF; gen. sg. m. sylfes 9, 27, 434. nom. sg. m. wk. sylfa myself 280, himself 542

gesyllan, w.v. (1c), [I-¹ + SELL]; give 400. p.t. sg. gesealde 20, 141, entrusted 16

syllic, adj., [SELLY]; wonderful 109

syn(don), see bēon

synfull, adj., SINFUL. gen. pl. as sb. synfullra 497

synn, f. jō-stem, SIN. dat. pl. synnum 336

gesynto, f. ō-stem, success, salvation; gen. sg. 272

T

tācn, n. a-stem, TOKEN; symbol; dat. sg. tācne 281n.

-talu, see folctalu

tǣcan, w.v. (1c), TEACH 528

-getæl, see folcgetæl, rincgetæl

getēag, tēah, see (ge)tēon

getellan, w.v. (1c), [I-TELLE]; count. p.t. pl. getealdon 224. pp. geteled 232, 372

tempel, n. a-stem, TEMPLE¹; acc. sg. 391

getenge, adj. w. dat., oppressing. nom. pl. m. 148

tēon, v. (2), [TEE¹]; draw, pull. p.t. sg. tēah 491

getēon, v. (2), [I-TEON]; draw. p.t. sg. getēag 407

-tēonde, see tuddortēonde

tēonhete, m. i-stem, [TEEN¹ + HATE¹]; malicious hate; dat. sg. 224

tiber, n. a-stem, sacrifice; acc. sg. 416. See also sigetiber

tid, f. i-stem, [TIDE]; time; acc. sg. 288. See also ūhttid

getimbrian, w.v. (2), [I-¹ + TIMBER]; build. p.t. sg. getimbrede 391

tirēadig, adj., [+ EADI]; glorious. gen. pl. tirēadigra 232, as sb. 184

tirfæst, adj., [+ FAST]; glorious. acc. pl. tirfæste 63

tō, adv., [TO]; in that direction 278

tō, prep. TO, w. dat. 277, 325, 397 etc., w. inflected inf. 438, for 88, 425, 548, as 319, 402, 405, 509, among 197, on 263, at 198; w. gen. towards 192

-toga, see folctoga

-torht, see heofontorht, meretorht

-torr, see meretorr

tosomne, *adv.,* [TO-*SAME*]; together 207

tredan, *v.* (*5*), TREAD; traverse 160

trēow, *f. wō-stem, TRUCE*; covenant; *acc. sg.* **trēowe** 423, **trēowa** 366; *gen. sg.* **trēowe** pledge 426. *dat. pl.* **trēowum** pledges 149. See also **hēahtrēow**

-trod, see **witrod**

trum, *adj.,* *TRIM*; strong 554

-getrum, see **angetrum, fyrdgetrum**

trymman, *w.v.* (*1a*), TRIM; be arrayed. *p.t. pl.* **trymedon** 158

-trȳwe, see **ortrȳwe**

tuddortēonde, *adj.,* [TUDDER +]; producing descendants. *gen. pl.* as *sb.* **tuddortēondra** 372

getwǣfan, *w.v.* (*1b*), put an end to. *p.t. sg.* **getwǣfde** *119*

twēgen, *num. adj. m.,* TWAIN; *TWO* 94; *f. acc.* **twā** 63, *n. acc.* 184

twelf, *num. adj., TWELVE. acc. pl.* **twelfe** 225

twēonum, see **be**

-twīgðu, see **antwīgðu**

tȳn, *num. adj.* TEN; *acc. n. 232*

þ

þā, *adv.,* [THO]; then 22, 30, 33 etc. *conj.* when 48, 202, 319 etc. *correl.* then . . . when 276–7

þā *dem. adj./pron., rel. pron.,* see **se, sē**

geþāh, see **geþēon, geþicgan**

þām, see **se**

þan, see **se, sē** *dem.*

-þanc, see **orþanc**

þanon, *adv.,* [THENNE]; after that 516

þāra, þāra þe see **sē** *dem.* and *rel.*

þās, see **þis** *adj.*

þā þe, see **sē** *rel.*

þǣr, *adv.,* THERE 71, 89, 91 etc., on that occasion 24. *conj.* where 272, 330, 458 etc., when 16, if 152

þǣre, see **se**

þǣs, *adv.,* [THES]; (*anticipating clause*)

with respect to that 49, to such an extent 439. **þǣs þe** *conj.* in as much as 51. See also **se, sē** *dem.*

þæt *adj./pron.,* see **se, sē** *dem.* and *rel.*

þæt, *conj.,* THAT 23, 91, 270 etc., so that 143, 206, 264 etc., in that 123; **þætte** so that 151, 510

þe, *indecl. rel. particle,* [THE]; see **sē** *dem.* and *rel.* *conj.* see **þēah**

þēah, *adv.,* THOUGH in *swa þeah* nevertheless 339

þēah, *conj.,* al*THOUGH* 29; **þēah þe** 141, 209, 259, 571

þearf, see **þurfan**

þeccan, *w.v.* (*1c*), [*THATCH*]; cover. *pr. 3 pl.* (*fut.*) **þeccað** *288*

þegn, *m. a-stem,* THANE[1]; retainer. *nom. pl.* **þegnas** 170. See also **meteþegn**

-þegnung, see **hēahþegnung**

þencan, *w.v.* (*1c*), THINK[2]; intend. *p.t. pl.* **þōhton** had intended 51

þenden, *conj.,* while 255

þengel, *m. a-stem,* ruler 173

þēod, *f. ō-stem,* [THEDE]; people; *acc. sg.* 160, **þēode** 357, 487. *gen. pl.* **þēoda** 326. See also **werþēod.** Cf. **ingeþēod**

þēoden, *m. a-stem,* leader 277, 363, Lord 432

þēodenhold, *adj.,* [+ HOLD]; loyal to one's lord. *nom. pl. m.* **þēodenholde** 182; *acc. pl. m.* as *sb.* the faithful 87

*þēodmægen, *n. a-stem,* [THEDE + MAIN[1]]; company 342

þēodscipe, *m. i-stem,* [THEDE + -SHIP]; fellowship; *gen. sg.* **þēodscipes** 529

-þēof, see **regnþēof**

geþēon, *v.* (*1*), [I-THEE]; prosper. *p.t. sg.* **geþāh** 143

þēos, see **þis** *adj.*

-þēow, see **lātþēow**

geþicgan, *v.* (*5*), [I-[1] + *THIG*]; receive. *p.t. sg.* **geþāh** 354

þider, *adv.,* THITHER, (to) there 46, 196

þin, *poss. adj.,* [THINE]; THY, your: *acc. sg. n.* 419; *gen. sg. n.* **þines** 435. *nom. pl. m.* **þine** 445. See also **þū**

þis, *dem. adj. m.,* THIS, *f.* **þēos** 280, 431, 554; *acc. sg. m.* **þysne** 535, *f.* **þās** 25, 274, 555; *dat. sg. m.* **þissum** 263

þis, *dem. pron. m.,* THIS 273, 532

þōhton, see **þencan**

þolian, *w.v.* (*2*), [THOLE]; endure 324

þon, see **sē** *dem.*

þone, see **se, sē** *dem. and rel.*

þonne, *conj.,* [THEN]; when 325, 544; (*w. compar.*) THAN 373, 429, than that 410

þraca, *f. ō-stem,* onrush 326

*þræcwig, *mn. a-stem,* [+ WI]: violent combat; *gen. sg.* **þræc-wiges** 182

-þrēat, see **gūðþrēat, hereþrēat, mægenþrēat, mearcþrēat**

þridda, *adj.,* THIRD; *nom. sg. n.* 87, **þridde** 342

þrie, *num. adj. m.,* THREE; *dat.* **þrim** 363

þrymfæst, *adj.,* [THRUM[1] + FAST]: glorious 363

-þrymm, see **mægenþrymm**

þrysmian, *w.v.* (*2*), suffocate, *p.t. sg.* **þrysmyde** *40*

þrȳðe, *f. pl. i-stem,* might; *dat.* **þrȳðum** 340

þū, *pron.,* THOU, you 419 422; *gen.* **þin** 421; *dat.* **þē** *432*. See also **þin**

þūf, *m. a-stem,* standard. *nom. pl.* **þūfas** 342; *acc. pl.* 160n.

þūhton, see **þyncan**

-þungen, see **hēahþungen**

þunian, *w.v.* (*2*), be lifted up 160

þurfan, *pret. pr.* (*3*), [THARF]; *w. gen.* need. *pr. 3 sg.* **þearf** 426

þurh, *prep. w. acc.,* THROUGH 262, 480, 573, by 434

þurstig, *adj.,* THIRSTY; greedy (for). *nom. pl. m.* **þurstige** 182

þūsend, *num.,* THOUSAND. *acc. pl.* **þūsendo** 184

þūsendmǣlum, *adv.,* [THOUSAND + -MEAL]; in thousands 196

þȳ, see **se, sē** *dem. and rel.*

þyncan, *w.v.* (*1c*), [THINK[1]]: seem. *p.t. pl.* **þūhton** 573

þysne, see **þis** *adj.*

U

ūhttid, *f. i-stem,* [+ TIDE]; dawn: *acc. sg.* 216

uncūð, *adj.,* [UNCOUTH]; unfamiliar: *acc. sg. n.* 313. (*prob.*) *acc. pl. n.* 58

under, *prep. w. dat.,* UNDER 228; beneath 376, 537; protected by 236. *w. acc.* below 572

unforht, *adj.,* [UN-[1] +]; dauntless: *nom. sg. n.* 335. *nom. pl. m.* **unforhte** 180, 328

ungeāre, *adv.,* [UN-[1] + YORE]; soon *33*n.

*ungrund, *adj.,* [UN-[1] + GROUND *sb.*]; measureless, immense. *gen. sg. m.* **ungrundes** 509

*unhlēow, *adj.,* [UN-[1] + LEE *sb.*[1]]: unprotective; *acc. sg. m. wk.* **unhlēowan** 495

unnan, *pret. pr.* (*3*), [UNNE]; give. *pr. 1 sg.* **on** 269

unrim, *n. a-stem,* [UN-[1] + RIME[3]]: countless number; *acc. sg.* 261

unswiciende, *adj.,* [UN-[1] + *pr. p.* of SWIKE *v.*]; unswerving, loyal; *nom. sg. f.* **unswiciendo** 425

unweaxen, *adj.,* [UN-[1] + WAXEN *ppl. a.*]; young; *acc. sg. m.* **un-weaxenne** 413

up, *adv.,* UP[1] 200, 253, 282 etc.; up above, on high 248, 462

uplang, *adj.,* [UP[1] + LONG[1]]; up-right 303

uprodor, *m. a-stem,* sky 430; *acc. sg.* 26, heaven 4, 76, 545

ūs, see **wē**
ūt, *adv.,* OUT 187

W

wāc, *adj.,* [WOKE]; *WEAK. acc. pl.*
m. as *sb.* **wāce** *233*
wacian, *w.v.* (*2, orig. 3*), [WAKE];
WATCH. pr.p. **wæccende** 213
wadan, *v.* (*6*), WADE; advance.
p.t. sg. **wōd** 311n.
gewadan, *v.* (*6*), [I-¹ + WADE]:
pervade. *p.t. sg.* **gewōd** 463
wāfian, *w.v.* (*2*), look on with
amazement. *p.t. pl.* **wāfedon** 78
Waldend, *m. nd-stem,* [WALDEND]:
controller, Lord 16, 433, *487*;
acc. sg. 422
wand, see **windan**
wāt, see **witan**
gewāt, see **gewītan**
waðum, *m. a-stem,* wave. *gen. pl.*
waðema 472
wæccende, see **wacian**
wǣg, *m. i-stem,* [WAW¹]; wave; *acc.
sg.* 495n.; *gen. sg.* **wǣges** *467*; *dat.
sg.* **wǣge** 458. *nom. pl.* **wǣgas**
484. See also **mōdwǣg**
*****wǣgfaru,** *f. ō-stem,* [WAW¹ +
FARE¹]; passage through the sea
298
wǣgon, see **wegan**
*****wǣgstrēam,** *m. a-stem,* [WAW¹ +
STREAM]; sea; *acc. sg.* 311
wælbend, *f. jō-stem,* [WAL+BEND¹];
deadly *BOND¹* (of the sea).
nom. pl. **wælbenna** 492n.
*****wælcēasega,** *m. n-stem,* [cf. WAL-
KYRIE]; raven 164n.
*****wælfæðōm,** *m. a-stem,* [WAL +
FATHOM]; deadly clutch. *dat. pl.*
wælfæðmum 481
*****wælgryre,** *m. i-stem,* [WAL +];
terror of death 137
wælhlencan, *f. pl. n-stem,* [WAL +
LINK²]; coat of mail; *acc. 176*
wælmist, *m. a-stem,* [WAL + MIST¹];
deadly mist 451

*****wælnet,** *n. ja-stem,* [WAL + NET¹];
coat of mail. *nom. pl.* 202n.
wælsliht, *m. i-stem,* [WAL +
SLEIGHT²]; death-blow. *nom. pl.*
wælslihtes carnage 328n.
wǣpen, *n. a-stem,* WEAPON. *gen. pl.*
wǣpna 20, 328, 451
wǣpnedcynn, *n. ja-stem,*
[WEAPONED + KIN¹]; male sex;
gen. sg. **wǣpnedcynnes** 188
wǣr, *f. ō-stem,* [WARE⁴]; treaty;
acc. sg. **wǣre** 140, 147, covenant
387, 422. See also **freoðowǣr,**
wērbēam
wǣre *p.t. subj.,* **wǣron, wæs,** se
bēon
wæstm, *m. a-stem,* [WASTUM]; sta-
ture. *dat. pl.* **wæstmum** 243
wæter, *n. a-stem,* WATER 451; *acc. sg.*
283. *gen. pl.* **wætera** 572
wǣðan, *w.v.* (*1b*), hunt. *p.t. sg.*
wǣðde 481
wē, *pron. pl.,* WE 1, 529; *dat.* **ūs** US
530, 531, *556*
wēa, *m. n-stem,* WOE, misery;
acc. sg. **wēan** 140; *gen. sg.* 213
gewealc, *n. i-stem,* rolling 456
geweald, *n. a-stem,* [I-WALD]:
power; *acc. sg.* 20, control 383
wealdan, *v.* (*7*) *w. dat., WIELD*:
control. *p.t. sg.* **wēold** 105
wealhstod, *m. a-stem,* interpreter
523
weall, *m. a-stem,* WALL¹. *acc. pl.*
weallas 572. See also **foreweall,**
holmweall, sǣweall
weallan, *v.* (*7*), [WALL¹]; seethe.
p.t. pl. **weollon** 492n.
weal(l)fæsten, *n. ja-stem,* [WALL¹
+]; rampart; *acc. sg.* 283. *nom. pl.*
484
wēan, see **wēa**
weard, *m. a-stem,* [WARD¹]; guard-
ian 486, 504, 524. *nom. pl.*
weardas watchers 221. See also
**burhweard, flōdweard, gūð-
weard, hordweard, lāstweard,**

**mearcweard, nihtweard, yrfe-
weard**

wearð, see **weorðan**

-weaxen, see **unweaxen**

-web, see **godweb**

wēdan, *w.v.* (*1b*), [WEDE]; rage.
p.t. sg. **wēdde** 490

weder, *n. a-stem,* WEATHER; storm.
dat. pl. **wederum** 118

wederwolcen, *n.* *a-stem,*
[WEATHER + *WELKIN*]; cloud 75

weg, *m. a-stem,* WAY[1]; path. *nom. pl.*
wegas 283, 458. See also **bǣð-
weg, flōdweg, forðweg, lifweg,
norðweg, sūðweg**

wegan, *v.* (*5*), [WEIGH[1]]; carry 157.
p.t. pl. **wǣgon** 573, moved
(*intrans.*) 180

wēn, *f. i-stem,* [WEEN]; expectation.
dat. pl. **wēnum** 176, 213, **wēnan**
165

-wende, see **hātwende**

-wēne, see **orwēne**

wēold, see **wealdan**

wēollon, see **weallan**

-weorc, see **dǣdweorc, dæg-
weorc, handweorc, sigor-
weorc**

weorðan, *v.* (*3*), [WORTH[1]]; become
424. *pr. 3 sg. subj.* **weorðe** 439;
2 pl. **weorðen** 294. *p.t. sg.* **wearð**
142, 154, 349, 455, (as *auxil. w.
pp.*) was 506; *pl.* **wurdon** 144

geweorðan, *v.* (*3*), [I-WORTH];
happen. *p.t.* *?* *sg. subj.* **gewurde**
365n.

geweorðian, *w.v.* (*2*), [I-WURTHI];
honour. *pr. 2 pl. subj* **gewurðien**
270. *p.t. sg.* **geweorðode** 86,
gewyrðode exalted 10. *pp.* **ge-
weorðod** ennobled 581, *acc. sg.
m.* **gewurðodne** exalted 31

wer, *m. a-stem,* [WERE[1]]; man 518.
nom. pl. **weras** 572, 577; *gen. pl.*
wera 3, 149, 236 etc. See also
lēodweras

wērbēam, *m. a-stem,* [*WARE*[4] +

BEAM[1]]; covenant-pillar; *gen. sg.*
wērbēamas 487n.

wērig, *adj.,* WEARY. *nom. pl. m.*
wērige 130

-wērig, see **ealdwērig**

werigean, *w.v.* (*1a*), [WERE]; de-
fend 237. *pr. 3 sg.* **wereð** protects
274. *p.t. pl.* **weredon** hindered
202

werigend, *m. nd-stem,* protector.
nom. pl. 589n.

werod, -ud, *n. a-stem,* [WERED];
troop, host, army 100, 204, 221
etc.; *acc. sg.* 123, 194, 568; *gen. sg.*
werodes 31, 65, 230, 258; *dat.
sg.* **werode** 170. *gen. pl.* **weroda,
-eda** 23, 92, 137 etc., **werode** 8;
dat. pl. **weredum** 117. See also
lēodwerod

-werod *adj.,* see **scirwerod**

werþēod, *f.* *ō-stem,* [WERE[1] +
THEDE]; people. *nom. pl.* **wer-
þēode** 520; *gen. pl.* **werþēoda**
383

wēstengryre, *m. i-stem,* [*WEST-
ERN*[2] +]; terror of the desert·
117

wēstenn, *n. ja-stem,* [*WESTERN*[2]];
desert, wilderness; *dat. sg.* **wē-
stenne** 8, 123

wic, *n. a-stem,* [WICK[2]]; camp 87,
133. *dat. pl.* **wicum** 200. See also
fyrdwic

wican, *v.* (*1*), give way. *p.t. pl.*
wicon 484

wician, *w.v.* (*2*), [WICK[1]]; dwell 117

-wicing, see **sǣwicing**

wicsteal, *m. a-stem,* [WICK[2] +
STALL[1]]; camping-place; *acc. sg.*
92

wid, *adj.,* WIDE. *dat. sg. n. wk.* **widan**
infinitely long 548. *dat. pl.* **widum**
widespread 75. *compar. acc. pl. n.*
(*uninflected*) **widdra** more exten-
sive 428

wide, *adv.,* WIDELY 39, 481, far and
wide, everywhere 42

wideferð, *adv.,* [WIDE *a.* +]; for
ever 51

wif, *n. a-stem,* WIFE; woman. *nom. pl.*
577

wig, *mn. a-stem,* [WI]; battle; *gen. sg.*
wiges 176. See also **witrod,**
þræcwig

wiga, *m. n-stem,* [WYE¹]; warrior;
acc. sg. **wigan** 188. *nom. pl.* **wigan**
311. See also **lindwiga, rand-**
wiga

***wigblāc,** *adj.,* [WI + BLOK(E)];
bright in arms 204

wigbord, *n. a-stem,* [WI + BOARD];
shield. *nom. pl.* 467

wigend *m. nd-stem* warrior. *nom. pl.*
180, 328. See also **randwigend,**
sweordwigend

wighēap, *m. a-stem,* [WI + HEAP];
troop of warriors; *acc. sg. 243*

***wiglēoð,** *n. a-stem,* [WI + LEOTH];
battle-cry; *acc. sg.* 221

wiglic, *adj.,* [WI + -LY¹]; warlike
233

willa, *m. n-stem,* WILL¹; *gen. sg.*
willan 552

willan, *anom. v.,* WILL¹; wish. *pr. 3*
sg. **wile** 523, 528, wishes and
intends 558, intends 261; *subj.*
wille 7. *imper. pl.* **willað** be will-
ing 266. *p.t. sg.* **wolde** 244, 256,
415, 505, intended 400, 412; *pl.*
woldon 323, 454, intended 150
wind, see **sūðwind**

windan, *v. (3),* WIND¹; move for-
ward. *p.t. sg.* **wand** 80; *pl.* **wun-**
don 342

-wine, see **mægwine**

winnan, *v. (3),* [WIN¹]; fight. *p.t. pl.*
wunnon 515

wis, *adj.,* WISE. *nom. pl. m.* **wise**
learned 377. *superl. nom. sg. m. wk.*
wisesta 393

wisa, *m. n-stem,* leader 13, 258. See
also **herewisa, mægenwisa**

wisian, *w.v. (2),* [WISE¹]; direct.
p.t. sg. **wisode** 348

wislic, *adj.,* [WISELY]; wise. *acc. pl.*
n. **wislicu** 527

wisse, see **witan**

wist, *f. i-stem,* food; *dat. sg.* **wiste**
130. See also **onwist**

witan, *pret. pr. (1),* [WIT¹]; know.
pr. 1 sg. **wāt** 291; *3 pl.* **witon** are
aware of 536. *p.t. sg.* **wisse** con-
sidered 409; *pl.* **wiston** 29, 69

gewitan, *v. (1),* [I-WITE²]; depart.
p.t. sg. **gewāt** 41, 346, mounted
460

wite, *n. ja-stem,* [WITE²]; punish-
ment, torment. *dat. pl.* **witum** 33,
140. See also **gyrdwite**

witig, *adj.,* WITTY; wise 25, 80.
dat. pl. wk. **witgan** 390

witod, *adj.,* ordained, appointed;
gen. sg. m. **witodes** 552; *dat. sg. f.*
witodre 472

witon, see **witan**

***witrod,** *n. a-stem,* [WI + TROD];
path of battle; *acc. sg.* 492n.

wið, *prep.,* WITH, *w. acc.* 172, 422,
against 237, 515; *w dat.* by 303,
against 20, 72, 224

***wiðfaran,** *v. (6),* [WITH-+FARE¹];
escape. *p.t. pl.* **wiðfōron** 574

wlanc, *adj.,* [WLONK]; audacious;
acc. sg. f. **wlance** 487. *nom. pl. m.*
wlance 170; *acc. pl. m.* as *sb.* 204

(ge)wōd, see **(ge)wadan**

wolcen, *n. a-stem,* [WELKIN];
cloud 93; *dat. sg.* **wolcne** 350n.
gen. pl. **wolcna** sky 298; *dat. pl.*
wolcnum sky 80. See also
wederwolcen

wolde, woldon, see **willan**

wōma, *m. n-stem,* uproar 202;
acc. sg. **wōman** battle-cry 100n.
See also **dægwōma**

womm, *mn. a-stem,* [WAM, *WEM*];
sin. *dat. pl.* **wommum** 533

wonn, *adj.,* [WAN]; dark 164

wōp, *m. a-stem,* [WOP]; lamentation
42, 200. See also **herewōp**

word, *n. a-stem,* WORD. *acc. pl.* 418,

428, 527; *dat. pl.* **wordum** 23, 299, 377 etc.

wordriht, *n. a-stem*, [WORD + RIGHT[1]]; law. *acc. pl.* 3

(ge)worhte, see **(ge)wyrcan**

worn, *m. a-stem*, large number; *acc. sg.* 56, 195

woruld, *f. ?i-stem*, WORLD; *acc. sg.* 25

worulddrēam, *m. a-stem*, [WORLD + DREAM[1]]; earthly joy. *gen. pl.* **worulddrēama** 42

woruldrice, *n. ja-stem*, [WORLD-RICHE]; world; *dat. sg.* 365, 393

wrāð, *adj.*, [WROTH]; hostile. *gen. pl.* as *sb.* **wrāðra** 20

wræc, *n. a-stem*, [WRACK[1]]; or **wracu**, *f. ō-stem*, [WRAKE[1]]; exile; *dat. sg.* **wræce** 383

wræclic, *adj.*, [WRACK *sb.*[1] + -LY[1]]: extraordinary, wonderful. *acc. pl. n.* **wræclico** 3

*****wræcmon**, *m. monos. stem*, [WRACK *sb.*[1] + MAN[1]]; exile 137

wrǣtlic, *adj.*, [+ -LY[1]]; splendid; *nom. sg. f.* **wrǣtlicu** 298

wrecca, *m. n-stem*, WRETCH; fugitive, exile. *dat. pl.* **wreccum** 533

gewrit, *n. a-stem*, [I-WRIT]; book. *dat. pl.* **gewritum** scriptures 520

wrōht, *m. a-stem*, strife; *acc. sg.* 147

-wudu, see **gārwudu**

wuldor, *n. a-stem*, [WULDER]; glory; *acc. sg.* 387; *gen. sg.* **wuldres** 100, 270, 418 etc.; *dat. sg.* **wuldre** 86

Wuldorcyning *m. a-stem* [WULDER + KING] glorious king (God); *acc. sg.* 548

wuldorfæst, *adj.*, [WULDER + FAST]; glorious 390

wuldorgesteald, *n. pl. a-stem*, [WULDER +]; glorious possessions; *acc.* 589

wulf, *m. a-stem*, WOLF. *nom. pl.* **wulfas** 164

gewuna, *adj.*, *w. dat.*, [I-[1] + WONE]; accustomed (to) 474

-wund, see **licwund**

wundon, see **windan**

wundor, *n. a-stem*, WONDER, miracle 108; *acc. sg.* 552. *gen. pl.* **wundra** 10. See also **eallwundor, fǣrwundor, lyftwundor, sōðwundor**

wunnon, see **winnan**

gewurde, wurdon, see **(ge)weorðan**

gewurðien, gewurðodne, see **geweorðian**

wurðmynd, *f. ō-stem*, [WORTH-MINT]; honour. *dat. pl.* as *adv.* **wurðmyndum** honourably 258

-wurðung, see **halswurðung**

-wylm, see **heaðowylm**

-wynn, see **lyftwynn**

wyrcan, *w.v.* (*1c*), WORK; make. *pr. 3 sg.* **wyrceð** 282. *p.t. sg.* **worhte** 25

gewyrcan, *w.v.* (*1c*), [I-WURCHE]; build. *p.t. pl. subj.* **geworhte** 396

wyrd, *f. i-stem*, [WEIRD]; course of events 458; *dat. sg.* **wyrde** *472. gen. pl.* **wyrda** events 433n. See also **eftwyrd**

wyrm, *m. i-stem*, WORM; serpent 537

wyrnan, *w.v.* (*1b*) *w. dat. of person to whom and gen. of thing denied*, [WARN[2]]; keep from 51

wyrpan, *w.v.* (*1b*), recuperate. *p.t. pl.* **wyrpton** 130

gewyrðode, see **geweorðian**

Y

yfel, *n. a-stem*, EVIL. *gen. pl.* **yfela** 538

ylde, *m. pl. i-stem*, men; **yldo** 437, *gen. pl.* 28

yldo, *f. ō-stem*, [ELD[2]]; age 540

yldra, see **eald**

ymb, *prep. w. acc.*, [UMBE, EMBE]: about 63, 145; around 180

ymbhwyrft, *m. ja-stem*, [UMBE +]: orb, circuit 430; *acc. sg.* 26

*****ymbwicigean**, *w.v.* (*2*) *w. dat..*

[UMBE + WICK[1]]; encamp around 65

-ypping, see **brimypping**

yrfeláf, *f. ō-stem,* [*ERF*[1] + LAVE[1]]: heir; *acc. sg.* **yrfeláfe** 403

yrfeweard, *m. a-stem,* [*ERF*[1] + WARD[1]]; guardian of the inheritance 142

yrmðu, *f. ō-stem,* [*ERMTH(E)*]; misery. *dat. pl.* **yrmðum** 265

yrre, *adj.,* [IRRE]; angry 506

ȳð, *f. jō-stem,* [YTHE]; sea 282. *nom. pl.* **ȳðe** waves 288; *acc. pl.* **ȳða** 442; *gen. pl.* 456; *dat. pl.* **ȳðum** 450, 473

*ȳðholm, *m. a-stem,* [YTHE + HOLM[1]]; sea-water; *gen. sg.* **ȳðholmes** *304*

ȳðláf, *f. ō-stem,* [YTHE + LAVE[1]]; shore; *dat. sg.* **ȳðláfe** 586

Glossarial Index of People and Places

This list gives the names of all personages, peoples and places found in the text and the references are complete. Notes on the scansion of some personal names that might cause metrical difficulty are included in square brackets at the end of the appropriate entry.

Abraham, *m. a-stem*, founding-father of the Israelites 380, 398, *411*, 419; *gen.* **Abrahames** 18, 273, 379. [Metrically disyllabic]

Afrisc, *adj.*, see *Glossary*

Æthan, *n. a-stem*, Etham, unidentifiable third stopping-place of Israelites on exodus; *gen.* **Æthanes** 66

Cananēas, *m. pl. a-stem*, Canaanites; *gen.* **Cananēa** 445, 556. [Scans ÚxxX]

Dāuid, *m. a-stem*, David, king of all the Israelites (d. 1016 BC); *gen.* **Dāuides** 389

Égypte, *m. pl. i-stem*, Egyptians 452; *gen.* **Égypta, Égipte** 50, 145, 444, 501; *dat.* **Égyptum** 506. See also *Glossary* **ingefolc, ingemen, ingeþēod, landmann**

Faraon, *m. a-stem*, PHARAOH, ruler of Egypt 259, 502; *gen.* **Faraones, -is** 14, 32, 156. [Scans Úxx]

God, *m. a-stem*, GOD 23, 71, 80, 152, 273, 292, 314, 380, 433; *acc. sg.* 515; *gen.* **Godes** 15, 268, 345, 358, 493, 503, 529, 569; *dat.* **Gode** 12,

391. See also *Glossary* **Āgend, aldor, Alwalda, cyning, Drihten, Flōdweard, Frēa, hālig, Heofoncyning, Liffrēa, mægenwisa, Metod, mihtig, þēoden, Waldend, weard, Wuldorcyning**

Hālig Gāst, *m.*, HOLY Spirit; *gen.* **(Hāliges) Gāstes** 96, 525. Cf. *Glossary* **gāst**

Iōsep, *m. a-stem*, Joseph, son of Jacob; *gen.* **Iōsepes** 588

Īsaac, *m. a-stem*, son of **Abraham**; *acc.* 398. [Metrically disyllabic or trisyllabic; the former gives a commoner verse-type]

Isra(h)ēlas, *m. pl. a-stem*, ISRAELites; *gen. pl.* **Isra(h)ēla** 91, 198, 265, 358; *dat. pl.* **Israhēlum** 303, 516. [Scans ⌣xx] See also *Glossary* **flota, sǣmann, sǣwīcing**

Iūdas, *m.*, Judah, son of Jacob 330. See also *Glossary* **Iūdisc**

Mōyses, Mōises, *m.* (*indecl.*), Moses 61, 101, 215, 352, *517*; *gen.* 2, 52, 152, 480; *dat.* 124. [Metrically disyllabic]

Nōe, *m.*, Noah 362; *dat.* 378. [Metrically disyllabic]

Rēad Sǣ, *m.,* Red Sea; *inst. sg.*
  Rēadan Sǣ 134. See also *Glossary*
  rēad, sǣ
Rūben, *m. a-stem,* Reuben, son of
  Jacob; *gen.* **Rūbenes** 332

Sēon, *? f. ō-stem,* Zion; *gen.* **Sēone**

386n. [Inflected form may be
metrically disyllabic or trisyl-
labic; the former gives a com-
moner verse-type]
Sigelware, *m. pl. i-stem,* Ethiopians;
  gen. **Sigelwara** 69
Simeon, *m. a-stem,* son of Jacob;
  gen. **Simeones** 341. [Scans ú̱xx]